D0882613

WITHDRAWN

PIERS PLOWMAN AND THE PROBLEM OF BELIEF

WITHDRAWN

BRITTON J. HARWOOD

Piers Plowman and
the Problem of Belief

UNIVERSITY OF TORONTO PRESS
Toronto Buffalo London

© University of Toronto Press 1992
Toronto Buffalo London
Printed in Canada

ISBN 0-8020-5799-3

Printed on acid-free paper

Canadian Cataloguing in Publication Data

Harwood, Britton J.
Piers Plowman and the problem of belief

ISBN 0-8020-5799-3

1. Langland, William, 1330?–1400? Piers the Plowman. I. Title.

PR2015.H37 1992   821'.1   C92-093221-5

To
the honour of my parents,
Frank W. and Marjorie E.A. Harwood,
and to
the happy memory of
Lulu M.C. Ackerman

Contents

Preface

The thesis and organization of this book are explained in the first chapter. I believe all work, including teaching and writing about literature, has a theory behind it, whether or not that theory is ever made explicit. Although I want to say here what kind of criticism this book attempts, I do not think one can account in a mere conception for any practice, especially one's own. Neither (to adapt the Talmudic saying) is it permissible to desist from trying to do that.

This is an essay in formalist historicism of the kind theorized most fully and perhaps best by E.D. Hirsch, Jr, in *Validity in Interpretation* (New Haven and London: Yale University Press 1967). Hirsch had recourse in this book to intentionality, in the Husserlian sense, in order to provide a consciousness that might intend – might hold in place as its object – the 'intrinsic genre' of a particular literary work. By this recourse, Hirsch moved to re-establish on European grounds critical procedures closely identified with American New Criticism.

While the fullest theorization of New Criticism appeared just when the latter was waning as a dominant practice, New Criticism, like many other liberal forms, has not disappeared. That perdurance could not justify in itself, of course, another New Critical book. Nevertheless, it seems obvious at least to me that the techniques of New Criticism – the construction of redundancy by (for example) taking some portions of a text as figurative or ironic restatements of other portions – are assumed by subsequent critical practice. The same may be said of the New Critical idea of an 'implied author' (in Wayne Booth's famous phrase), the subject of meaning in Hirsch's phenomenological account. What can there be to deconstruct unless, for a text, the kind of organization that Hirsch called an 'intrinsic genre' already is 'in place'? In deconstructing Rousseau's *Essay on the Origin of Languages*, for example, Jacques Derrida repeatedly made use of Rousseau's 'deep intention' there. Moreover, a materialist criticism like Pierre Macherey's, which starts with textual fissures that open up when a 'project' cannot subdue history to its purposes, necessarily uses 'intention' and the redundancies that exhibit it.

A distinguished materialist criticism of *Piers Plowman* has been initiated already by David Aers and others. Nevertheless, I have written this book because, despite more than a century of scholarly explication, no satisfactory formalist-historical reading of the poem has yet, I think, been published. The narrator of *Piers* says he began to write in order to fill a gap: 'Ac if þer were any wight,' he tells the character Imaginative,

> þat wolde me telle
> What were dowel and dobet and dobest at þe laste,
> Wolde I neuere do werk, but wende to holi chirche
> And þere bidde my bedes but whan ich ete or slepe.

Although I try to describe the poet's understanding of this gap and of the 'werk' he thinks might fill it, my principal point about *Piers* certainly will not 'save' all the 'appearances' of the poem. *Piers*, a quest that presents itself as repeatedly making fresh starts, shows to just a limited degree the kinds of redundancy that New Criticism has prized. Moreover, Langland betrays only a moderate anxiety, as in his rueful acknowledgment in passus 11 of the B text, when he fails to eliminate every detraction from a single aesthetic effect: 'This lokynge on lewed preestes haþ doon me lepe from pouerte, / The which I preise, þer pacience is, moore parfit þan richesse.' If *Piers* is a narrative, nonetheless, it has an 'action,' and this book exists because I have not been convinced by other accounts of it. I hope it may give materialist and other kinds of criticism something to presuppose in *Piers*. It is not intended to refuse them.

In this essay, I follow the 'action' in the B text because, as George Kane and E.T. Donaldson observe in the introduction to their edition, B is 'the one form of *Piers Plowman* which at some moment in history its author might have considered finished.' Nonetheless, I do not hesitate to consider changes from A to B or from B to C when I think they help to explain the 'action' of B. I cite the poem from these editions: A.G. Rigg and Charlotte Brewer eds *'Piers Plowman': The z Version* (Toronto: Pontifical Institute of Medieval Studies 1983); George Kane ed *'Piers Plowman': The*

A Version (London: Athlone Press 1960); Kane and Donaldson eds *'Piers Plowman': The B Version* (London: Athlone Press 1975); and Derek Pearsall ed *'Piers Plowman': An Edition of the C-Text* (Berkeley and Los Angeles: University of California Press 1979). Although their significance has been contested, I use the traditional terms *Visio* (for the prologue and passus 1 through 7) and *Vita* (for the rest of the poem). Even if these rubrics are merely scribal, critics need a means for designating the stations (or aporias) reached in the movement of *Piers*. The question is still open, of course, whether the traditional rubrics have served to reveal these or to hide them. When I italicize *Dowel, Dobet,* or *Dobest,* I mean the *Vita de dowel* or one of the other subdivisions of the *Vita.*

For generous financial support in the publication of this book, I thank Ronald J. Henry, Provost, and Gary H. Knock, Dean of the Graduate School and Research at Miami University. The Committee on Faculty Research at Miami provided time for some writing with a summer grant; and I am grateful to them.

Earlier versions of parts of this study have been previously published – portions of chapters 1 and 3 in *Modern Philology,* some other portions of the same chapters in *ELH: English Literary History,* a number of paragraphs from chapter 3 in *Medium Aevum,* and several from chapter 4 in *Philological Quarterly.* For permission to reuse this material, I thank the editors of these journals.

For help of many other kinds, personal and professional, I will remain profoundly indebted to Natalie Roghaar Harwood. The late Ruth Fisher Smith, a wry, discreet, unfailingly kind teacher, first guided me through *Piers Plowman.* And the late Talbot Donaldson, with his usual courtesy, had an encouraging word at a crucial point. I have tried to acknowledge in the notes my use of the immense learning and intelligence that he and others over the decades have focused on this astonishing poem. For work I have absorbed and somehow misunderstood to be my own, I offer here a plenary expression of gratitude.

Trudi Nixon prepared the final manuscript with diligent care. Margaret Allen edited for University of Toronto Press tactfully and perspicaciously.

I am always obligated to a handful of colleagues, present and former, who perhaps have nothing in common but an ability to make their friends think better than they otherwise would and a perennial gift for unselfish support. Affectionate thanks, then, to Don Daiker, Jane Gallop, Tom Idinopulos, Constance Pierce, Jack Reardon, Peter Rose, Jack

Wallace, and – first and last – Jim Sosnoski. I thank Lea Idinopulos, a warm and loyal friend. And for unequalled companionship and more, I thank my wife, Lauri.

No man has ever been luckier in his children. Suffice it to say, with Hamilton, Kelley, Joshua, Gareth, Miranda, and Elihu it is always 'a somer seson.'

PIERS PLOWMAN AND THE PROBLEM OF BELIEF

1

The Narrator in *Piers Plowman*: The Object of His Search, the Form of His Poem

When William Langland begins to write the poem we know as *Piers Plowman*, does he think of himself as beginning a process of discovery? Or does he think of himself as acting primarily on a moral duty to say what he knows? Does he begin with what he considers an adequate idea of contemporary corruption, notwithstanding a possible doubt about his authority to denounce it? Or does he represent in his poem the desire for a change in himself? These motives do not exclude each other, of course. Langland's indignation over the social costs of avarice and sloth does not mean that he never thinks of himself as guilty (as slothful, for example) or that he never wonders what sort of experience might change his course of behaviour. If his impetus in beginning and resuming his poem is to discover, then, like everyone, he has no choice but to say what he knows – to proceed from the known to the unknown. And in doing so, he may – in fact he surely does – write didactically for long passages.

While these motives are compatible, they relate to different 'levels' of thinking. One motive – sometimes satiric, sometimes didactic, often both at once – applies the moral law as Langland understands it. The other, represented as motivating a quest, relates to the moral law only as an interrogation of its grounds. In seeking the authority for sanctions, it is the motive to discover how the grounds of human existence might be known and thus how the moral law, as it stands on these grounds, might be something that one comes to obey.[1]

Though not mutually exclusive, these motives are unlikely to be perfectly balanced or present to an equal degree at every moment of composition. And readers of *Piers Plowman* construct the poem for themselves by assuming that one and not the other of these motives is dominant.[2]

The earliest readers of the poem 'evidently perceived it as a compendiously didactic work,' if we judge from other texts in the manuscript books where *Piers* survives.[3] In whatever form the rebellious priest John Ball knew the poem, he invokes it because, for him, it can be relied on to teach 'do wel and bettre,'[4] as if *Richard the Redeless* and *Mum and the Sothsegger* had established a generic context for understanding the poem. When *Piers* is read as chiefly didactic, it does not suffer some avoidable misfortune. As Anne Middleton has observed, its situation is that 'of all literature as distinct from instrumental discourse: the poem must be open to misprision if it is also to be open to its intended affective use. Its heteroclitic nature, its capacity to become a property of public discourse in several incommensurable ways at once, defines its social power and its wholly *ad hoc* authority.'[5]

This earlier reception notwithstanding, my enabling assumption as I write this book is that Langland wrote *Piers* not in order to teach but to find out. Specifically, he wrote it to find out how he might come to believe in Christ. This is not a new idea within criticism of the poem.[6] None the less, for whatever reasons, critics have not steadily read any part of *Piers*, much less the whole of it, in light of such a possibility.

Very early in the poem Langland represents himself as impelled by just this desire to believe. The very first of Will's interlocutors is Lady Holy Church. Once she has identified herself, he says that he falls to his knees and begs

> hire pitously to preye for my synnes;
> And ek kenne me kyndely on crist to beleue,
> That I my3te werchen his will þat wro3te me to man.   (1.80–2)

Just as many readers have constructed the object of the whole poem as essentially moral, so Holy Church understands Will as asking for essentially moral instruction. She ignores any soteriological meaning his request might have that does not simply ask about right conduct. Perhaps without exception, critics have constructed the question as she does. In following Holy Church in her approach to the narrator's request, they have already begun to assign a particular value – in fact, a negative one – to this narrative voice and thus to limit the kinds of relationship that could exist between the narrator and his interlocutors. They begin to assume as well a certain 'action' – a certain 'mythos,' in Aristotle's sense – for the poem as a whole. Prior to the questions of narrative voice and of possible trajectories for *Piers*, we might consider what Holy Church may be leaving out.

1

One of the conclusions of Augustinian theology is that faith can exist without hope and charity, but that hope and charity cannot merit salvation without faith. If we set aside for the time being Langland's handling of Trajan, the righteous pagan emperor (11.140–66, 12.283–94), other parts of the poem seem to insist that love without faith does not suffice for salvation. The Jews themselves, Anima points out, 'lyuen in lele lawe'; *'Dilige deum & proximum* is parfit Iewen lawe' (15.582, 584). Nevertheless, if they are to be saved, they must learn to believe 'litlum and litlum ... in *Iesum Christum*' (15.610). Belief rather than living perfectly is decisive. Ignorant folk like shoemakers and shepherds

> passen Purgatorie penaunceless at hir hennes partyng
> Into þe parfit blisse of Paradis for hir pure bileue,
> That inparfitly here knewe and ek lyuede.   (10.469–71)

As Augustine wrote in the *Enchiridion*, faith is a necessary condition for charity, not the other way around.[7] It is not a particular (loving) choice that will give people the knowledge they need. Rather, for Bernard of Clairvaux, for example, through the knowledge of Christ, people recover 'liberum consilium' in its lower degree – the freedom to be able not to sin.[8]

Just as there were Jews who witnessed the marvels performed by Christ and yet denied him as Messiah (15.587–603), so, from what may have been the earliest version of the poem, there is a crucial sense in which (so the narrator claims) he does not yet believe in Christ, however much he would like to (Z 1.24–7). Critical debate during the last ten years on whether Langland inclines towards a nominalist or an Augustinian position has actually helped to silence the narrator's plea. The two positions have been summarized by Marilyn McCord Adams, in her recent study of William of Ockham: 'theologians debated whether God decided whom to predestine on the basis of their foreseen good use of free will, which seemed to lead in a Pelagian or semi-Pelagian direction; or whether God first determines who shall receive grace and thereby do good works, and then rewards and punishes accordingly, which seemed to raise the question of how God's choice can be reasonable, wise, or good.'[9] Yet the two traditions agree that an infusion of the theological virtues is a prerequisite for salvation. For example, Ockham held that God has in fact ordained 'that only acts performed by means of created [grace or] charity in the soul ... merit eternal bliss.'[10] Because there is for Ockham a constant conjunction between receipt of the sacraments and the infusion of grace,[11] and because the validity of a sacrament depends in part on the existence of the relevant intentions, there appears to be nothing in Ockham to suggest that, under the ordinances of God, someone can merit salvation who does not believe in Christ. The debate on whether Langland thinks that works lead to grace or grace leads to works has drowned out the confession by Will that faith has become a problem for him.

I take Will's request to Holy Church ('kenne me kyndely on crist to bileue') to mean that he needs a sign of the reality of Christ the person, God-with-us. Then he will be able to repent. Repentance is dramatized early enough in the poem: Robert the robber, for instance, when he prays, seems geniunely faithful and contrite: 'for thi muchel mercy mitigacion I beseche: / Dampe me noght at Domesday for that I dide so ille!' (5.470–1). And the narrator observes that Robert 'wepte water with hise eighen, / And knowliched his coupe to Crist yet eftsoones' (5.473–4). That Langland can dramatize repentance, nevertheless, does not mean that he has attained it. Like a prophet, Langland is preoccupied with people who are themselves 'bisie ... about þe maȝe' (1.6), oblivious of the judgment to come. But where critics have stressed that Will's shortcomings give figures like Holy Church the occasion to preach justice and love (as in another time and country Dostoevsky's Father Zossima will tell a lady who has lost her faith, 'If you attain to perfect self-forgetfulness in the love of your neighbor, then you will believe without doubt, and no doubt can possibly enter your soul'),[12] so these critics may neglect the power of Will's first questions; for part of Langland's greatness is his undercutting of his own prophecy by searching for its grounds. In short, Will is also Ivan: if one does not believe in God, then everything becomes lawful. Raving in his 'folie,' 'looþ to reuerencen / Lordes or ladies' (15.5–10), he has something in him of Flannery O'Connor's Misfit: 'Jesus was the only One that ever raised the dead ... If I had of been there I would of known and I wouldn't be like I am now.'[13] The repentant thousands 'cride upward to Christ' (5.511) but don't know how to find him.

Belief, as M.-D. Chenu has written, is a 'type d'adhésion, de connaissance, [which] se construit en effet inévitablement en dépendance

et en contre-partie de la connaissance par évidence, directe ou indi-
recte, donc en face d'une théorie de la science.'[14] To propose that *Piers*
is chiefly motivated by the problem of the knowledge of God of
course does not imply that Langland is agnostic or Laodicean; it
would be absurd to maintain that he doubted the historicity of God's
having become flesh while someone like Hobbes did not doubt it.
Will (to adopt Walter Ong's phrasing) has opinion (belief that) but
not faith (belief in). Belief *that* is directed towards an object and re-
gards objective existence, even though one may have no direct knowledge of it. In this way Will always accepts 'the existence of God as
a truth,' believes *that* God exists, a Being who can do everything.
'Belief as faith, on the other hand, is belief *in* and faces toward a person ... [It] is ultimately an invitation to the person to respond.'[15] It
submits 'to the power of God exercising pressure upon me here and
now ...'[16] Although the narrator, *pace* Holy Church ('It is a kynde
knowyng þat kenneþ in þyn herte' 1.143), cannot see Christ in the
pressure he feels, he has not despaired:

> Ac ȝut, I hope, as he þat ofte hath ychaffared
> And ay loste and loste, and at þe laste hym happed
> A bouhte suche a bargayn he was þe bet euere,
> And sette all his los at a leef at the laste ende,
> Suche a wynnyng hym warth thorw wordes of grace.
>> *Simile est regnum celorum thesauro abscondito in agro.*
>> *Mulier que inuenit dragmam, etc.*
> So hope y to haue of hym that is almyghty
> A gobet of his grace, and bigynne a tyme
> That alle tymes of my tyme to profit shal turne.   (c 5.94–101)

He looks to meet God as a power that will embrace and sustain him
'even in his fallen, self-assertive state.'[17]

Belief in Christ as a person was often thought to require the knowledge of oneself as a person. In one of the classic dilemmas of epistemology, one cannot know what is not oneself.[18] Augustine desired
to know the soul as well as God, nothing more,[19] because understanding the three powers of the soul can lead to knowledge of the
Trinity. So far as the immanent God is to be known, he needs to be
univocal with something in the self. And yet, 'By what craft' in one's
body (1.139) does that knowledge come? Langland does not deduce
the difficulty of knowing Christ on philosophical grounds. He does
not deduce it at all. Rather he starts with the facts of his own sinful-

ness and his unbelief and understands these as reciprocal causes for each other. Because the mind has been damaged by sin, he has no confidence in a person's ability to know anything, much less Christ. 'The first mischief that afflicts man through sin,' wrote Aquinas, 'is disorder in his mind ...' More than half a century later, Gregory of Rimini (d 1358), defending tradition, held that human beings in their fallen state could not know even 'what is morally right and circumstantially requisite.'[20] This obstacle is dramatized in passus 19 of *Piers* as the dawn of that stage of Christian history beginning with Pentecost goes down to day. The minions of Pride warn Christians that

> youre caples two,
> Confession and Contricion, and youre carte þe bileeue
> Shal be coloured so queyntely and couered vnder oure Sophistrie
> That Conscience shal noȝt knowe who is cristene or heþene.   (345–8)

As Anima points out, greed has infected the Church, and even simple things now baffle the mind:

> Now faileþ þe folk of þe flood and of þe lond boþe
> Shepherdes and shipmen and so do þise tilieris.
> Neiþer þei konneþ ne knoweþ oon cours bifore anoþer.
> Astronomyens also aren at hir wittes ende;
> Of þat was calculed of þe element þe contrarie þei fynde.
> Grammer, þe ground of al, bigileþ now children ...   (15.367–72)

At times radical doubt of the ability to know confers on the dreamer almost an absurdity: 'Here is wil wolde wite if wit koude hym teche' (8.129). Having met characters named Faith and *Spes*, he wonders whether 'eny of ȝow be trewe / And leel to beleyuen on' (c 20.25–6). The sinful narrator offers the only mirror in which Christ can be seen (15.160–1).

The narrator, then, is alien from most of his world, not because he needs to act on his faith, but because he cannot, when he thinks of it, bring himself to perform the act that constitutes faith. Will appears to mean by his request 'kenne me kyndely on crist to bileue' that he wants a 'kynde knowyng' of Christ. Rather than assume that he must become good if he is to obtain this, we can read the poem by taking him at his word: he needs to *know* Christ before he can become good ('werchen [Christ's] wille'). What, then, does Will mean by a 'kynde knowyng'? Personifying the household of faith, Holy

Church herself of course believes: for example, she holds that 'who is trewe of his tonge, telleþ noon ooþer,

> Dooþ þe werkes þerwiþ and wilneþ no man ille,
> He is a god by þe gospel, a grounde and o lofte,
> And ek ylik to oure lord by Seint Lukes wordes.   (1.88–91)

If 'belief that' is at least sometimes an act of will by which one assents to a proposition like 'Deus est incarnabilis,' such an act is necessary because the proposition is not evident in itself. It does not detract from such a proposition, William of Ockham pointed out, that it can be held only 'propter firmiorem adhaesionem' – because one adheres to it, not because it is evident ('non sciuntur evidenter').[21] Nevertheless, knowledge of some sort is the condition for any act of the will, including adherence. As Gordon Leff paraphrases a comment by Ockham on the second book of the *Sentences* of Peter Lombard, 'The intellect can be said to be prior to the will; for an act of knowing connoted by the intellect is a partial efficient cause of an act of willing connoted by the will. The first can be without the second but not the converse ...'[22] And the narrator even seems to demand that this knowledge conditioning love somehow be evident knowledge. It may not become evident for him simply because it once was so for someone else – 'Seint Luke' or the Thomas who was able to touch Christ's 'flesshliche herte' and say, '*Dominus meus & deus meus*' (19.172a).

Evident knowledge is knowledge that a proposition is true because its terms (subject and predicate) are evidently known.[23] They are known, that is, through intuitive cognition. 'Intuitive' here means nothing instinctive or mysterious; rather, it derives from 'intueri,' 'to gaze at, pay attention to.' While Langland is not a systematic philosopher, I believe his crucial term 'kynde knowyng' resonates with – conceivably replaces for him – 'notitia intuitiva,' one of the terms essential to philosophy for the previous hundred years. In effect, Will makes intuitive cognition the psychological test for his knowledge of Christ. In evident knowledge of Christ, the concept signified by 'Christ' would be caused by an existing and present object.[24] 'Intuitive cognition of a thing ... enables us to know whether the thing exists or does not exist, in such a way that, if the thing exists, then the intellect immediately judges that it exists and evidently knows that it exists ...'[25]

By natural means in this life a person apparently cannot have intuitive knowledge of God. Propositions like 'deus est incarnabilis' cannot be evidently known, for neither of their terms, it seems, can be known intuitively.[26] To the proposition that human love is the image of God's own love, where at least one of the terms cannot be known intuitively, Holy Church personifies that act of will nevertheless compelling assent (1.88–91, 163–8). In passus 5, Repentance assents as well to the proposition that God made 'man moost lik to' himself (481). And Kynde will take the dreamer up the mountain called Middle Earth so that he might discover the vestiges of his 'creatour' in 'ech a creature' (11.326). Knowing that a portrait, say, is a good likeness of one's mother depends upon what Ockham called abstractive cognition, the quidditative knowledge of one's mother without respect to whether she now exists or not. But abstractive knowledge in turn presupposes that one once had intuitive knowledge.[27] If God himself cannot be intuitively known, 'there can be no habitual knowledge of him, regardless of the similarity between hypothetical accidents in God and creatures.'[28] If Holy Church, for example, cannot know evidently that the person 'who is trewe of his tonge' is 'ylik to oure lord,' she must know it 'propter firmiorem adhaesionem.'

I suggest, then, that the object (Christ) sought by Will from the beginning must be one that gives itself as existing. That others, including Piers, report (not necessarily reliably) that Christ is or was known intuitively by them is no help to Will in his unprivileged, natural state. Of two *kinds* of knowledge ('duae notitiae'),[29] one brackets altogether the question of whether a particular does or does not exist. The other, which the poet calls 'kynde knowyng,'[30] is how the narrator, having no faith, needs to know Christ: 'kenne me kyndely on crist to bileue ...' While both Scotus and Ockham agreed that 'notitia intuitiva' might be supernaturally provided, 'kynde knowyng' has not come so for Will.

Our understanding of *Piers* may have been hindered less by the occasional anachronistic imposition of modern assumptions than by the anachronism of supposing that the poet's theology was *tout court* that of his favourite doctors, 'Austyn and Ambrose ... / Gregori þe grete clerk and þe goode Ierom' (19.269–70). As complaint, much in the poem looks back to better days,[31] including better theologians, not the logicizing friars of the dreamer's experience. It would not follow, however, that the poet was immune to the effects of the last century of philosophy and theology simply because he disliked them. Janet Coleman rightly remarks that, 'The poem is to a large extent a vernacular expression of coming to terms with the *moderni*.'[32] As pervasive as the distinction between the absolute power of God and God's ordered power, which has now been applied to some of Will's speeches in *Dowel*,[33] was the doctrine that 'notitia intuitiva' underlies all knowledge. An Augustinian element,[34] the concept although not the name had already appeared in the preceding century when Vital du Four argued that 'la connaissance expérimentale de l'existence actuelle de la chose est le fondement de toutes les autres connaissances et comme le germe, *vis seminaria*, d'où elles dériveront.'[35] The difference between the 'duae notitiae' had spread sufficiently throughout clerical culture by the early fourteenth century that Nicholas of Lyre, for example, was using it in his commentary on the whole Bible.[36] In naming intuitive cognition, Scotus went beyond his predecessors. He held for the direct contact of the mind with the particular and the certain apprehension of the existence of a present object.[37] A modern historian has seen Scotus's 'emphasis upon the presence of the object in intuition' as following from one of the qualitative differences in human experiences. Where pre-established classifications generally dominate our pragmatic experience, intuition has to do with 'a full-fledged encounter.'[38]

Ockham, too, sought to explain this cognition of the individual as the source of all knowledge. The singular is the first thing known by the intellect: 'Intellectus pro stato isto cognoscit singulare et primo ... et est primum cognitum primitate generationis.'[39] Ockhamism, including the notion of intuitive cognition, already played the conservative role even in the same statement of the Parisian Faculty of Arts in December 1340 that prohibited certain nominalistic theses.[40] The notion was known to Wyclif, who discussed, in connection with faith, how the 'intuitiva sensitiva' bears on the 'intuitiva intellectiva.'[41] In fact, the 'epistemology of intuitive cognition' was 'adopted by almost everyone in the late Middle Ages.'[42] Although 'intuition' has not been traced in English before the mid-fifteenth century, the notion already may have fed what Heiko Oberman perceives as the fourteenth-century 'hunger for reality in respect to the created world ... What in another context could be called the eschatological awareness in Nominalism can from the point of view of the God-man relationship be called the quest for immediacy.'[43]

To entertain the possibility that Will's request to Holy Church – 'Kenne me kyndely on crist to bileue' – asks for the same kind of present, existing object that was available to Thomas the disciple makes it possible to understand his dissatisfaction with her answer. On first descending from the castle, Holy Church asks Will whether he, unlike those 'bisie ... aboute þe maȝe,' pays any attention to a reality other than the shadows of this world (1.5–9). Evidently such a reality is 'truþe.' But 'truþe' is adduced by Holy Church only to be defined as a source – 'of feiþ,' the human body and intelligence, clothing, food, and drink. 'Truþe,' rather than pointed out as a particular that Will could not help but know intuitively, is defined connotatively (as I shall explain) through particulars which *he* has produced ('wollen,' 'lynnen,' and so on); and Holy Church, with her ethical bias, begins at once lengthily to persuade the dreamer to a 'mesurable' use of these.

If he wishes to know God intuitively, this will not do. His next question should be considered in light of that: 'Ac þe moneie on þis molde þat men so faste holdeþ, / Tel me to whom þat tresour appendeþ' (1.44–5). This question would redirect Holy Church's own glance to the source. Men would not be involved in the identification of the money ('þat men so faste holdeþ') if they were also to be the ones to whom it 'appendeþ.' The question is constructed to lead Holy Church to someone else. She produces Caesar (1.50–1). Then she moves to her long suit, the regulated use rather than the enjoyment of one's 'tresor' (1.54–7).[44] Again Will attempts to move her away from the 'bona temporalia' to what conditions them, 'the dongeon in þe dale þat dredful is of siȝte'; for if, as Peace claims elsewhere, some things become knowable in some sense only through knowledge of their opposites (18.205–29), Will may be forced to try to get Holy Church to help him apprehend the 'fader of feiþ' by way of the 'fader of falshede' (1.64). Him too Holy Church simply defines connotatively, through those 'he egged to ille.'

Knowing what is 'good to þe goost' and what 'ille,' she appears wonderfully wise. Will asks her identity, and when he hears it he puts the object of his search in what I take to be its plainest form (1.81). Nevertheless, assuming that because she has 'tauȝte' him the 'feiþ' he has therefore learned it, she passes over his need to believe to the need to be 'buxom' at God's bidding (1.110). No doubt he needs to obey. But 'oboedire' has to do with listening, and rather than listen to Will, Holy Church speaks as if to a crowd: after his request to be taught to believe in Christ, she replies for fifty-three lines without once using a second-person pronoun or otherwise addressing Will specifically. An ethical answer again does not satisfy him ('Yet haue I no kynde knowyng ... ye mote kenne me bettre' 1.138). Further, Holy Church once again had *defined* 'Treuþe,' and defined it, perhaps, in the wrong way.

Ockham distinguished between terms with real definition ('quid rei') and those with only nominal definition ('quid nominis'). A definition 'quid rei' signifies 'the whole nature of a thing without indicating anything extrinsic to the object defined.' This can be accomplished either by 'signifying essential parts of the thing' or by signifying the distinguishing difference of a thing, 'but only in the way in which "white" expresses whiteness.'[45] If 'Treuþe is in Trinitee' (1.133), then the Trinity may be at least partly extrinsic to it; if 'truþe is þe beste' of 'alle tresors' (1.135), then all treasures but one are extrinsic to it. Holy Church defines God only connotatively also, through what he acts upon (1.122–3).

Definitions in a broader sense, 'nominal' definitions, simply state what a conventional sign implies.[46] They do not, as Leff has pointed out, 'directly signify things as real definitions do; for that reason they can also be of what is impossible as well as possible …'[47] Thus, 'who is trewe of his tonge' may be defined nominally as 'a god by þe gospel' (1.88, 90) without prejudice to the possibility that such a person does not exist. Again, the term 'Treuþe' designates, or means, 'tresor þe trieste on erþe' (1.137). But such nominal definitions are distinguished from real ones precisely as connotative are different from absolute terms. And only the latter 'directly stand for real things.'[48] More importantly, all definitions are second-intentional, not signifiying anything outside the soul.[49]

If Holy Church provides not a definition of 'Treuþe' but a description, that would have no existential importance either. Ockham quotes from the *Logic* of John of Damascus: 'A description is composed of accidents, i.e., properties and accidents. For example, "Man is a risible thing, who walks erect and has broad nails." All of the elements of this description are accidents. Because of this it is said that a description conceals or fails to make manifest the substantial existence of the subject; it focuses only on the consequences of that substantial existence.'[50] By contrast, intuitive cognition meant for both Scotus and Ockham that the senses, particularly the visual sense,[51] knew the presence of the object concomitantly and immediately just as the intellect did.[52] Just so, when Will, having told Holy Church he has no 'kynde knowyng' of her definitions and description of 'Treuþe,' asks her to teach him the power in his body ('craft in my cors') whence 'kynde knowyng' begins, he may ask for something not only evident to him as a viator but also something that he can see.[53] Perhaps I need to make clear again that I am not advancing the least claim that Langland is a systematic logician, epistemologist, or semanticist. Nor do I assert that he conceives of differences between real and nominal definition, absolute and connotative terms, and the like. The narrator typically announces what he did not get ('I haue no kynde knowyng'). If 'kynde knowyng' means intuitive cognition, then Ockham's names for forms of language that do not imply intuitive cognition should cover the answers that Will finds unsatisfactory. This keeps open the possibility that the preoccupations of professional philosophy during the preceding hundred years may help to account, however indirectly, for the nature of his quest.

After Will asks to be taught to believe in Christ, Holy Church teaches about a 'tresor' that does not serve even to distinguish Christians from non-Christians: 'The clerkes þat knowen it [namely, Truth] sholde kennen it aboute / For cristen and vncristen cleymeþ it echone' (1.92–3). In the fifty-three lines following Will's request, Holy Church mentions Christ only twice: 'Crist, kyngene kyng, knyȝted ten,' and Lucifer 'was þe louelokest of liȝt after oure lord' (1.105, 112). Holy Church may here report imperfect intuitive cognitions she now has, propositions that once were evident for her. Otherwise, 'crist' and 'oure lord' are relative terms and therefore second-intentional – connotative names that refer principally to the thing they stand for but secondarily also to something else (for instance, knights, the knighting of whom defines a king nominally, as the secondary reference to a child defines 'father').

Will demurs: 'Ye mote kenne me bettre' (1.138). Serenely imperceptive of his plight, her new answer looks neither right nor left of ethics: love cures sin, authenticates faith, opens the way to heaven. Christ is adduced only as an example of one who 'was myȝtful and meke and mercy gan graunte' (1.173). Picking up Will's repetition of 'kynde knowyng,' Holy Church transforms the phrase as she works it into her answer. 'And for to knowen [love] kyndely,' she says, 'it comseþ by myght,'

And in þe herte þere is þe heed and þe heiȝe welle.
For in kynde knowynge in herte þer comseþ a myȝt,
And þat falleþ to þe fader þat formed vs alle ...   (1.163–6)

This – what Robert W. Frank calls 'the inherent desire of the soul for the good'[54] – is the conformity of every created will to what God wills, a habit based on prior knowledge. Where such prior knowledge exists, giving the moral virtues their ends,[55] it is a cause of love. By calling love a 'knowyng,' Holy Church names this cause, familiar in the Dominican tradition as 'synderesis.'[56] Even if it were possible for Will to experience God immediately as the one who wills, however, he would remain with the conviction of his own unjustness and the continued need to know Christ.

While I shall not go on to consider in this second half of Holy Church's speech what is not evident for her (such as definitions) and what is evident (such as existing singulars), we may note that she refers to, even

if she does not honour as such, a hunger for sensible experience: 'For
heuene myȝte nat holden [love], so heuy it semed, / Til it hadde of þe
erþe yeten hitselue' (1.153–4).

We have been trying to come to terms with the narrator's understanding of what he needs. Setting aside for the time being the rest of
the *Visio*, including the famous claim by Piers that he knows Truth as
'kyndely as clerc doþ hise bokes' (5.538), we may move from Will's difficulties with Holy Church to his next rejection of authority, his telling
the Franciscans that 'I haue no kynde knowyng ... to conceyuen þi
wordes' (8.57). To understand this, however, we must back up a moment to Will's reaction when Piers tears the pardon.

Piers had been expecting something ('which a pardon Piers hadde
þe peple to conforte' 7.152) that he did not get: 'þe preest preued no
pardon to dowel' (7.174). This shows not only in his 'pure tene' (7.119)
but in his self-conviction for a kind of mistake:

'I shal cessen of my sowyng,' quod Piers, '& swynke noȝt so harde,
Ne aboute my bilyue so bisy be na moore;
Of preieres and of penaunce my plouȝ shal ben herafter.'   (7.122–4)

If Will has sought an existing, present singular, then the best response
available to him, as the second vision disperses with an exchange of in-
sults between Piers and the priest, is Piers. While one might doubt that
the poem began with the search for a person,[57] indisputably that is the
way it concludes. When Will awakens from the inner dream in passus
16, he wipes his eyes and 'after Piers þe Plowman pried and stared'
(16.168). Envisioning later the entry into Jerusalem of 'Oon semblable to
þe Samaritan and somdeel to Piers þe Plowman,' Will is evidently sur-
prised to learn that Piers is 'in þis place' (18.21) because he has been
looking for him and did not recognize him. Faith has been 'after a segge'
(16.178); *Spes* has sought 'after a Knyght' (17.1). And although Will drags
about apparently objectless as passus 20 begins, the poem of course concludes with (his) Conscience going in search of Piers (20.382, 385). In
entire consistency with this, then, in passus 7, Will for 'loue' of a person, 'Piers ... þe Plowman,' is 'pencif in herte' (151). Nevertheless, this
person has just undergone an important change of mind, moved by
the intractable imperative 'Do wel and haue wel, and god shal haue þi
soule, / And do yuel and haue yuel' (7.116–17). (His mind may change,
of course, not about the content of the Law but about his standing in
relation to it.) Accordingly, the narrator goes on to ponder not only a

person but a conditional act (doing 'wel'), which is unfortunately separable from people.⁵⁸

Piers's self-disqualification, his exchanging the effort to work justly for the plow 'of penaunce,' is simultaneously a conversion, and Clergy will await him (13.133), as the narrator, who has not ceased to desire him, swoons in the Tree of Charity scene upon hearing 'his name' (16.19). Nevertheless, while continuing to seek a person, Will bows to the standard that has broken Piers and personifies this: he wishes for grace so 'that, after oure deep day, dowel reherce / At þe day of dome we dide as he hiȝte' (7.205–6).

Because the Law implies a lawgiver, who is also the one who imparts grace ('criep god mercy ... That god gyue vs grace'), he too, however, may be implicit in the personification when Will inquires at the start of passus 8 'where dowel was at Inne, / And what man he myȝte be' (4–5).⁵⁹ This language cannot be explained merely as Will's seeking here the sorts of acts coming under the type 'do wel,' since Truth has already glossed the pardon extensively, ordering, for example, merchants to spend their profits on hospitals and bridges. To the contrary, Will's personification of the Law tends to decompose into a person. If 'dowel' were chiefly one or more related acts, part of the narrator's apology in passus 12 would be inexplicable:

'Ac if þer were any wight þat wolde me telle
What were dowel and dobet and dobest at þe laste,
Wolde I neuere do werk, but wende to holi chirche
And þere bidde my bedes but whan ich ete or slepe.'   (12.25–8)

If 'dowel' were simply a norm for behaviour, logically it could exclude going to church or praying. But it does not. And the fact that Will knows that going to church or praying would still be possible means that he knows at least that 'dowel' is not an activity that might then displace others.

When Will meets the two friars early in passus 8, he will reject them because one friar argues in effect that he himself does well: 'amonges vs he dwelleþ' (8.18). If Will has been seeking a person, then it may be this person's non-appearance – the absence of the existing particular – that causes Will to say, 'I haue no kynde knowyng ... to conceyuen þi wordes' (8.57), thus rejecting the friar as a candidate. Someone's occasionally doing well – Will allows that the friar is sometimes 'rightfulle' (8.21) – does not make doing well a real thing. For the friar, 'dowel' is an attribute, which Ockham, for one, treated as only a connotative term.⁶⁰

To the contrary, when the dreamer objects 'that dowel and do yuele mowe not dwelle togideres' (8.23), he means that one substance – for example, one person – cannot be another. Obviously, he could not be ruling out the possibility that conceptions of opposite acts may signify the same person, for Will himself insists on that (8.21).

If Will cannot for very long think of an attribute as real, Thought, personifying the intellect with its universals, makes possible that very mistake. As if in illustration of the error of identifying 'grammatical and logical forms with ontological realities,'[61] Thought claims that the three degrees of 'dowel,' 'dobet,' and 'dobest' 'ben noʒt fer to fynde' (8.79). What may well have signified a person is now, together with its higher degrees, in simple supposition, in Ockham's phrase, to 'þre faire vertues' – simple, not personal, because 'vertues' are 'habitūs,' not real and only nominally definable (for instance, 'someone is likely to behave in a certain way'). Because a virtue is not a human being, Wit can misleadingly reify it as something making a home in the physical body: 'Sire Dowel dwelleþ ... In a Castle þat kynde made' (9.1–2). Further, Wit sometimes makes 'dowel' a genus, a term of second intention, like definition: 'Dowel in þis world is trewe wedded libbynge folk' (9.110). Small wonder that the narrator is drawn, at least temporarily, into the orbit of his interlocutors. Having begun by wishing to perform the will of him 'þat wroʒte me to man,' he is now prepared to work Study's 'wille while my lif dureþ' (10.150). And what he seeks from her in the next line ('kenne me kyndely to knowe *what* is dowel') may or may not be a person.[62]

Will is not permanently deflected. Scripture, preaching that Christians who wish to be saved must love the Lord and then 'alle cristene creatures' (10.362), states moral obligation clearly enough. Nevertheless, Will rejects her lesson as obscure. He does so, I think, because, in the jargon of the philosophy of the day, she gives him accidents while he seeks a substance. Much later, having met Reason, Imaginative, Conscience, Patience, and others, he awakens with Haukyn's weeping and reports that it was long 'er I koude kyndely knowe what was dowel' (15.2). After all the 'sermons' of the *Vita de dowel*, as Jusserand once called them, he could not possibly mean that he doubts what he *ought* to do. Rather, he still has not found the person he is after: 'I seiʒ neuere swich a man' (15.158).

Anima takes up the abiding object of Will's quest – 'Clerkes kenne me,' says Will, 'þat crist is in alle places / Ac I seiʒ hym neuere sooþly' – but uses Christ in simple supposition for charity, a concept. Conversely,

Anima also takes a series of concepts – being indifferent to clothing, being patient in adversity, and so on – and constructs the semblance of a person. For Anima, charity is a genus of such acts. One or another may once have belonged to Anthony or Egidius or 'oþere holy fadres' (15.272). Now he assembles them as if they were the difference that could make a person identifiable:

> For whoso myȝte meete wiþ hym swiche maneres hym eileþ:
> Neiþer he blameþ ne banneþ, bosteþ ne preiseþ,
> Lakkeþ ne loseþ ne lokeþ vp sterne,
> Craueþ ne coueiteþ ne crieþ after moore ...   (15.251–4)

While charity as a genus is really a second-intentional term used in simple supposition for other abstractions, Anima treats it as an incomplex, a subject known evidently at the same time one knows evidently that the subject acts in a certain way. A subject is known like that, however, only in an intuitive cognition, which does not occur just because a number of notes, abstracted in experience, are composed into what one would like to be a subject. The detachability of such signs was parodied in the *Visio* when a pardoner said he would have to go home to fetch 'my box wiþ my breuettes & a bulle with bisshopes lettres' so he might be recognized (5.640). In his commentary on the *Sentences*, Ockham showed that one could abstract from creatures certain concepts – concepts of wisdom, for example, or of goodness – and compose them into a single concept, 'proprium Deo.' But God would not really be known by this means.[63] Anima is generally clear that he speaks figuratively, that charity is not a person but something to which Christians should conform themselves (15.344). Yet the composite portrait fetches Will: 'By crist! I wolde I knewe hym ... no creature leuere' (15.195). And Anima for the moment speaks of the will itself, really the same as the soul and therefore as the substance. He ceases for a bit, that is, to speak of the acts of the will: 'Wiþouten help of Piers Plowman ... his persone sestow neuere'; 'Piers þe Plowman parceyueþ moor depper / What is þe wille' (15.196, 199–200). The narrator is left 'in a weer what charite is to mene' (16.3) at least partly because Anima's language is marked sometimes by simple, sometimes (more congenially) by personal supposition.

If Piers sees the 'persone' now, has that always been the case? Will, who need not be told that he lacks all Piers's industrious qualities, seeks a 'kynde knowyng' from the beginning. If he seems to doom a quest for Christ by demanding an ocular proof, then it may turn out to be important for Langland that 'notitia intuitiva' included the certain, immediate knowledge of the mind's own acts. 'Intellectiones, affectiones, delectationes, tristitiae et huiusmodi sunt intelligibles et nullo modo sensibiles, et aliqua notitia incomplexa earum sufficit ad notitiam evidentem utrum sint vel non sint ...'[64] Whether Langland achieves a 'kynde knowyng' – in passus 18, for example, or elsewhere in the *Dobest*, where the term 'kynde knowyng' all but disappears[65] – is the question of the rest of this book. But we cannot learn whether he discovers what he needs if we are unclear on the *kind* of question motivating his search.

2

When readers join Lady Holy Church in patronizing Will, they assume that the conventions of literacy were much less problematic for Langland than they may have been. To concur with Holy Church that Will is ignorant ('Thow doted daffe!' 1.140) or with Scripture that he is self-ignorant ('*Multi multa sciunt et seipsos nesciunt*' 11.3) implies that Will's voice must be kept separate from the narrator's and Langland's, just as Lord Jim's voice is not Marlow's or Conrad's.[66] If Will is really self-ignorant, he cannot describe himself as such; hence he is not the narrator or poet. The representation of the author as a character engaged with other characters and marked with deficiencies that separate him from the author is, of course, a convention available within literacy. For those who see *Piers* as the education of such a *naif* and therefore the gradual convergence of dreamer and author, the movement illustrates the 'interlacing of two personalities' made possible by written texts.[67] Yet in fact this is not a convention that Langland appropriates: dreamer cannot be separated from author, and not simply because Langland is unavailable to us except as he is everywhere represented within *Piers*.[68] Langland may decline to take this convention up – or, at least, he takes it up imperfectly – partly because of his ambivalence towards literacy itself.

This ambivalence consists first, perhaps, in his doubts about the abstractions that literacy makes possible. With literacy, Latin grammar becomes a model of models–the ground of everything, in Langland's phrase (15.372). Anselm and others had perceived that 'man's intellectual apparatus was highly influenced by the structure of language.'[69] In a comparable way, 'relacoun rect' (c 3.343) for Langland is a structure no less linguistic than moral. The very idea of structure ('relacoun') depends upon literacy's having made a theme of abstraction: through the review that rereading makes possible, 'things' as events in particular contexts are compared until the reader isolates (in Plato's formula) 'the thing *per se*.'[70] One kind of literary character emerges in this way, as a poet becomes the reader of his own text, revising what he writes, giving to the character the kind of coherence that, in psychoanalytic thought, the process of secondary revision confers upon the ego. Abstraction having created a 'thing' that is nowhere but internal to a human being, it creates as well the difference between internal things and external ones, a difference not yet clear in preliterate culture (for example, in the Homeric words that named both the physical organ and its psychological function).[71] The abstractness that necessarily arises with literacy had already been a theme for centuries by the time Langland wrote, as in the anonymous eleventh-century letter from Speier cited by Brian Stock that separates 'the attitude of repenting' from 'the expiation, which among other things, included confession and satisfaction.'[72] Accordingly, it is natural for Langland that priests can judge only the penitent's 'werkes and wordes,' but that Piers Plowman 'parceyueþ moore depper / What is þe wille and wherfore þat many wight suffreþ' (15.198–200). Even when Langland depreciates literacy in favour of the 'liber conscientiae,' the only book that the primitive hermits needed (15.536), literacy has made the difference between an outer book and an inner one conceivable.

However, literacy creates not only the possibility of an integration of abstractions but also suspicion of the motive behind such a goal and uncertainty about its relevance.[73] Literacy suppresses the parataxis of story in favour of the kind of integration epitomized by a mathematical equation. As Stock notes, a 'consequence of the rise in general levels of literacy was the new appeal of a systematic, reflective theology.'[74] In Langland's frequent expositions of the Trinity – when he describes, for instance, the props of the Tree of Charity (16.23–52) – he draws on systematic theology. Yet systematic theology is the 'contemplacion' that fosters the pride of friars who have gone 'to scole' (20.273–4), the 'Sophistrie' that will colour 'the bileeue' so quaintly that no one will be able to tell Christian speech from heathen (19.346–8). The poet himself uses what has been, since the twelfth century, the chief technique of systematic theology, the Abelardian 'sic et non,' which harmonized contrary views by a 'dialectical hermeneutic.'[75] The character Imaginative, for example, attempts to account for opposite views on the necessity of baptism to salvation (12.280–94). The Samaritan harmonizes the views of Faith and Hope (17.134–298). Nevertheless, as we have seen, Will himself abandons a pair of Franciscans who try to resolve the contradiction between their claim to do well and his objection that even the best person sins seven times daily.

Moreover, as we have also seen, literate culture opened an epistemological space between sensory experience and what Eric Havelock has called the 'non-visualness ... of the sheer idea.'[76] The poet exploits this readily enough – in the distance, for example, between a visible mark made by Christ in the sand and the idea of forgiveness simultaneously held in mind (12.72–7). Interpretive activity bridges the space between the visible manifestation ('sacramentum') and invisible reality. Yet this gap becomes the page on which nominalism writes the unknowability of God. In the absence of a literate culture, the problem of a 'kynde knowyng' of Christ could not have arisen for Will. Even an orthodox opponent of the nominalists, Gregory of Rimini, was ready to grant that, in a person's present state, there is no means open to her or him of immediate knowledge of God. While Will never doubts that the world stands under the judgment of Truth in his tower, his periodic demand for a 'kynde knowyng' seems to express the untimely wish that God might again be part of sensible experience. The narrator represents himself as having 'ay loste and loste' (c 5.95), as one might who had been condemned to try to wring from experience what he could not see that experience would yield.

Finally, it is in relation to eternity, a conception that because of its negativity is first of all linguistic, that literacy itself is brought into question.[77] How will the 'rusticus' fare at the Day of Judgment? Whether he is advantaged or handicapped remains, perhaps, undecided in the poem. Will argues that it is 'well ylettred clerkes' who seldom live as they teach, while no one is sooner saved than 'lewed laborers' (10.403, 478). (Ironically, Recklessness, who speaks these lines in the c text, has made this discovery by reading 'registres and bokes.') Anima declares that faith all by itself suffices 'to saue wiþ lewed peple' (15.389). (He makes this point by quoting a Latin hymn.) If Imaginative pities the person who must get by without literate help (12.186), the poem leaves in doubt the value of such help as the literate priest could give Piers the plowman. Piers offers the only sure example of conversion in the poem. And there is no reason to believe that he has ever learned to read.

An ambivalence in Langland towards the consequences of literacy would not entail a refusal of the kind of characterization that literacy makes possible, but it would certainly be consistent with it. For all his revisions, no one, I think, has ever proposed that he made changes towards the creation of more coherent or realistic characters.[78] Haukyn, for example, one of Langland's more vivid figures, is not coherently composed even in B. How is it that an English wafer-seller provides food for the Pope and his horse? What would he do with a prebend or a parsonage in return? And yet Haukyn is even less realistic or coherent in C. Within the novel, M.M. Bakhtin has pointed out, the reader 'is confronted with several heterogeneous stylistic unities,' among the basic types of them being 'stylization of the various forms of oral everyday narration' and 'various forms of literary but extra-artistic authorial speech (moral, philosophical or scientific statements, oratory, ethnographic descriptions, memoranda and so forth).' No doubt there is heteroglossia in *Piers*: its concerns are filtered through the voices of Cheapside on the one hand, as in the lines closing the Prologue, and, on the other, through Anima's long quotation from Isidore of Seville. Yet it would be hard to show the presence of that basic type of compositional-stylistic unity that Bakhtin calls 'the stylistically individualized speech of characters.'[79] In fact, Will/narrator shares the viewpoints and voices of Lady Holy Church, Conscience, Repentance, Truth, Wit, Dame Study, Clergy, Scripture, Reason, Imaginative, Patience, Haukyn, and Anima, among others.

So far as the narrator is distinct from any other character in the poem, that is because he introduces certain facts into the process of the poem. There is perhaps no reason not to say facts about the poet. Because Langland creates the other figures too, there is nothing strange in their often looking at Langland's society as the narrator himself does. Because Langland does not think of them as so many life-worlds, it does not follow that they fail as characters or that *Piers* becomes incoherent. As we shall see, they simply enter the process of the poem in a different way than the narrator does.

That the narrator occupies many of the same subject-positions as other characters can be readily shown. He objects that 'Iaperes and Iangleres, Iudas children,' make fools of themselves in fantastic entertainments, when they might work productively if they chose (Prol 35–7). Such fools, flatterers, and liars bring a person 'to muche sorwe' (13.426). Wit and Dame Study sound much like him when they deplore wasted speech (9.103–6) and those who pretend they are 'foolis,' spitting, spewing, speaking 'foule wordes,' drivelling, causing people 'to gape' (10.39–42). In a similarly disapproving vein, the narrator warns workmen, 'Wynneþ whil ye mowe' (6.321). While he looks back rather than forwards, Haukyn too thinks that it takes a famine to chasten workmen (13.259, 267). Where Wit and Dame Study blame lords for neglecting the poor (9.92–4,

10.97–103), the narrator thinks that lawyers should plead for the poor without requiring gifts (7.41–60). (Like Conscience [3.252–4], he thinks that wise priests would make no charge for singing mass [11.283–4].) Anima has never seen a beggar who lived in charity (15.227); the narrator denounces at least those beggars who are able-bodied (7.67–9). Like Repentance, who counsels Sloth (for instance) to say to God, 'I am sory for my synne' (5.445), the narrator advises 'alle cristene to crie god mercy' (7.201). He rebukes the avidity of friars for the profitable duty of burying people (11.75–9), where Reason had preached against covetous monks and bishops (4.119–25). Like Scripture (10.346–8), he believes that the poor can lay claim to heaven (10.467–71); and like Imaginative (11.175), he believes that contrition suffices for salvation (11.81). Few people, the narrator allows, 'ben goode' (10.444); and Reason agrees: 'man was maad of swich a matere he may no3t wel asterte / That som tyme hym bitit to folwen his kynde' (11.402–3). Although Patience tries to silence Will's criticism of the gluttonous friar at Conscience's dinner party, Patience and Will finally complain about him in much the same language (13.65–96). The Samaritan will contend that no one is so wretched 'that he ne may louye, and hym like,' all manner of men, wishing them 'mercy and for3ifnesse' (17.351, 353). The narrator himself, however, has already insisted on this: God commands 'ech creature to conformen hym to louye / Hir euencristene as hemself and hir enemyes after' (11.181–2).

Nevertheless, if we mean by 'abstraction' a unified idea abstracted from the text, at certain points the narrator is no doubt as much an abstraction for Langland as other characters sometimes are. The idea of the narrator is neither simple nor, apart from a view of the process of the poem as a whole, intelligible. Reciprocally, of course, how we understand the process depends upon how we understand the narrator. This poet represents himself as having a bad conscience and thus as sometimes doing things that guilty people do. Pre-eminent among these is the search for what might make possible a change in his life, make him able to love. No doubt at points – for example, when he is writing of the poor, most remarkably in the c text (9.72–97) – the poet writes compassionately enough. This, however, like the compassion and otherwise lawful behaviour shown by Saracens or Jews, is irrelevant. It does not matter that Langland at times finds himself instinctively loving. He represents himself as searching for Christ – an experience of being loved perfectly, unconditionally, forever. He looks to encounter love as some final truth about the nature of existence, so that human love is not one response among many possible, but evoked by the character of reality.

Piers can scarcely be thought to bring the narrator to a knowledge of his own sinfulness, since this is something he insists on from the beginning, when he compares himself with a gyrovague, 'vnholy of werkes' (Prol 3). Because the poet represents himself in the poem as uneasy about his extra-regular status and about his disapproval of contemporary bishops and beggars alike (11.86) (an attitude that sets him apart from other Christians), he must intend at least some of the stains on Haukyn's coat to tar him as well:

> inobedient to ben vndernome of any lif lyuynge;
> And so singuler by hymself as to si3te of þe peple
> Was noon swich as hymself, ne noon so pope holy;
> Yhabited as an heremyte, an ordre by hymselue,
> Religion saun3 rule and resonable obedience;
> Lakkynge lettrede men and lewed men boþe.   (13.281–6)

The narrator tells a story in which any sin, unexpectedly, can turn out to be his. '*Esto sobrius!*' Repentance interrupts the confessions of the personified sins to urge him, 'and assoiled *me* after, / And bad *me* wilne to wepe *my* wikkednesse to amende' (5.184–5). Whether Langland actually had a bad conscience is not presently the issue; but he would not represent himself as defensive if he did not also mean to represent himself as guilty: 'I sei3 wel,' he says, that Imaginative is correct in rebuking him, 'and somwhat me to excuse' goes on to cite 'Cato' (12.20). He snaps at Scripture that baptism is enough to save rich men–and perhaps himself as well. Aware as he is of his own shortcomings, he writhes with anguish when Scripture suggests that he is self-ignorant (11.3), then falls into an inner dream where he sees himself as preterite, desperate, and given over to concupiscence, avarice, and 'pride of parfit lyuynge' (11.33). He seems to admit to Imaginative his close acquaintance with shame (11.435–7) and jokes nervously with Anima (15.40). Thus, when this narrator, who depicts himself as 'auctor,' reports that characters within his poem accuse him of delinquency (Imaginative, for instance, reproaches him for criticizing Reason [11.420–4], and Anima taxes him with illicit curiosity [15.45–6]), they are not surprising a certain character called the Dreamer; they repeat what the narrator is ready to say about himself. And hence they do not appear in the poem chiefly to level these rebukes.

His quest for Christ, which becomes one in his poem with his fictional account of his life, troubles him in itself. His search for a renewal of faith ('kenne me kyndely on crist to bileue') aggravates the bad conscience that inspired the search to begin with ('that I myȝte werchen his wille'). To use language to conduct such a quest would arrogate to himself the privilege of clerical discourse; and periodically in the poem, as Anne Middleton has persuasively argued, the narrator reports that his interlocutors contest his right to do this.[80] He gives to Imaginative the clearest objection:

> þow medlest þee wiþ makynges and myȝtest go seye þi sauter,
> And bidde for hem þat ȝyueþ þee breed, for þer are bokes ynowe
> To telle men what dowel is, dobet and dobest boþe ...   (12.16–18)

While he may sometimes represent himself as supercilious and self-congratulatory ('And somme lakkede my lif – allowed it fewe' 15.4) and sometimes so sure that his interlocutors have missed his point that he can permit them to abuse him ('Wel artow wis,' says Study to Wit, 'any wisdomes to telle / To flateres or to fooles þat frenetike ben of wittes' 10.5–6), he thinks it entirely possible that this quest of his, not to mention the long moments of prophetic satire that interrupt it,[81] is marked by 'pryde ... and presumpcion' (11.423). As a vocation but not a recognizable profession, it leaves him hard to distinguish from the voluntary beggars, the 'lollers,' that he reprehends.[82] When it does not go well he holds himself responsible, as if it were within his power to sleep more soundly and see more than he does (5.3–4). 'Allas!' he says to Faith, 'þat synne so longe shal lette / The myght of goddes mercy þat myȝte vs alle amende' (16.270–1).

The bad conscience, even the meanness of spirit, that the narrator imputes to himself (he tells *Spes* that *Spes*'s 'lawe' is hopeless [17.49]) is not *tour de force*. To the contrary, it initiates the quest; it is part of the problematic of the poem. If this quest is, as Middleton suggests, 'repeatedly disrupted and transformed by encounters that humiliate this ambition,'[83] these are not mishaps that befall Will as a character separable from the poet. They mark the narrator's doubt about a course that he cannot finally give up, at the same time that they mark dead ends in it, new beginnings, and always its reason for being. If Will as 'poetic "I"' (in Leo Spitzer's phrase), the rational appetite, the homesick pursuer of '"heart-ravishing" knowledge,'[84] raves with a divine madness (15.10) or swoons when he hears the name of Piers (16.19), the test of what he seeks will be its capacity to move the 'empirical "I,"' the poet as he represents himself in his limitations. Spitzer's well-known essay seems worth quoting at length for the light it sheds on the narrator of *Piers* no less than the narrator of the *Divine Comedy*: 'How,' Spitzer asks, 'could the medieval public have accepted as genuine the supposedly eye-witness report ... on the supermundane world, unless the "poetic I" of Dante represented, for this medieval community, the human soul as such with all its capacity to attain to the Beyond and to reach out of space toward its Creator?' The 'empirical "I,"' the historical Dante, is also included in this 'poetic "I"' by necessity:

on the one hand, he must transcend the limitations of individuality in order to gain an experience of universal experience; on the other, an individual eye is necessary to perceive and to fix the matter of experience ... This personality which Dante, the beholder, the experiencer, retains, is in direct correspondence with the personal character of divinity: according to Augustine, it is the personality of God which determines the personal soul of man: only through God's personality has man a personal soul – whose characteristic is its God-seeking quality. Thus Dante in his report of his quest performs artistically the basic endeavour of the Christian: to seek a personal relationship with divinity ...

Thus Dante must take care to establish his own personality in the *Commedia*: his own figure cannot be less graphically portrayed than are the vigorous shades of Ugolino or Cato or Saint Bernard. It is only for this reason that we find ... the insertion of autobiographical material ... Dante is not interested, poetically, in himself *qua* himself ... but *qua* an example of the generally human capacity for cognizing the supramundane – which can be cognized only by what is most personal in man. It is only when the quest for the supramundane can no longer be taken for granted as uniting author and public, that an insistence on the individual 'I' becomes quite simply a matter of the 'empirical I' ...[85]

The 'poetic "I"' in *Piers* both allegorizes an appetitive power (Will the 'voluntas')[86] satiable by nothing short of a certain kind of mental object, and, more broadly, represents all human beings so far as they are moved by this 'God-seeking quality.' Will's interlocutors demonstrate the inability of such powers as Wit and Reason to satisfy 'wille' in this sense. Nevertheless, these are all rooted within Will the 'empirical "I,"' the persona assimilated to the implied author, such self-knowledge as he can proceed with; for they are all points of view taken by a living, limited person.

Unless we are ready to grant, within the economy of the poem, the importance of the narrator's demand for a 'kynde knowyng' of Christ – a demand made not less but more compelling by the narrator's representation of his own sometimes desperate and shabby behaviour – we shall be hard pressed to understand the process, the movement, of the poem. At one point, Dame Study heaps contempt upon lords who debate the justness of original sin by way of an after-dinner entertainment (10.104–18). The narrator, too, raises the question of the justness of God and is rebuked by Reason for doing so (11.374–9). Yet from the beginning he represents himself as incurring a great many inconveniences by his raising of such questions (rebukes of his presumptuousness not least among them), with the consequence that he establishes his own earnestness. There is no possibility of finally distinguishing a poet who is in earnest from a Dreamer who is not. Because he is in earnest, even his jokes have a context. He passes on unsatisfied through Thought, Wit, Clergy, and others. If this journey is only Will's, 'an Everyman figure who receives Langland's teaching on behalf of the audience,'[87] we would be left not simply with the problem of his inseparability from Langland, as we have seen, but with the scandalously non-cumulative, unsynthesizable character of this 'teaching.' Moreover, if Thought, Wit, and the others give Will what he should have rather than the 'theoretical' knowledge he wants, they must nevertheless in some important sense personify capacities of his own mind. Whatever theoretical knowledge is, in other words, they are likely his powers of acquiring it. And if he seeks theoretical knowledge, it would appear to be unintelligible that he should be at odds with them.

Once we grant the importance for the narrator of a 'kynde knowyng' of Christ, the movement of the poem can be understood. Should a 'kynde knowyng' be one *kind* of knowledge, then an important problem in relation to Thought and the other interlocutors is dissolved; for just as Boethius urges that everything is known 'nat aftir his strengthe and his nature, but aftir the faculte ... of hem that knowen' and distinguishes such ways as 'wit,' 'ymaginacioun,' 'resoun,' and 'intelligence,'[88] so the narrator may find himself at odds with Thought, Wit, and the others not because they are not his own capacities but because they give him no 'kynde knowyng' of Christ.[89] The Boethian convention of the erring but corrigible dreamer, of which *Pearl* offers the most familiar Middle English example, may be distorted in *Piers* for one purpose, just as, for another (the recovery of the Man in Black), Chaucer distorts it in *The Book of the Duchess*. In *Piers*, the 'spiritual teachers' may be put to the test of a problem more basic than ethics. When Clergy, for instance, is telling Will of the threat to 'Monkes and Chanons' from a king who will violently return them to their original purposes ('*ad pristinum statum*'), the narrator responds with a question that is not naïve: 'Thanne is dowel and dobet ... *dominus* and knyȝthode?' (10.336). However deeply the poet (who has written the speech of Clergy, after all) may regret the worldliness of contemporary monks, or however brightly this speech illuminates 'clergye,' it finally does not inscribe the object of the narrator's quest; and the narrator redirects events by taking Clergy *au pied de la lettre*. When Scripture then responds, 'I nel noȝt scorne,' she is contrasting herself with the narrator. This reply does not mean that the narrator's scorn does not spring from the most fundamental motive of the poem. The narrator faces his interlocutors ambivalently. They do not give him what he needs; hence he resists them. Perhaps none of them is negligible in itself, however; many point up his lack of moral authority. Hence, he is guilty – sometimes guiltily defensive before them – and his need for what they do not provide is intensified the more.

3

Narrators, like a 'discipulus' in one of Anselm's dialogues, can elicit an orderly course of instruction. There is no reason *a priori* why Will's request, 'Kenne me kyndely on crist to bileue' (1.81), could not have worked throughout *Piers Plowman* much like Conscience's request to Clergy ('Now þow, ... carpe what is dowel' 13.119), soliciting from one 'magister' after another parcels of instruction that Langland had planned to unpack. Because the May morning and the pregnant sleep signal a 'chanson d'avanture,' readers expect a dreamer whose wonderful visions they will be left, at their leisure, to total up.[90] In fact, if Langland began with chiefly didactic intentions, then he hardly succeeded. Maureen Quilligan points to 'vast formless stretches of verse.' John Norton-Smith describes a 'scientific disorganization' in the third vision, calls passus 15 a 'quagmire,' and concludes that 'the poem, however closely and skilfully annotated and explicated, seems to lack a convincing controlling *idée*.' Hugh White has lately understated the same point: 'I take Langland to be a poet not securely in control of his material.'[91] Readers adjust their expectations: the narrator undergoes revelations that can scarcely be summed up.

Besides this extreme difficulty when we try to synthesize what Will hears and sees, there are good reasons for revising any notion that the genesis of the poem is didactic. First, by the end of his poem the narrator's life is still oblique to the Law:

'Counseille me, kynde,' quod I, 'what craft is best to lerne?'
'Lerne to loue,' quod kynde, 'and leef alle opere.'
'How shal I come to catel so to clope me and to feede?' (20.207–9)

Such solicitude about clothing and food is not what Scripture, Patience, or Anima taught. Conscience, who must in some way be the narrator's conscience, will close the poem by crying for grace, as if he is still bad conscience. The poem cannot exist chiefly to instruct when it ends with the absorbing point that instruction has not been efficacious, and thus with the question of what, finally, might suffice.

Second, because the poet represents himself as conducting a search at a considerable cost ('Wolleward and weetshoed wente I forþ after / As a recchelees renk þat reccheþ of no wo' 18.1–2), it would not be perverse to read with the assumption that Langland writes less to teach than to find out. The request of his that goes by Holy Church, as it eludes other interlocutors who also supply ethical answers to an ontological question, is the motor of the poem. While Elizabeth Salter argued for the 'compilatio' genre as important to *Piers*, where she saw Langland manipulating and rearranging 'large quantities of traditional material ... with an eye to their accessibility to varied classes of readers,' she nevertheless insisted on Langland's 'ultimate undervaluing of anything except the search for the heart of the matter.'[92] My claim is that 'the heart of the matter' will escape us if we assume that only a modern writer, not a medieval one like 'longe wille,' could find it difficult to believe in Christ.

This 'search for the heart of the matter' determines the form of the poem. In practice, it is more usual to speak, not of the form, but of the forms of *Piers* – stages in the poet's process of revision or genres suggested by parts of the poem. Some, perhaps even most or all, of *Piers* might be distributed among the six genres adduced by Morton Bloomfield: the allegorical religious romance (recalling the *Romans de carité* or Grosseteste's *Chasteau d'amour*), the 'consolatio' debate, the encyclopaedic satire, the complaint, and so on.[93] And yet, having named these and others, we might be no more satisfied than if we had described the form of Joyce's *Ulysses* by calling the 'Nausicaa' and 'Penelope' episodes romance and confession. There are clearly marked sections: the manuscripts strongly attest a division into a *Visio*, *Vita de dowel*,

Vita de dobet, and *Vita de dobest*.[94] These subdivide into dreams, ten altogether in the B-text, nine in the C.[95] The question of the relationship of these parts poses the question of the form of the whole poem. While some critics answer it by specifying the conceptual relations among the four sections,[96] the late Northrop Frye treated it boldly by calling *Piers* 'the first major English treatment of the contrast-epic,' an epic framework 'where one pole is the ironic human situation and the other the origin or continuation of a divine society.'[97]

The inadequacy of this suggestion, however, becomes clear from Frye's own discussion of literary form, basic to which is Aristotle's distinction between 'mythos' and 'dianoia.' 'Mythos' denotes plot and narrative, 'dianoia' the idea or theme. 'The word "narrative" or *mythos* conveys the sense of movement caught by the ear, and the word "meaning" or *dianoia* conveys, or at least preserves, the sense of simultaneity caught by the eye. We *listen* to the poem as it moves from beginning to end, but as soon as the whole of it is in our minds at once we "see" what it means ... The *mythos* is the *dianoia* in movement; the *dianoia* is the *mythos* in stasis.'[98] After two decades and more of deconstructive criticism (Jacques Derrida's of Rousseau, for example, or Pierre Macherey's of Jules Verne), it is difficult for us to think of a literary work as ever controlled by the author as a unified whole – a whole that unfolds without rupture. It is also difficult to believe that such a unifying intention could be communicated so that a reader might repeat it. No doubt, written under erasure, so to speak, 'contrast-epic' describes some of the striking polarities of *Piers Plowman* – the hill and the field, Holy Church and Meed, Piers and the wasters, the Tree of Charity and the pillaging devil, the Harrowing of Hell and the fall of Unity, Will as ironic questioner and Will as a seedy layabout. But in certain respects Langland apparently has the project of mediating these.[99] And in any case 'contrast-epic' does not begin to describe the linear movement. For the narrator is a searcher; his quest – cumulative and self-correcting – is governed by the nature of the question he begins with, although quest-as-plot surely does not subdue the text. So far as Langland does control it, he keeps recentring it, imitating the act of the mind attempting to find what will suffice, discarding with sad and guilty jokes what will not do.[100] 'Contrast-epic' does not say enough about the structure of the poem even in any provisional simultaneity.

The poet himself makes free enough with 'dowel,' 'dobet,' and 'dobest'[101] for us to rule out the narrow notion that the *Vitae* move up three steps. I propose first that the four separate starts signalled by the rubrics (the *Visio* and each of the *Vitae*) in fact correspond to movements in the poem, but that these are not progressive. Each takes to its conclusion the sort of thinking present in its starting point. Second, these end points constellate in a manner that, when the last one is in place, constitutes a solution to Will's problem. For this conception of the 'dianoia,' however, an optical metaphor seems more useful than a grammatical one.[102] The *Visio* ends with an event, but it is not understood; in this it is like something too small for the naked eye. *Dowel* and *Dobet* grind two lenses, and when at the end of *Dobest* they have been ground and placed over each other and over the fact of the *Visio*, that fact becomes visible in *Dobest*. At the end of *Dobest* the image is as sharp in its own way as the cry of Conscience. In chapter 5, I attempt to make good such a description of the poem's form.

The following chapters proceed from the assumption, then, that the dynamic of the poem arises with a problem of belief and that the perspective and material shift as the poem turns from one mode of knowledge to another. The difficulty we have in situating *Piers* within one genre or another is no evidence that the narrator does not begin with a search that he continually resumes. To the contrary, this difficulty may be a sign of the nature of the search. As James Druff has remarked, the formal experiments 'that so often announce significant generic change ... are usually directly concerned to locate themselves within a tradition whose terms the authors confront as epistemological ones.'[103] The next four chapters each have two general features. First, because the vernacular does not supply the poet with a stock of unambiguous psychological terms[104] and the poet's milieu furnishes the critic with no single, received psychology, one must see what Langland means by the numerous psychological terms dotting the poem – many of them, indeed, personified as such principal characters as Conscience. A good personification is a persona, and, accordingly, I suppose initially that there is a bias in its speeches and actions. If this proves to be so, I use it with other evidence in trying to find out what the character means. Second, in interpreting the episodes where each of the terms, whether personified or not, seems important, I see how far an emphasis on the problematics of belief adheres to the complexities of these episodes. The chapters are arranged so that the episodes they chiefly deal with occur in their sequence in the poem.

Piers and his 'pardon' do not, it seems evident to me as to some others, provide the reader with clear concepts exploitable in lighting up the dark places. Rather, these puzzling symbols lie close to the heart of the blooming, buzzing confusion of the poem. It is the rest of the poem that must illuminate them, and not the other way around. Accordingly, in my last chapter, I assume the truth of my conclusions to that point and bring them to bear on the two famous cruxes – which I earlier try to leave alone. There, too, in relation to Piers and the 'pardon,' I shall discuss briefly the action of the rest of the *Visio*.

In the thick, strident, disorderly world of the *Visio*, Reason is soon invoked as the most promising candidate for setting matters right. We may thus begin with him.

2

Mentality in the *Visio*:
The Burden of the Law and
the Limits of Reason

More than sixty years ago, remarking that 'The chief problem in the Story of Lady Meed is man's well-being in this world' and that the 'chief problem debated in the *Vita de Do-well* is man's eternal well-being,' H.W. Wells saw Reason as central in each case to a solution.[1] The character who counsels the king on handling Meed and who, at the beginning of Will's second dream, moves the kingdom to repentance with a sermon has been generally understood simply to allegorize what T.P. Dunning called 'the intellect ... directed towards the moral aspects of action.'[2] However that definition of 'reson' might serve for the A text (to which, of course, Dunning was directing his attention), it will not do for the later versions, where, from the vantage of Middle Earth, for example, Will grieves to find 'That Reson rewarded and ruled alle beestes / Saue man and his make' (11.370–1). Brute creation may naturally obey divine precept, but not through intellect; and 'reson' must therefore mean something else.[3]

Before concluding that the poet has left us 'not sure of Reason's inherent value,'[4] we might see if we can perceive family resemblances from one use of 'reson' to another. Although these so vary that certainly no single definition from a *De anima* could cover all of them, the plot of the *Visio* depends heavily upon Reason's being given a free hand. This would not likely have been the case if the poet lacked a coherent sense of 'reson.' Rather, the *Visio* tests the relevance of such a notion to the narrator's abiding question, 'But tel me þis ilke, / How I may saue my soule' (1.83–4); and while 'reson' may prove futile, that is not the same as saying that the poet's notion has become incoherent.

The mentality named by 'reson' has as a sort of ground-colour a preoccupation with causality. Laid over this are such variants as physical causation or the apprehension of that; divine precept as a partial cause of human rectitude; justice as something thus determined, and as affecting in turn positive law; and equity ('mesure') as the form of these. Because the narrator wants to know Christ, 'reson' understood in this way fails, as we shall see. It proves unsatisfactory because it apprehends something verbal, a conception or a precept, which, nevertheless, expounded with sufficient power, may influence anyone to behave lawfully. However, the corpus of Christian precepts can exist independently of the person of Christ – for example, in the 'magisterium' of the Church. Precisely the detachability of this is satirized in the 'doctour' who one moment stuffs himself with pudding and the next teaches that one should do 'noon yuel to þyn euencristen' (13.105). Moreover, since the object of 'reson' is pre-eminently moral in import, it implies rewards and punishments; but the hope it motivates does not flow from faith that morality has any meaning beyond itself.

As a power, pervasively and fundamentally in *Piers*, 'reson' knows the relationship between cause and effect, a relationship that the word 'reson' connotes. This is not quite the same as naming the cause itself, as when Chaucer, translating Boethius, calls 'purveaunce' 'thilke devyne resoun that is establissed in the sovereyn prince of thinges.'[5] As distinct from this sense, in the Canon's Yeoman's Tale, when the silver 'lemaille' falls out of the rigged coal after the wax plug melts, the narrator says that 'it moste nedes, by resoun, / Syn it so evene above couched was.'[6] Here 'resoun' names not the cause (the coal's being poised above the crucible) but the *relation* between that and the descent of the filings.

In *Piers*, evidently just once does 'reson' mean a cause, and the c text will revise the line in a manner that changes the signification: Christ will recover Adam and all his issue 'þoruȝ raunsoun and by no reson ellis' (18.352). By contrast, one reveres a rich man, Anima remarks, 'by reson of his richesse' (14.207). Here 'reson' is something predicable *of* riches and not the riches themselves, even as cause; 'reson' here signifies an attribute of the riches – their capacity to produce certain effects, such as the appearance of flatterers – rather than denotes them. It connotes the cause only because of its causing. 'Reson ... sheweþ,' says Langland's Samaritan, that, having been hurt in the palm of the hand, one cannot grip anything (17.187–8). Here Reason knows not so much one phenomenon or the other as the non-reversible relationship between the two.[7]

Within the field of causal relations known to Reason, more interesting links appear, however, than those binding one material phenomenon to another. 'The sense in which saying something produces effects on other persons, or causes things, is a fundamentally different sense of cause from that used in physical causation by pressure, &c.,' J.L. Austin has remarked. 'It has to operate through the conventions of language and is a matter of influence exerted by one person on another: this is probably the original sense of "cause."'[8] The causative power of language underlies one of the most puzzling appearances of 'reson' in the poem, one that introduces in effect the conception of 'rectitudo' developed by Anselm more than three centuries earlier and that opens the way to understanding the place of Reason within Will's quest. In the 1350s, interest revived at Oxford in at least some of Anselm's theological writings.[9]

In passus 11, Will is lifted to a mountaintop to survey the earth and learn through examples – 'Thorugh ech a creature kynde' – to love his creator. Lacking a rational appetite (having been made so that their happiness, unlike humanity's, rests entirely in the useful), the teeming creatures Will sees cannot help but do what they ought. In this sense 'reson' characterizes their habits 'In etynge, in drynkynge and in engendrynge of kynde' (11.336).[10] Like fire, which 'does rightness' ('facere ... rectitudinem')[11] when it does what it ought ('debet'), the birds who skilfully make nests and hide their eggs and the stallions and dogs who keep apart from their mate once she is pregnant act this way out of necessity ('necessariam'). They do what they ought in the sense that 'they are what they are in the highest truth.'[12] Out of necessity, the animals remain faithful to their essence, conform themselves to their idea in God.[13] This notion of rightness from the beginning of scholasticism reappears in Thomas Aquinas: 'res naturales dicuntur esse verae, secundum quod assequuntur similitudinem specierum quae sunt in mente divina.'[14] 'Truth of thing' is caused by the First Being, just as the 'truth of intellect' is caused by the First Truth.[15]

Desire for the useful inheres in human beings as in birds and horses, but humans also have the ability to choose; and happiness for them is free choice, free as long as it is right. Imelda Choquette, drawing upon Anselm's *De voluntate*, writes: 'There are two principal affections of the will: the affection of willing the useful, *commodum*, and the affection of willing justice. The affection for the useful is always and inseparably present in the instrument; the affection of justice is not always thus present ...'[16] Because God has created all things capable of attaining their end, the affection for the useful in brutes adheres to the divine plan by instinct. In human beings, however, justice, or the rectitude of the will, which a person chooses or not, mediates between the ultimate rule of the divine plan and a person's own affection for the useful. Aware of his sins, Will grows angry because only humanity has been permitted to lose this rightness; it is only humanity that 'Reson' no longer rules:

Ac þat moost meued me and my mood chaunged,
That Reson rewarded and ruled alle beestes
Saue man and his make; many tyme me þouʒte
No Reson hem ruled, neiþer riche ne pouere.
Thanne I rebukede Reson and riʒt til hym I seyde,
'I haue wonder in my wit, þat witty art holden,
Why þow ne sewest man and his make þat no mysfeet hem folwe.' (11.369–75)

The rightness of a thing consists in the conformity of the direction of its specific activity with the mind of God, 'whose infinite and self-subsisting truth is the norm and measure of all things.'[17] 'Reson' as that rightness is a metonym as well for the idea, or 'ratio,' thought to exist in the divine mind, inflecting human rightness.[18] 'Reson' thus seems very close to what another Catholic poet, Hopkins, called 'inscape.'

Each mortal thing does one thing and the same;
    Deals out that being indoors each one dwells,
    Selves – goes itself; *myself* it speaks and spells,
Crying *What I do is me: for that I came.*[19]

As the rightness, the inscape, of a thing instresses itself upon people, by an act of love they may move to their own right inscape. Intuition of inscape opens them to grace, Hopkins thought.

Rightness – the effect that Reason in *Piers* can grasp in its determinateness and that humanity has been permitted to lose – consists, morally speaking, in the truth of opinion and the truth of the will. In *De veritate* Anselm claims: 'nothing is more properly called the truth of thought than its rightness. For the power has been given us to think that something is or is not, to the end that we think that that which is, is, and that that which is not, is not. Wherefore, whoever thinks that that which is, is, thinks as he should, and consequently the thought is right.' This is 'de opinionis veritas.' There is also truth of the will, 'nothing except rightness,' 'to wish' what one 'should.'[20] This 'rectitudo voluntatis' receives the name 'iustitia' when one wills to preserve it because of itself: 'Quod vero addidimus "propter se," ita necessarium est, ut nullo modo eadem rectitudo nisi propter se servata iustitia sit.'[21] Parallel to the specific act of a bird – weaving twigs together, for instance – choosing to will justly for the sake of justice is the specific rightness of man: 'the just man justices,' in Hopkins' phrase. That Reason does not 'follow' people points to a failure in action. Where the divine will is a sufficient cause for the rightness of brute creation, for people, in whom right action depends in any case upon truth in knowledge, the divine will is only a necessary cause for justice. Not simply by instinct does the just person act 'in God's eye what in God's eye he is.' 'Reson' in *Piers*, then, knows the various kinds of causality holding between 'Truþe' (as God is called in *Piers* when he is known as the source of rightness) and human action.[22]

This rightness of will and the rightness of opinion on which it relies make up 'right reason,'[23] that coalescence of judgment and good will that, in Christian humanism, is the form taken by the Stoic notion of 'recta ratio.' In the human mind, this coalescence is contingent: a thing known rightly can be desired or not in the way it ought to be. In the mind of God, however, reason and desire are one: he wills what he knows to be good. Despite a logical difference, 'objects of will fall under intellect, and objects of intellect can fall under will.'[24]

'Riȝt' and 'reson' coincide in *Piers* with a frequency that probably cannot be explained simply by the existence of an alliterative formula.[25] Although such a fact must be regarded diffidently, very few instances disappear between the B text and the C; in fact more than a third occur in C for the first time. Examples of the combination include Conscience's caution that receiving payment before one earns it is 'nother resoun ne ryhte.'[26] and that only those who act 'wiþ right and wiþ reson' (3.239) will dwell with the Lord. *Spes* tells of his commission to rule all kingdoms 'in riȝhte and in resoun' (C 19.3), Lucifer claims the souls of the damned 'by right and in reison' (B 18.278), and so on. The conjunction may be a hendiadys for right reason, in the sense just considered. More likely, 'riȝt' being cognate with 'rectitudo'[27] and 'reson' meaning rectitude in *Piers*, 'reson' draws 'riȝt' into a formula replenished with significance because each now designates indifferently both rightness of will and that knowledge of the unified idea and will in God that causes – in the sense of placing under obligation – human volition.[28]

Further, 'riȝt' signifies straightness, metaphoric for 'reson' because thereunder always lies the notion of causality. The flow from cause to effect appears as an unarguable straightness, asking only that anything relevant to it fall into line. It resembles the plumbline signifying in the prophecy of Amos the judgment coming upon Israel. Rectitude ('reson' or 'riȝt') is merely causality as that is known (by 'reson') to operate in moral matters. Unlike the 'straightness of a rod,' which Anselm put to one side,[29] 'riȝt' is only metaphorically straight; for rather than by material continuity, the terms – the cause and the effect – of rectitude are connected as speaker and hearer. In Austin's words, this causality 'has to operate through the conventions of language ...' The cause is ultimately a precept, communicated by the Church. Hence the bond between 'ratio' and 'oratio' (and in Middle English between 'reson' and speech)[30] is not lost. The precept may also be written, as when Imaginative, despite the bias of his own mode of knowledge, refers to rectitude: 'riȝt as siȝt serueþ a man to se þe heiȝe strete, / Riȝt so lereþ lettrure lewed men to Reson' (12.102–3). 'Lettrure' – or the light shining through it, God's love – teaches the rightness to which human beings must conform, a unity construed as the continuity of nature and grace ('þe heiȝe strete').

   Having considered this moral overlay to the ground notion of causality, we may consider Reason's role in the *Visio*; for not only is his mode of knowing nowhere clearer than when he speaks for himself, as he does there, but also his way is crucial in the *Visio* narrative, an influence that cannot be fully appreciated until Piers and his 'pardon' are finally taken up. Reason's first opportunity to speak comes in passus 4, when the king raises him to the bench to help adjudicate the matter of Lady Meed. This crops up sordidly in allegations made by a small freeholder against some purveyors. Caught at crimes ranging from rape to the restraint of trade, Wrong attempts to divert any penalty from his person to his purse by making it worthwhile for Peace to drop the charges. The king will not forgive Wrong so easily, however, fearing his greater insolence in the future. 'But Reson haue ruþe on hym,' says the king, Wrong 'shal reste in þe stokkes / As longe as I lyue, but lowenesse hym borwe' (4.108–9). Where Piers, later in the *Visio*, will feel for a moment the dilemma of trying to exact justice from his 'blody breþeren,' the well-intentioned king insists upon reform and turns to Reason. And 'reson,' rectification, excludes any possibility of an arrangement between the unrighteous:

'Reed me noȝt,' quod Reson, 'no ruþe to haue
Til lordes and ladies louen alle truþe
And haten al harlotrie to heren or to mouþen it;
Til pernelles purfill be put in hire hucche,
And childrene cherissynge be chastised wiþ yerdes,

And harlottes holynesse be holden for an heþyng;
Til clerkene coueitise be to cloþe þe pouere and fede,
And Religiouse Romeris *Recordare* in hir cloistres
As Seynt Benyt hem bad, Bernard and Fraunceis;
And til prechours prechynge be preued on hemselue;
Til þe kynges counseil be þe commune profit;
Til Bisshopes Bayardes ben beggeris Chaumbres,
Hire haukes and hire houndes help to pouere Religious;
And til Seint Iames be souȝt þere I shal assigne,
That no man go to Galis but if he go for euere;
And alle Rome renneres for Robberes of biyonde,
Bere no siluer ouer see þat signe of kyng sheweþ,
Neiþer grotes ne gold ygraue wiþ kynges coyn
Vp forfeture of þat fee, who fynt hym at Douere ...'   (4.113–31)

If he were king, says Reason, no wrong would go unpunished, and
he would 'for no Mede haue mercy but mekenesse it made.' Everywhere in *Piers*, Reason knows the relationship between an antecedent
utterance (or idea or thing) and its consequence. Therefore, to know
lords and ladies as the divine idea would determine them is to know
the kind of behaviour this idea implies.[31] Being a lord or a lady implies an obligation to love the truth. When people deviate from the
order in which the single divine rightness determines them, then a
divine precept obligates others to hate this deviation:

Sholde neuere wrong in þis world þat I wite myȝte
Ben vnpunysshed at my power for peril of my soule,
Ne gete my grace þoruȝ giftes, so me god helpe!
Ne for no Mede haue mercy but mekenesse it made.   (4.139–42)

Thus Reason perceives the relationship between harlotry and odi-
ousness; he knows that whoredom implies being stripped of one's
furs and having one's piety detested as impudence. Knowing the
idea of a child entails loving him or her with discipline. The right
idea of a priest entails solicitude for the poor, that of a monk entails
claustration. Even for a coin to be stamped with the king's likeness
entails a species of behaviour: the coin is to stay in England.

Once 'reson' is understood as the power to make out causation
generally and, specifically, to see the relationship running between
the divine rightness and the rightnesses of created things that it

would stabilize, then much of the difficulty disappears from the sometimes disparaged grammatical metaphor by which Conscience in the c text divides 'mede' from 'mercede.'[32] Meed offers something for nothing and attracts the greedy; 'mercede' promises only an exchange of value, 'a permutacion apertly, a penyworþ for anoþer' (3.258). 'Mercede,' therefore, is always deduced – for example, from labour already performed. As a power of the soul, Conscience subtends 'reson'[33] and argues for 'mercede' because he does so.[34] That is, as a power of the soul Conscience subtends as a major premise the just relationship between work (of a certain magnitude) and payment (of a certain magnitude). From an instance of work, therefore, Conscience (as the power of the mind that makes such moral deductions) infers the rightness of the sequent reward. However, if Conscience meant simply to distinguish fair reward from theft or bribery, then the passage would seem to be cluttered with irrelevances to the 'mede-mercede' issue:

> thow the kyng of his cortesye, cayser or pope,
> ȝeue lond or lordschipe oþer large ȝeftes
> To here lele and to lege, loue ys the cause ...   (c 3.314–16)

[A person] acordeth with Crist in kynde, *Verbum caro factum est*;
In case, *Credere in ecclesia*, in holy kyrke to bileue;
In nombre, rotye and aryse and remissioun to haue,
Of oure sory synnes to be assoiled and yclansed ...   (c 3.355–8)

> Ac relacoun rect is a ryhtful custume,
> As a kyng to clayme the comune at his wille
> To folowe and to fynde hym and fecche at hem his consayl
> That here loue to his lawe thorw al þe lond acorde.
> So comune claymeth of a kyng thre kyne thynges,
> Lawe, loue and lewete, and hym lord antecedent,
> Bothe heued and here kyng, haldyng with no parteyȝe
> Bote standynge as a stake þat stikede in a mere
> Bytwene two lordes for a trewe marke.   (c 3.373–81)

> þat lordes loue that for oure loue deyede
> And coueytede oure kynde and be kald in oure name,
>   *Deus homo*,
> And nyme hym into oure noumbre now and eueremore.   (c 3.401–2)

By 'relacoun rect'[35] he means both rectitude and a grammatical metaphor for rectitude. Grammar, the vehicle of the metaphor, shares the abstractness of rectitude. More importantly, so far as a relative pronoun repeats the number and gender of its antecedent, it unites with its antecedent; analogously, the rightness of the human mind – the rectitude of intellect and will[36] – unites with the divine rightness. As the relative is inflected subsequently to its antecedent, so human rightness depends upon the divine 'ratio.'

This interpretation can be tested against some of the intricacies of the passage. Conscience has explained 'mede' and 'mercede' 'as two maner relacions,'

Rect and indirect, reninde bothe
On a sad and a siker semblable to hemsuluen,
As adiectif and sustantif vnite asken
And acordaunce in kynde, in case and in nombre,
And ayther is otheres helpe – of hem cometh retribucoun,
And that þe gyft þat god gyueth to alle lele lyuynge ...   (c 3.332–8)

'Relacion rect and indirect aftur, / Thenne adiectyf and sustantyf' are two different relationships. The first involves nouns and relative pronouns that may be either definite or indefinite ('certeyn' or 'vncerteyn').[37] The distinction is clear in Latin, with its indefinite relatives 'quicumque' and 'quisquis'; for example, the poet elsewhere quotes, 'Quodcumque petieritis in nomine meo, dabitur enim vobis' (c 7.260a). The poet, then, braids several metaphors, of which the differences in detail emphasize their singleness of tenor. Although a distinction between the 'qualities' of relative pronouns is the figure controlling the others, the explicit simile of 'adiectif and sustantif' supports it. Declined in number, gender, and case, relatives of course do not necessarily agree with their antecedents in the latter; agreement between adjective and noun includes all three. But the tenor of the metaphor of accordance is neither two nor three specific points of Christian belief or behaviour, but rather 'reson,' on which Conscience finally and specifically bases his disapproval of Meed.[38] Only briefly, near the end of the long metaphor, will Conscience move beyond 'reson' by speaking of him who 'for oure loue deyede / And coueytede oure kynde and be kald in oure name' (c 3.400–1). In that passage, God will commit himself to *our* 'noumbre.' But this inversion of the metaphor, like the Incarnation, follows from all the failed attempts at human justice that only Reason can perceive. Justice, then, or 'reson' in its metonymic sense of rectitude,[39] is the tenor of all the metaphors. Justice condemns meed; it allows a king, the immediate source of justice, to give large gifts to loyal men and withdraw them again from evil ones. It requires persons to subordinate themselves to Holy Church and the son who wishes his father's wealth to honour his father by also taking his name;[40] and it obligates a king to give his people love and guidance and them to support him in turn.

'Reson' in its metonymic sense of rectitude underlies the comparable passage in the B text as well. The reward of those whose conduct is stabilized by the divine idea of them is lawful. Limitless reward ('mede mesurelees' 3.246) can be either lawful or unlawful. The only lawful reward that is limitless is the boundless enjoyment of heaven by the righteous: 'Lord, who shal wonye in þi wones' (3.235). Meed is unlawful, not because it is unending (because then the unending enjoyment of heaven would be unlawful too), but because the action it is meant to prompt or that occasions it is conduct inconsistent with the divine idea of the recipient. When 'maistres' maintain 'mysdoers,' the former depart from the divine idea of them and of their office (3.246–7). The maintenance thus consists of unlawful meed. The divine idea of a priest excludes his taking money for singing masses (3.253). In the B text, limited reward ('mesurable hire' 3.256), meaning a lawful payment calibrated in some way to the behaviour it supports, occupies only a minor place.

While in the C text there is still a distinction between a lawful and an unlawful meed, the notion of limitlessness seems to have suggested the idea of pronouns that are 'infinita' or 'vncertyn' to Langland. The 'relacoynes indirect' (C 3.387) involving indefinite pronouns can figure either meed or 'mercede': 'Thus is mede and mercede as two maner relacions, / Rect and indirect ' (C 3.332–3).[41] Because limitlessness in C is restricted in its meaning to a failure of rectitude or justice (that is, a failure to allow the divine idea to be determining), the difference between the meed given by a human sovereign, which necessarily is not unlimited, and the endless enjoyment that makes up the meed of God is not mentioned in C, although C refers both to the large gifts given by kings (3.325) and the 'gret ioye' that God gives to all just people (3.338–9).

In C, limitedness, by contrast, follows first of all from the limits imposed by the divine idea of us, the 'fundement' of our strength

(3.343, 344), the knowledge and choice of which are the 'treuthe' that we need to record in our conduct and the rectitude ('ryhte') that gave Solomon his strength (3.323–4). Analogously, it is the limits imposed by other sources of wealth, whether fathers or kings. Limitlessness means the rejection of these limits and hence the eventual loss of fruition (a loss that may or may not be unlimited). The elaboration in c of the 'mede' and 'measurable hire' found in B does not emerge from some failure of these categories to include all varieties of gifts and payments. The elaboration arises as a kind of meditation on what it would mean for 'Reson' to 'regne' (B 3.285). 'Reson' is otherwise unmentioned in the B passage. As the power, however, to make out the relationship running between the divine rightness and the rightnesses of things, and as that relationship itself, it is the idea that in c organizes the domain of reward.

'Reson' as 'rectitudo voluntatis' – 'justice' – presupposes equity, an inference about the rightness of any specific act. Defined by Aquinas as a habit for rendering persons their due,[42] one sense of the motif 'Redde quod debes,' justice is the doing well set by the Law as the price of eternal life. It is, like grammatical agreement, both a unity and an exchange. As justice or rectitude, the human 'semblable' (c 3.334) of the divine rightness, 'relacion rect' is single and entire; but as the equity that constitutes justice it is as much an exchange as the interdependence of adjective and noun (for God may receive praise as a noun may receive qualification). Thus, 'ayther is otheres helpe' (c 3.337).

'Reson' grasps not only the idea of oneself as determined by the divine 'ratio' but the idea of other people as similarly determined. Traditionally unique among the virtues in being desired for its own sake, justice – 'reson' as the perception of causality in the moral domain and, metonymically, the rectitude of the will – differs from the other virtues also in having as its object not oneself but one's relation with others. The poet links 'reson' with proportion and measurement because 'reson' grasps the necessary relationship binding the known terms of a proportion (others as God thinks of them)[43] with the term (the specific act of will) yet to be determined. Like 'mercede,' then, this term is deduced.

Thus, Reason brings to the narrator's quest the power of discerning equity. For instance, frequently in *Piers* there are precepts about eating, drinking, and so on 'in reson.'[44] Modern readers may assume that these enjoin moderation. A friar, for example, says that Will cannot be absolved of his sin until he is able 'To restitue resonably for al vnrihtfole wynnynge' (c 12.17). A splotch on Haukyn's coat represents the unruliness of hermits who live without 'resonable obedience' (B 13.285). But restitution cannot be satisfied by a 'moderate' return – say, forty cents on the dollar. Of the regular clergy, more than a moderate degree of obedience, and for more than part of the time, is to be expected. Rather, in each case 'reson' means the determination of what is owing. Imaginative contends, accordingly, that it would be 'neiþer reson ne riȝt' to seat the thief who was saved on Good Friday in the same rank as the martyrs and confessors (12.208–9). Similarly, at another meal – the disastrous one taking place, in c, at Conscience's house – Reason distributes the honours ('stoed and styhlede, as for styward of halle' c 15.40). Reason likewise is the equity in the Old Law: 'þe olde lawe graunteþ / That gilours be bigiled and þat is good reson' (B 18.338–9).[45]

Langland often uses 'reson,' then, to signify the just idea (the knowledge of specific obligations that is the form of the just act). In contrast with life under the capricious rule of the cat, where each wise mouse looks out for himself ('wite wel his owene'), 'lawe and leaute' enable 'ech lif to knowe his owene' (B Prol 122) in the sense of possessing and enjoying what is due him. Langland's understanding of 'reson' *qua* justice is basically Aristotelian: 'Now each person's own,' wrote Aquinas, 'is that which is due to him in proportion ... That is why the proper activity of justice is none other than to render to each his own.'[46] Because the just act in *Piers* very often takes its rightness from 'mesure,' or proper apportionment, the 'mesurable' is not helplessly relative and imperfect before God's justice;[47] and it may be worthwhile to recall Aristotle's treatment of justice and its prerequisite knowledge, both called 'reson' in *Piers*:

Now equality implies at least two things. The just, then, must be both intermediate and equal and relative (i.e., for certain persons). And *qua* intermediate it must be between certain things ... The just, therefore, involves at least four terms; for the persons for whom it is in fact just are two, and the things in which it is manifested, the objects distributed, are two. And the same equality will exist between the persons and between the things concerned; for as the latter – the things concerned – are related, so far the former; if they are not equal, they will not have what is equal ...

This, then, is what the just is – the proportional; the unjust is what violates the proportion. Hence one term becomes too great, the other too small, as indeed happens in practice; for the man who acts unjustly has too much, and the man who is unjustly treated too little, of what is good.[48]

The remark of Chambers that Langland 'believes in the old world of feudal obligations'[49] should be placed in the light of the distinction between just and unjust, 'resonable' and 'vnresonable,' that binds even a king. Justness, rectitude of the will, is the 'leute' enjoined upon the king by the 'lunatik' in the Prologue and then desired by the king himself as 'leaute in lawe' (4.180). When people work first and draw their pay accordingly, 'ther is resoun as a reue rewardynge treuthe' (c 3.308). For the sake of equity, Reason does proportions – calculates from three of the four terms (to use Aristotle's language) the value of the fourth term:

> Why sholde we þat now ben for þe werkes of Adam
> Roten and torende? Reson wolde it neuere!
> *Vnusquisque portabit onus suum, &c.*   (10.115–16)[50]

Such calculation is impossible if the third term is also missing: to give payment 'bifore þe doynge / ... is nother resoun ne ryhte ne in no rewme lawe' (c 3.292–3). Reason can measure more than wages – for example, the tolerable difficulty of lessons to be set for the unlettered.[51] The poor person gets into heaven more easily than the rich, in Patience's view, because the poor can call upon 'reson.'[52]

When the causality perceived by 'reson' operates in the moral domain, 'reson' means, as we have just seen, the knowledge of specific obligations; and not surprisingly, therefore, 'reson' is personified in the B text as a judge and in C as a chancellor,[53] an adviser whose work, from the reign of Edward III, was increasingly judicial.[54] Moreover, 'reson' bears on positive law. For example, when Meed subverts the civil service, brewers, butchers, and the like are suffered to 'selle somdel ayeins reson' (3.92) – a word that C replaces with 'lawe.'[55]

These links between 'reson' and equity (forged when the knowledge of causality is used to conceive of law), and consequently between 'reson' and both the judiciary and positive law, constrain the role played by Reason in the *Visio*, particularly in his influence on Conscience, as appeared in the large grammatical metaphor given to Conscience in the c text. Whatever the role of Conscience later, in the *Visio* he yields when Reason implacably derives from the nature of a thing the only kind of conduct that can save it from punishment. So, with Conscience merely as his crozier, Reason mounts the pulpit as a bishop to ring his changes on the theme of rectitude. The simplicity and rigour with which he draws the consequences of 'unity,' the 'one wit and one will' (c 5.189, 185) that alone spell safety at doomsday, have little in common, notwithstanding their homiletic force, with the doubleness of vision attained by the narrator later in the poem, his subtlety, or his experience of sin. Reason makes a good reformer because he can move briskly from one earthly thing to another, treat the idea of each as a cause, and point to a single mode of conduct as its unarguable effect. From his perspective, nature may never have separated from grace, for, whatever the case with the world he addresses, his own mentality is prelapsarian.[56]

Reason orders the idle man to go to work at whatever he can do best,

> And preide Pernele hir purfil to leue
> And kepe it in hire cofre for catel at nede.
> Tomme Stowue he tauȝte to take two staues
> And fecche Felice hom fro wyuen pyne.
> He warnede watte his wif was to blame,
> That hire heed was worþ a marc & his hood noȝt a grote.
> He bad Bette kutte a bouȝ ouþer tweye
> And bete Beton þerwith but if she wolde werche. (5.26–33)

Having begun by expounding the regularity in natural phenomena – sin as the sufficient condition for an extraordinary windstorm – Reason goes on to preach the enforcement of regularity everywhere. He is the essence of 'regula.' So he rules that idle men must work to eat. Pernele's uneven living, her fluctuation between extravagance and need, must stop; Tom Stowe, Wat, and Betty need to re-establish order in their households; and parents generally must regain control over their children. In glossing this passage, Skeat attempted to explain the 'two staves' as useful 'in dispersing the crowd' that has gathered around the cucking stool, since he did not believe Reason would give advice so bad as to urge Tom to beat his wife.[57] But Reason had earlier promised he would be merciless until the realm dwelt in rectitude. Always signifying causality, Reason in moral and social matters infers punishments rather than invents them.

That Reason helps set rather than solve the poem's pivotal problem seems nowhere plainer than in the well-known transitional passage added in the c text between the two dreams of the *Visio*. In the first dream, Will's question to Holy Church – How may I know the false? – was answered by the debate on 'mede' and a demonstration of the nature of 'reson.' On awakening, Will meets Reason, who applies to him what he has been applying to others.[58] Has Will's first question – how he might save his soul – been answered through this turnabout? To the contrary, the fact of sin in the world is here reinforced by the fact of sin in himself, just as it will be elaborated by the confession of the sins. These episodes intensify the search for Christ, not close it.

In the presumptively autobiographical passage (c 5), the fictiveness of Will's poem about the 'lollares of Londone and lewede ermytes' dissolves, and he proceeds to lie to Reason about the causes of his own laziness. In one sense, the poem, like the personification allegory, is still going on; but in another, the poet has incorporated his readers into Will's search for a way 'on crist to bileue' – first by associating them with him in his detailed and critical vision of sin, then by leaving them tied to him still when the dream dissolves and those who conspired to dream it are themselves brought to judgment before the norms of rectitude. Thus tied to Will in feeling the requirements of righteousness, the reader is tied to him as well in looking for a way to *become* righteous.

For better or worse, however, Will evades the literal-mindedness of Reason and Conscience in this transitional passage: there are more ways to be hurt than in the limbs. Will is a casualty in the society of 'mesure' from having, as a youth, 'wyste witterly what holy writ menede' (c 5.37). Having learned that one needs more than bread, Will has never discovered 'Lyf þat me lykede but in this longe clothes' (c 5.41); and he sustains himself by saying psalms and paternosters – as someone presumably in minor orders doing religious odd jobs. (Reason says only that he *looks* like a beggar.) At a moment in b resonant with this passage, Piers, having learned that the priest can find no pardon in the Latin, vows to cease sowing and working so hard, except with prayers and penance.[59] The ironic similarities between Will's situation and that of Piers point up the moral disparity. But that moral disparity is exactly what, in effect, has motivated Will's erratic quest from the beginning.

That Reason can identify these sins of Will's does not mean he can remove them. Will requires not moral direction but a perception of reality that makes sense of the inadequacy of Reason. The first dream and the waking interval afterward restate the *donnée* of the poem from the viewpoint of Conscience, who, against Will's asseveration that he is throwing himself into dependence upon the Lord ('*Fiat voluntas dei* – þat fynt vs alle thynges'), complains that Will is unaccountable 'to prior or to mynistre' (c 5.91).[60] This irregularity, the object of 'reson' in many senses, presses the point of human ignorance of a way out of sin's magic circle. When, somewhat earlier, Conscience was (superfluously) advising Reason to avoid crooked lawyers, he cited scripture: 'Contricio & infelicitas in viis eorum ... non est timor Dei ante oculos eorum &c.' At first glance, this seems less than apt; the shysters Warren Wisdom and Witty do not seem to have lived calamitously. But the quotation may make better sense if not Psalm 13 but Romans 3 is taken as its source, where texts from Proverbs, Isaiah, and Psalms are conflated to carry Paul's point that 'Judaeos et Graecos omnes sub peccato esse': 'There is not one just man; there is none who understands; there is none who seeks after God.' Likewise *Piers* puts forward no reasonable person, if we take 'reson' in the senses developed in this chapter. Dunning was right to interpret Reason's entry into the vision of Meed and his sermon in passus 5 as showing that, where in unfallen man reason would have ruled, it no longer serves to perfect the soul.[61] Reason points out to fallen humanity only that the 'via pacis' has been missed. To the Lamb of God, the Three Kings impute rectitude of opinion and will ('Reson and Rightwisnesse') with their symbolic gifts of frankincense and gold (19.83–90). But fallen man, says Reason,

> was maad of swich a matere he may noȝt wel asterte
> That som tyme hym bitit to folwen his kynde;
> Caton acordeþ þerwiþ: *Nemo sine crimine viuit.*   (11.402–4)

To the general uselessness of 'reson' to fallen humanity, the poem may offer one or two exceptions. Justice in Romans is equivocal, for it saves humanity as well as condemns it; and here Paul does not speak 'secundum hominem': 'But now the justice of God has been made manifest ... the justice of God through faith in Jesus Christ upon all who believe' (3.21–2). Similarly, towards the end of *Piers*, 'reson' becomes ambiguous. It is not simply implicative and judicial. The Samaritan is explaining how only a failure in love is damnable:

And þouȝ þat men make muche doel in hir angre
And ben inpacient in hir penaunce, pure reson knoweþ
That þei han cause to contrarie by kynde of hir siknesse;
And lightliche oure lord at hir lyues ende
Haþ mercy on swiche men þat so yuele may suffre.
Ac þe smoke and þe smolder þat smyt in oure eighen,
That is coueitise and vnkyndenesse þat quencheþ goddes mercy;
For vnkyndenesse is þe contrarie of alle kynnes reson.   (17.342–9)

This is not the Reason who wanted to hear nothing about mercy until a whole series of rather unlikely conditions had been met. He still conceives the 'causa causans,' but the knowledge from which he proceeds is of human weakness: 'pure reson knoweþ / That þei han cause to contrarie.' Finally, 'reson' stands opposite here, not simply to inequity (failure to forgive one's debtors, having had one's own debts forgiven), but also to 'vnkyndenesse,'[62] the failure to pardon being failure to give *more* than is due. For the Samaritan at least, who has some knowledge of another sort, 'reson' both does and does not function in the old way.

A second important exception to the uselessness of 'reson' in the search for salvation lies in its several uses near the end of the poem to mean a faculty for perceiving analogy. Significantly, the clearest examples of 'reson' used in this sense also come from the Samaritan. Having shown that the diverse acts of the fist, fingers, and palm are nevertheless the work of a single hand, he says that 'Right so, redily, Reson it sheweth / How he þat is holy goost sire and sone preueþ' (17.157–8). Similarly, in the next passus, asked why Jesus is also called the Christ, Conscience responds that 'Thou knowest wel … and þow konne reson, / That knyght, kyng, conquerour may be o persone' (19.26–7).[63] Conscience is asking Will not only to make an induction by combining past experiences but to move from one kind of experience (political and empirical) to another. Analogy seems to be a small model for the knowledge of God, which must somehow begin with the self, if the language that describes God is not to be utterly equivocal, and yet apprehend the otherness of God, thereby ruling out univocity.

The poet's understanding of 'reson,' then, is fairly complex. He seems to use it fundamentally to name the grasp of causality – for example, physical. When this flows as the moral imperative exerted by the divine idea of a person, 'reson' means rectitude. The conformity of the human will to the divine will is justice, a further meaning of 'reson,' like the formal cause of justice, equity. In certain senses, then, 'reson' is the point of the command *'Redde quod debes,'* which some, and perhaps all, people do not obey. 'Reson' constitutes the Law rather than knows the Christ. And as it informs the moral conscience, it becomes the knowledge of a scene where, for salvation, only the knowledge of Christ will do.

3

The Action of the Third Dream:
Division, Ingenuity, and Allegory

While Gerard Manley Hopkins evidently never recorded the point he had reached in *Piers Plowman* when he decided that the poem was not worth reading, the first vision of the *Vita de dowel* (the third of the poem)[1] makes a likely candidate. By then, the passions of the pardon scene that woke Will from his last dream have given way to the clever but somehow unfructifying talk of two Franciscans, whom he meets in the waking world. Alone again, he falls asleep to bird-song. The dream that now follows has not been easy to understand within the whole structure of the B text, and critics have been hard on it. Jusserand thought it was full of sermons. John Norton-Smith must speak for many readers in calling it 'a depressing sequence of false turnings, cul-de-sacs, and miles of boot-sucking mud.' Malcolm Godden finds it 'muddled in its thought, uncertain in its tones, lacking in momentum or direction.'[2]

Because the pardon scene has not only redirected Will's search but intensified it, the search is probably not – as Nevill Coghill once proposed – interrupted for the duration of the third vision so that the narrator might gloss other parts of the poem.[3] Nevertheless, if Will is looking for something, he evidently does not find it in this third dream. Despite the view of a good many critics that 'the reconciling speech by Imaginatif' brings the whole confusing vision 'into accord,'[4] Will's interview with Imaginative in fact seems to leave him little the wiser. He will awaken afterwards 'witlees nerhande,' dead on his feet, and wander like a beggar for many years after (13.1–3). Will's sense of the guiltiness of all people – except, perhaps, for the very poor, who may never lose their innocence – and thus his knowledge of the moral law are present throughout the poem: 'nemo bonus, nemo sine crimine uiuit,' Piers tears the pardon with 'Si ambulauero in medio vmbre mortis'; the goliardic

Lyf (Will himself, that is) debauches himself for the sake of oblivion no less in the middle of *Dobest* than in the middle of *Dowel*; Unity falls, 'Sin is Behovely.' The first dream of *Dowel* marks no stage in this, one way or the other.

It serves instead to test the power of Thought, Wit, and Imaginative to apprehend Christ as present and existing. Thought is the first of these, met at the start of the vision, personified as a tall man 'lik to' the narrator himself, with whom he will 'dispute' for days on end (8.70, 118). This 'disputyng on dowel' begins what critics have frequently described as 'the intellectual search for Dowel,' a mistake by the narrator who has not yet confronted his 'own moral imperfection' or realized that 'dowel' cannot be 'known without being lived.'[5] To the contrary, if he did not know himself to be sinful, he would not be looking for 'dowel.' The Franciscans, after all, are not: 'amonges vs he dwelleþ' (8.18). Presumably the narrator wishes that he, no less than they, might become a good man (8.61). Will does not mistakenly postpone a search *with* the will (an 'affective search,' as it has been called),[6] because the will can choose only an object of knowledge that it cannot provide by itself. Will's 'disputyng' with the faculties of his own mind must be carefully understood, therefore, not as his conducting of some sort of 'intellectual' argument with them. Indeed, how would he argue with a mental faculty except by means of a mental faculty? Rather, he tests each mode of knowledge to see what it can do with the guilty conscience that he begins with.

1

In Thought's brief appearance, he gratuitously offers three answers when Will asks where 'dowel' is. Thought thereby introduces one of the chief, puzzling elements of the poem's form. 'Dowel ... and dobet and dobest the þridde,' he says, 'Arn þre faire vertues' (8.78–9). The conventional quality of these[7] – the dutifulness of lay labourers, active charity and evangelism, the prelatical power to discipline – could be illustrated from Augustine or Gregory.[8] Will nevertheless expresses himself as dissatisfied:

Ac yet sauoreþ me noȝt þi seying, so me god helpe!
More kynde knowynge I coueite to lerne ...   (8.112–13)

It is possible, of course, that the poet characterizes himself thus so that he might continue with his exposition.

However, the dissatisfaction might also arise with Thought itself as a mode of knowledge, at least at the point in the poet's life where he now finds himself. If someone was expecting a pardon for his sins, he would be disconcerted to hear the inflexible reminder, 'Et qui egerunt ibunt in vitam eternam; qui vero mala in ignem eternum.' Whichever the priest will mean – that indulgences do not sound like that, or that this 'pardon' hardly offers forgiveness – he is right. On waking from the argument between Piers and the priest, Will rejects any notion of doubting the pope's power to loose and bind. Yet he warns wealthy men not to trust their salvation to papal pardons, for at the Last Judgment these will not demonstrate that one has kept Christ's 'lawe' (7.195). We need so to work during our life that, when it ends, we shall have satisfied 'dowel' (205–6). Whether or not Will has contradicted himself in this by now impugning the power of the keys depends, of course, on how he relates 'dowel' to the Atonement.

Here two points seem clear: (1) any value a pardon has comes from agreeing with 'dowel'; and (2) 'dowel' is not entirely separable from the person of Christ. This latter point is made by an ambiguity in syntax and by the structure of the passage. Will prays for the grace to work in such a way that at Doomsday 'dowel' can 'reherce / ... we dide as he hi3te' (7.206). Although the nearest referent for 'he' is 'dowel' (in which case, 'dowel' declares on our behalf that we did what he had required), 'god' as it appears close above (7.201, 203) also makes a plausible referent. In this case, it is God who not only gives grace but who commands, and 'dowel' is what is commanded. Our good works respond – 'reherce' for us – to the one who has required them. Further, the passage obviously identifies God's law and 'dowel,' since both, in their reliability, are opposed to triennials. Thereupon to personify 'dowel' tends to equate it with Christ himself. And immediately, the next passus begins with Will's asking 'where dowel was at Inne; / And what man he my3te be' (8.4–5). We cannot assume that this is simply a figurative way of trying to identify a moral quality.

If Will is looking for Christ, he has no way at this point of seeing him in the two Franciscans he encounters. They defend themselves (incoherently)[9] as being helped by the habit of 'charite þe champion' (8.45), undefeated by the venial sins they admit. 'Dowel' for them – 'that is charite' – is an attribute; for Will it may be a person; and their readiness to admit imperfection shows that they would not be the right person, one whom the narrator must meet if he, like them, is to become ('worþe') a good man (8.61). Thus, still looking for 'dowel,' he rests awhile and then falls asleep.

Upon this scene appears 'Thou3t,' who, like Wit and Study to come, resembles Will himself and, like Imaginative, says he has accompanied the narrator for a number of years. His viewpoint is not easy to locate, partly because 'Thought' as a noun occurs in the poem only a few times.[10] This pale and momentary phantom has not drawn much critical interest. Because Otto Mensendieck's interpretation of *Dowel* as the autobiographical record of the poet's own schooling has never been widely accepted, only Helmut Maisack and Greta Hort have taken an interest in rejecting Mensendieck's specific view that Thought had been the most rudimentary stage of this education.[11]

However, not all movement is upward; and Thought seems to represent the highest faculty, short of 'intelligentia,' known to medieval psychology – the rational soul *qua* abstractive.[12] As we shall see, the personifications that follow in this third vision orient themselves much more to the sensible world than Thought does, who represents particularly the power to reason by compounding and dividing.[13] Because the friars as realities are not that reality called 'dowel,' Thought's appearance is a dramatic reaction to them; for through him 'dowel' becomes a 'vertue,' an abstraction from reality. Conversely, because an abstraction is not what Will needs, when Will tells Thought he is yet unsatisfied, he not only repeats the criterion of intuitive cognition ('kynde knowynge') but moves to bring himself back to earth, among realities present and existing – 'How dowel, dobet and dobest doon among þe peple' (8.114). And Thought himself, in turning the dreamer over to Wit, makes this demand explicit: 'Here is wil wolde wit ... / Wheiþer he [viz 'dowel'] be man or no man' (8.129–30).

'Thou3t' means a new modality of knowledge, not new information. He may seem to enlarge upon 'dowel' ('Et qui bona egerunt ibunt in vitam eternam'), but the 'pardon' itself merely reduced to 'two lynes' Truth's corollary instructions, which had occupied all the preceding portion of passus 7. These instructions, so far as Thought teaches ethics, he simply duplicates.[14] He says,

Whoso is meke of his mouþ, milde of his speche,
Trewe of his tunge and of his two handes,
And þoru3 his labour or his land his lyflode wynneþ,
Trusty of his tailende, takeþ but his owene,
And is no3t dronkelew ne deynous, dowel hym folweþ. (8.80–4)

Earlier, however, Truth had promised to anyone helping Piers to plow,

to erye or to sowe,
Or any maner mestier þat myȝte Pieres helpe,
Pardon wiþ Piers Plowman ...
...
Alle libbynge laborers þat lyuen by hir hondes,
That treweliche taken and treweliche wynnen
And lyuen in loue and in lawe, for hir lowe herte
Hadde þe same absolucion þat sent was to Piers.   (7.6–8, 61–4)

Thought teaches that 'dobet' does this and more:

He is as lowe as a lomb, and louelich of speche;
Whiles he haþ ouȝt of his owene he helpeþ þer nede is;
The bagges and þe bigirdles he haþ brok hem alle
That the Erl Auarous hadde, or hise heires,
And wiþ Mammonaes moneie he haþ maad hym frendes;
And is ronne to Religion, and haþ rendred þe bible,
And precheth þe people Seint Poules wordes,
Libenter suffertis insipientes cum sitis ipsi sapientes.   (8.86–93)

But Truth earlier promises the merchants they will be saved 'a pena et a culpa' if they take their profits,

And make Mesondieux þerwiþ myseise to helpe,
Wikkede weyes wightly amende ...
...
Pouere peple bedredene and prisons in stokkes
Fynden swiche hir foode for oure lordes loue of heuene,
Sette Scolers to scole or to somme kynnes craftes,
Releue Religion and renten hem bettre.   (7.26–7, 30–3)

And perhaps even Thought's advice to be good to 'fools' is anticipated by Truth's urging on behalf of 'lunatik lollers,' wandering in the cold 'With a good wil, witless,' that 'We sholde have hem to house and help hem when thei come.' Finally, Thought wishes 'dobest' to carry 'þe bisshopes crose,'

And halie with þe hoked ende alle men to gode,
And with the pyk pulte adoun *preuaricatores legis.*[15]
Lordes þat lyuen as hem lust and no lawe acounten,

For here mok and here mebles suche men thenketh
Sholde no bisshop be, here biddynges to withsite.
...
  Thus Dowel and Dobet demede as Dobest
And crounede oen to be kyng, to kull withoute synne
That wolde nat do as Dobest deuinede and tauhte.   (C 10.92–7, 99–101)

Truth, however, had already made a grant to bishops:

Bishopis yblessed, yf they ben as they sholde,
Lele and fol of loue and no lord drede,
Merciable to meke and mylde to þe gode
And bitynge in badde men but yf they wol amende,
Drede nat for no deth to distruye by here power
Lechery amonges lordes and here luyther custumes,
And such liue as þei lereth men, oure lord Treuthe hem graunteth
To be peres to þe apostles, alle peple to reule
And deme with hem at domesday bothe quyke and dede.   (C 9.13–21)[16]

That Thought has no new virtues to teach matters less than his power
to manipulate abstractions. Asked where 'dowel' lives, Thought can
refer at once to 'þre faire vertues' (8.79), because he apprehends 'dowel'
as an abstraction, and in this case the abstraction 'virtue' rather than
the abstraction 'person.' Having done so he continues with something
like the logical process of division. Thought takes the original division
in the pardon ('do wel' and 'do yuel') and proceeds by subdividing 'do
wel' into 'dobet' and its complement, and then by subdividing 'dobet.'
He projects Will's own capacity to think in this way, as when Will deployed against the friars the law of non-contradiction, on which 'divisio' is based: 'dowel and do yuele mowe noȝt dwelle togideres' (8.23).
The friars argue by dividing sins (deadly versus venial) and ways of
falling (falling out versus its complement, not falling out, which includes, however, falling down). This is what it means for Will himself
to 'disputen' 'as a clerc' (8.20); and the dream that follows, with Will's
encounter with Thought, therefore has some of the character of an 'insomnium' in Macrobius' classification, simply a repetition of waking
content.
  That Thought recollects so much of his material from the *Visio* may
be tell-tale, having to do with a certain poverty in the mode. That is,
although subclasses are treated as if they inhered in the main class, they

can never actually be inferred from it. Hence, 'divisio' as a process ob-scures the interests and information that actually determine the forma-tion of the subclasses. Division proves nothing about 'dowel,' least of all that it exists.[17] When Will demurs from Thought in order to learn 'How dowel, dobet and dobest doon among þe peple' (8.114), he may be objecting with Aristotle that division begs what it ought to prove and uses universals in such a way that it finally shows 'nothing clearly.'[18] In Thought's teaching, the attribute more general than 'doing well' is doing. In assuming the existence of this universal, division, which then divides this middle term into doing well and doing evil, never perceives that it is incapable of attaining to a statement of the existence of 'dowel.' It is a particular existent, none the less, that Will needs to find.

2

Thought at this point simply passes Will on to Wit, whom he introduces as uniquely able to show 'dowel,' 'dobet,' and 'dobest.' Because the nar-rator will still be asking, after Dame Study has berated and lectured him, for someone 'To kenne [him] kyndely to knowe what is dowel' (10.151), Wit, who speaks the whole of passus 9 without interruption in the B text, will seem not to have served. If Will in fact needs to know whether 'dowel' 'be man or no man' (8.130), it is perhaps a bad lookout that Wit immediately moves the question of a person into a question of personification: like the Franciscans and like Thought, Wit conceives of 'dowel' as a virtue – 'Sire Dowel,' who keeps the maiden Anima in a state of grace (9.1–11).

It is also unpromising for the narrator, perhaps, that, like Reason, Wit assumes the knowledge of God and makes applications predicated upon it. Where, however, Reason had known God as lawgiver, Wit appears to know God as the exemplary worker and the sponsor of work. Be-fore considering how Wit's understanding of the world gives his mono-logue a certain form and content, it may be useful to try to isolate his particular power by looking at some of the poet's frequent uses of the word 'wit' elsewhere. In this endeavour, the speech of Anima at the be-ginning of *Dobet* scarcely helps. (Anima in passus 15, masculine in gen-der, is, as we shall see, not so vulnerable as in Wit's construction.) Dilating a passage from Isidore of Seville's *De spiritu et anima*, Anima gives his version of the powers that he enjoys. He reports that 'whan I feel þat folk telleþ my firste name is *sensus*, / And þat is wit and wis-dom,[19] the welle of alle craftes' (15.29–30). While some readers have

seized on *'sensus'* here to identify the Wit of passus 9,[20] Anima's truism
that knowledge begins with sensation – that the sensorium is the 'welle'
where all the mental powers must drink – has little bearing on 'wit'
in *Piers*. Elsewhere in the poem, 'wit' simply does not mean sensation,
although the expression 'fyue wittes' does (c 15.256), sensation in
medieval psychology being plural because the diverse physical or-
gans must always be taken into account.[21]

In general, when characters in *Piers* speak from the viewpoint of nature, they designate by 'wit' the knowledge of means. Imaginative, for
example, uses 'wit' in its most basic way: 'wit and wisdom ... was some
tyme tresor / To kepe wiþ a commune' (12.295–6). Here the purpose is
assumed, and the ability to achieve it is the value of 'wit.' Similarly,
Piers denotes by 'wit' a talent for finding ways to convert an enemy into
a friend: 'Fond thorw wit and word his loue to wynne' (c 15.144). (When
Patience had the comparable lines in B, the means for doing this were
the more formulaic 'werk and ... word' 13.145.) Even, so far as he will
not be outmanoeuvred, God himself, who arranges that wealth accu-
mulated through false tricks slips away from the control of 'wikkede
men' at the last, is 'witty' (15.130).[22] The Son also has 'wit,' and controls
'manye sleightes,' as becomes a leader (19.99–100). To convince Mary of
his divine origin, Jesus, 'ful of wit,' 'inventiveness,' adopts the tactic of
turning water into wine (19.118).

Thus, wit as a power of the mind knows *how* to go to work: 'The wit-
tiore þat eny wihte is, but yf he worche þerafture, / The bittorere he
shall abugge' (c 16.219–20).[23] While this work often consists specifically
in finding the right forms of words,[24] words are not an adequate end in
themselves. Wit assigns to God a line that might be Wit's own motto:
'moore moot herto þan my word oone' (9.37). And the wittiest creatures
(Wit's wife, Dame Study, will develop this in her own way) may actually be those who are wordless – the birds, for example, who make their
nests more skilfully than any carpenter or mason could. 'Hadde neuere
wye wit to werche þe leeste' (11.346). 'Dere god,' asks Recklessness, one
of the shapes of Will, 'Where hadde thise wilde suche wit, and at what
scole?' (c 13.167–8). Because people can and do deviate from their tasks,
they appear to be ill made – as if, puzzlingly, 'Reson ... þat witty [is]
holden' had botched that particular job (11.374, 389–91, 396–404).

As the discovery of means, 'wit' narrows in *Piers* in three further
ways at least. First, it sometimes denotes inductive thinking, because
induction, too, moves from the known to the unknown: without enter-
taining one hypothesis rather than another, no one could know what

kind of phenomena to consider. Induction verifies rather than discovers an end. For instance, Conscience predicts that, when the millennial harmony arrives, Jews will interpret it as evidence ('shul wene in hire wit') of the coming of Moses or the Messiah (3.302).[25] Second, because Imaginative makes 'wit' metonymic for 'kynde wit' (the goal of which is material benefit)[26] and because, as we shall see, Imaginative thinks of both 'kynde wit' and 'clergye' as a knowledge of metaphors, our 'wittes' interpret the physical universe as if it were a vast and significant means to a profitable end:

> Dyuyneris toforn vs viseden and markeden
> The selkouþes þat þei seiȝen, hir sones for to teche.
> And helden it an heiȝ science hir wittes to knowe.   (12.130–2)[27]

Finally, 'wit' is related to rationalization: 'For hadde neuere freke fyn wit þe feiþ to dispute,' says Clergy, 'Ne man hadde no merite myȝte it ben ypreued' (10.255–6). 'Fyn wit' has nothing inquisitive about it; it merely locates appropriate evidence.

If 'wit' is distinguished by the discovery of means to an end, then it evidently coincides with the ancient faculty 'ingenium.' This power, wrote Isidore, 'investigat.'[28] According to Hugh of St Cher, the fourth duty of 'liberum-arbitrium' 'est inuenire media, et secundum hoc dicitur "ingenium."'[29] The 'ingenium' thus moves from the known – the present situation – to unknown means: 'Sensus vero de rationabilitate exsurgens, propter tempus praesens, praeteritum et futurum variatur, aut varie nominatur, "ratio," "memoria," "ingenium." Ingenium vero ea vis animae dicitur, sive intentio, qua se extendit et excitat ad incognitorum inventionem. Ingenium vero exquirit incognita ... Ingenium igitur quae adinvenit ad rationem adducit ...'[30] Choosing a means is a matter of judgment as well as discovery. Instead of the 'ingenium,' Ockham spoke of the 'intellectus consiliativus,' the 'deliberative intellect,' as he called the mind when it looks into the best means of achieving an end already determined.[31] If it were a 'habitus' rather than power, 'wit' would recall the virtue prudence as conceived by Albertus Magnus[32] and especially Aquinas, which devised 'fitting ways' to an end.[33] The poet himself on one occasion associates wit and prudence:

> And *spiritus prudencie* in many a point shal faille
> Of þat he weneþ wolde falle if his wit ne weere;
> Wenynge is no wysdom, ne wys ymaginacion ...   (20.31–3)

Although prudence is said to 'deuyse wel þe ende' (19.278), prudence does not settle upon an outcome; rather it discerns one outcome from one choice of means, another from another, as shown by Langland's example of the way cooks buy a ladle with a long handle before they try to skim the fat from a crock. These terms fall within a tradition in the history of psychology beginning with Aristotle, who had distinguished a faculty for carrying out the choices we have made. He called it δεινότης, 'cleverness.'[34]

On this basis, then, of Langland's use of 'wit' elsewhere in *Piers*, such is the mode of knowledge we may assume to be personified in the speaker of passus 9. While 'dowel,' 'dobet,' and 'dobest' appear at the beginning, middle, and end of the passus, Wit has an essentially simple notion of virtue: it does not connect with his first use of the triad at all; in his second use it links up with 'dobest'; then he relates it to 'dowel' without using the other members of the triad; and when he uses the triad to close the passus Wit's idea of virture connects indirectly with first 'dobest' and then 'dowel.' Wit's preoccupation causes him to model in turn the human psychology and the nuclear family (as we now call it) in identical ways. The result is that he establishes certain strong parallels, which run through the passus like threads, even when he interrupts one of his principal topics with another.

If 'wit' elsewhere in *Piers* is the discovery of means to an end, in passus 9 Wit emphasizes this knowledge as a praxis: the means is first known, then it is fabricated. 'Wit' issues in work; its personification returns again and again to the language of production: 'Dixit & facta sunt' (9.33a), '*faciamus*' (36), 'make' (39), 'made' (2, 3, 34, 45, 50, 119, 194), 'makede' (133), 'ymaked' (41, 53), 'werche' (21, 44, 52, 111, 209), 'wroȝte' (52, 157), 'ywroȝt' (116, 119), 'trauaille' (107). Accordingly, when Wit discusses the human psychology, the key actors in the allegorical castle of *Caro*, 'Inwit and alle wittes' (9.54), are organized towards production. At points, it is true, Wit describes 'inwit' as if it were an inborn knowledge of the natural law, a knowledge called 'synderesis' in Dominican tradition. Thus, for example, Wit says that 'after þe grace of god þe gretteste is Inwit' (9.61), and that the insane may lack, and the drunken overrule, this natural knowledge (9.68, 61–2).[35] Further, Sir Inwit's five sons ('Sire Se-wel, and Sey-wel, and here-wel þe hende,' and so on [9.20–2]) obviously recall the five senses, as we have already noted. Nevertheless, Wit understands 'inwit' even more as the knowledge that enables people to support themselves. So it is not simply the insane and infantile who 'fauten Inwit' (9.68) but widows who do not know how to earn their food (9.71). Then Wit dwells for twenty lines or so on the responsibility of godparents and prelates to care for every 'cristene creature' crying at the door, as they would be helped by everyone who actually feared God. With the idea of dreading God, Wit hooks up again with 'dowel' and 'dobet,' but comes into his own in dilating on 'dobest,' which is avoiding any loss of 'speche' or 'tyme':

Tynynge of tyme, truþe woot þe soþe,
Is moost yhated vpon erþe of hem þat ben in heuene;
And siþþe to spille speche þat spire is of grace ...   (9.101–3)

With 'dobest,' Wit returns to exactly the kind of industriousness impossible for those who lack inwit, and who are thus commended to our care. The 'loore' that they need (9.73), the inwit they lack, is equivalent to the speech that should not be wasted by those who have it. 'Speche' here means 'inwit,' the necessary condition for work, comparable to the 'word' or 'speche' that even in God must be supplemented 'wiþ werk' (9.38, 52). When 'word' is not wasted, it becomes Sir Inwit's five fair sons, who are less the senses than the good works performed with them: the sense of touch, for example, becomes 'Sire werch-wel-wiþ-þyn-hand,' and smell is simply replaced with Sir Godfrey Go-well (9.21–2).

Wit interrupts his version of the human psychology by his account of Kynde's having created this 'man wiþ a Soule' (9.51). Because Wit models Kynde entirely on this psychology, the interruption preserves certain continuities in the passus. The divine activity is productivity. From Wit's perspective, God is first of all 'creatour,' 'Fader and formour.' His 'word' is expressed through 'myȝt' and 'werkmanshipe.' Wit leaves the relationship of the persons of the Trinity imprecise. Possibly, the 'word,' or 'wit,' denotes Christ the Logos, and the 'showing,' then, a demiurgic power.[36] Both the 'word and werkmanship' may be Christ, considered (in Milton's phrase) as 'word ... wisdom, and effectual might.' Or – this is perhaps the likeliest – 'word' and 'wit' may refer to the first person, in whom the ideas of all things exist eternally. The showing, then, would fall to the servant son, whom the Samaritan in passus 17 likens to fingers that do the bidding of the fist. Any such correlation is less important for Wit, however, than the priority of wit and its issuing into action. This is so much the nature of God for Wit that he says it three times (9.37–8, 46, 52).

Kynde is maker twice over: he makes not only humankind but also marriages. Wit will revert to the term 'dowel' to name 'trewe wedded libbinge folk' (9.110). Whatever the later relevance in the poem of other grades of chastity, Wit does not ascend beyond 'dowel,' for married people 'mote werche and wynne and þe world sustene (9.111); and this is Wit's preoccupation. The knowledge of means, Wit thinks of marriage as beginning with a 'wye' who wants to get something done. The child is the product. The means is figured by the wife, made in order 'to helpe' the man 'werche' (9.115). Thus, wedlock is 'ywroȝt' precisely 'wiþ a mene persone' (9.116). (In God, by contrast, word and execution are one. No physical instrument is required. Hence God made Eve of Adam's 'ryb bon wiþouten any mene' 9.35). Since wedlock, like the soul, is for Wit a model of purposeful effort, 'Wercheþ in tyme' (9.187) is his advice to those who marry.

In C, this counsel is 'Worcheth nat out of tyme' (10.198); and although Wit here means prohibitions upon sexual intercourse, repeatedly called 'work,' he refers by extension to all labour ungoverned by 'word.' One who will 'werche wiþ his word and his wit shewe' bears abundant fruit – kings and knights, emperors and labourers, virgins and martyrs. But working in 'vntyme' (with a sort of 'false prudence,' or disoriented effort) botches the product, which is a child who grows up to be a rascal. Wit dwells on production, even when, as in most of the second half of his speech, production goes wrong: where in the first half he invokes aid for those who cannot work, in the second half he rehearses the unsatisfactory results when people work at the wrong times or with the wrong people. Such marriages yield not children but harsh words (9.171–2). Production is the point of his final reprise of 'dowel,' 'dobet,' and 'dobest': 'dobest' cares for everyone exactly by bringing down the 'wikked wille, þat many werk shendeþ.' When 'many werk' are destroyed, so is 'dowel' (9.208–10). C revises this ending to emphasize material enactment even more: 'For þe more a man may do, by so þat a do hit, / The more he is worthy and worth, of wyse and goed ypresed' (10.306–7).

One critic has described Wit's speech as rambling, acknowledged its obscurity, but concluded that 'some of Wit's definitions of Dowel, Dobet, and Dobest have given the Dreamer useful moral advice.'[37] While no one would mistake passus 9 for a lyric by George Herbert, it is unified at least by a certain preoccupation: Wit being the 'mene persone' (exactly so far as he finds the means that mediate between knowledge of a final cause and the deeds that achieve it), his morality emphasizes doing. His monologue has a certain balance. The first half takes up the mental movement from purpose to product and the fortunes of those who cannot produce; the second conceives of wedlock on a similar model and dwells on products ill-made. Wit touches on certain opportunities for sin – temptations, for example, to take too young a spouse or too old. Instead of discovering in the human soul a way to the God who is *other than* humankind, Wit seems simply to model God after the human soul so far as he knows that to be the principle of creativity. But Will does not need instruction on the occasions for sin. He has begun with the fact of it and seeks a 'kynde knowyng' of Christ.[38]

While 'wit' does not provide this, 'wit' will reappear later in the poem modified, like 'reson,' by characters already in a state of grace. When Patience, for example, tells the dinner party that he will conquer not through witchery but through 'wit,' the gluttonous doctor misconstrues this by taking 'wit' in its predominant sense. On that basis he dismisses Patience as a fabulist: 'Al þe wit of þis world [cf 'word'] and wiȝt mennes strengþe [cf 'werk']' could not reconcile the pope to his enemies (13.172–3).[39] No feat of political ingenuity can accomplish this, he means. The graces distributed at Pentecost will include the 'wit' to use language well or to teach people (19.229–33). And Conscience, as noted, talks of the miracles of Jesus' manhood as 'wiles and wit.' But 'wit' in all these cases becomes equivocal. Perseverance in faith displaces for Patience the usual significance of 'wit.' Similarly, Conscience can turn around and displace 'wit' itself: Jesus, he says, 'wroȝte þat by no wit' (19.122). And if those who, in *Dobest*, live in part by 'wit' make up a primitive Christian community that also stands for the Christian soul (as in 1 Corinthians 12), then the distribution of the graces would presuppose love, even as the growth of the virtues does. 'Wit' would thus be in part metonymic for its precondition, faith. The predominant sense of 'wit' is presupposed in each of these cases by its deformation. And the tension between the new and the displaced senses coincides with a tension between grace and nature.

For the narrator, constrained by his own unsanctified nature, 'wit' cannot show the Christ. Yet eventually, by thus entering into the paradoxes of *Dobest*, 'wit' may contribute to the knowledge that does.

3

For some time now, there has been little argument for the existence of any sort of order in the episodes composing the third vision of the poem. Here I want to concentrate on just a part of the sequence, the movement from Dame Study to her 'cosyn,' Clergy. Wit has been one modality of knowledge. Imaginative will be another. 'Clergye' names the body of knowledge that, as I shall want to argue later, Imaginative produces. In other words, from the viewpoint of medieval psychology, Wit and Imaginative are the faculties or 'potentiae' explored in the third vision. Nevertheless, the connection between Study and Clergy is something like a psychological one in the modern sense. Specifically, Study represents a necessary condition for Clergy because of her preoccupation with the voice. Further, if, as I proposed in my first chapter, the poet is ambivalent towards literacy itself, which has helped to make belief a problem for him, then it may be that Study functions in *Piers* not only as one condition for a body of knowledge of a certain kind but as a provisional reduction of the tension created by literacy.

Study herself has not, perhaps, been adequately identified. The disarmingly comic tirade that Wit's gaunt, earthy wife vents upon her husband may divert us from several evident inconsistencies about her. For example, while 'study' might recall Will's earlier use of the word to mean 'musyng on' difficult matters (c 9.298), she mentions reflection or investigation only to deplore it. She complains, for instance, that subtle clerics sometimes entertain rich men at dinner by defending theses about the most sacred of mysteries: 'Thus they dreuele at the deyes, the deite to knowe' (c 11.40).[40] This intrusiveness is the fourth of the modes that Aquinas discerned for 'curiositas,' a vice. While the second of these, studying to learn 'ab eo a quo non licet,' 'from an illicit source,'[41] is associated with Study herself in the B text, where she claims to have ordained such sciences as astrology, alchemy, and necromancy (10.212–21), no reference to these hazardous inquiries or her responsibility for them appears in c. John Lawlor rightly pointed out that she puts together on one side 'learning and dialectical subtlety ... gluttony, misuse of wealth, and heartless indifference to the poor; on the other, righteousness, compassion, an active charity ...' and poverty.[42] What is odd, however, is that a personification called 'Study' *takes the side she does*.

Actually, her point of view may be defined by her preoccupation with the voice. God or holy writ is, for better or worse, 'ay in [the] mouth,' 'muche in þe gorge,' 'muche in hire mouþ' (c 11.31, B 10.67, 71). This preoccupation is not *all* she personifies, any more than the virtue 'patientia' exhausts the meaning of 'Pacience' in passus 13 and 14. As 'close mental application to something,' for example, she makes a good wife for Wit, who, as we have seen, personifies the power of locating appropriate means towards a known end. Nevertheless, her dominant meaning shows already when she berates Wit for giving pearls – his 'wysdomes' – for swine to eat. Although Wit's discourse was demonstrably intricate and continuous, Study describes it as if it had been a collection of discrete apothegms, 'sooþ sawes' (10.16), as readily sorted as 'perye.' These can be put to bad use, as facetious men have appropriated Bernard's language; or these can be replaced with 'lesynges,' 'nugae,' and 'fals questes' told by dissolute or insidious men (10.22, c 11.19, 22). If short speeches can be thus prostituted, the disputed questions emerging within systematic theology are bad even in their origin:

> Clerkes and kete men carpen of god faste
> And haue hym muche in hire mouþ, ac meene men in herte.
> Freres and faitours han founde vp swiche questions
> To please wiþ proude men syn þe pestilence tyme;
> And prechen at Seint Poules, for pure enuye of clerkes,
> That folk is noȝt fermed in þe feiþ ...   (10.70–5)

Her preference for meaty sayings shows also in the recourse that she has to the wisdom books.[43] The 'sooþ sawes' were Solomon's, but she refers to Job's 'gestes' too, in particular some aphorisms on the prosperity of the wicked. She invokes Tobit twice (10.33, c 11.70–2a) and claims to have 'sette' Scripture 'to Sapience' (10.175).[44] These biblical 'groups of aphorisms, extended maxims, and didactic poems' existed as a class because they were thought to derive from oral instruction by a sage. Hence the tradition of attributing Proverbs, Ecclesiastes, and Wisdom to Solomon.[45] Study's recourse to the wisdom books, like her distaste for the systematic theology transmitted by writing, reinforces the orality essential to her performance.

Partial to spoken texts, Study nevertheless attacks people who talk a great deal, whom she thinks of as symbiotic with the rich and callous. On the one hand, she groups the silent poor with simple preachers who merely repeat 'holy writ' and describe Christ's passion. On the other, she assimilates to slavering buffoons the lawyers and friars who pervert justice for wealthy clients. By contrast with people who somehow embody Christ, others merely speak of him. They are voluble also with 'lesynges,' 'fykel speche,' 'gestes' (here meaning profane narratives rather than Job's pithy laments), spitting, spewing, 'foule wordes,' spiteful criticism, 'losengerye,' 'losels tales,' and 'grete oþes.' Those who 'lickne men' (10.43) are as likely to be licking, or fawning on, the rich as disparaging those who 'leneþ hem no ȝiftes.'

The oral imagery condenses in Study's attack on the suave cleric and the vulgar rich man. These two gratify each other, the friar glad to be recognized, Dives eager to adorn his table with learning. Having finished the chops, the company continues by gnawing God (10.58). First, in a poem where characters can change drastically because of what they discover, the pun on 'knowe'/'gnawen' points to a contrasting sort of knowledge that, based on logic (reasons and premises 'preue[n] þe soþe'), leaves the gnawers untransformed. In the mouth, many words follow much food.[46] The theme is elaborated with the hungry, who are carried into heaven by the few words of the paternoster (10.465–71).

Study's preoccupation with orality is unsurprising, because she characterizes herself not as receiving but as *giving* knowledge, like a teacher. The early portions of her speech divide between attacks on miserliness (10.13–29, 81–103) and attacks on vulgar or cynical entertainment, which has replaced edifying preaching (10.30–80). Then, after she softens towards Will, she describes herself as a teacher – one who can understand little about theology except that it teaches people to love (10.190). Thus, she allies herself to the grave preachers she has mentioned earlier, those who give lessons to lords on how they can care for the needy (10.94). As a teacher, she has set Scripture

> to Sapience and to þe Sauter glosed.
> Logyk I lerned hire, and al þe lawe after,
> And alle þe Musons in Musik I made hire to knowe.
> Plato þe poete, I putte hym first to boke;
> Aristotle and oþere mo to argue I tauȝte;
> Grammer for girles I garte first write,
> And bette hem wiþ a baleys but if þei wolde lerne.   (10.175–81)

She is the teaching voice, equivalent in modern terms to the auditory memory. The voice may be the teacher's or, whether audible or subaudible, the student's as used either in reading or in repeating to himself what he has read or heard. To learn, a student in the fourteenth century had to rely almost exclusively upon his ear. Hastings Rashdall has remarked that the theological student at the University of Paris 'passed the first six years of his course as a simple *auditor*.'[47] The expense and scarcity of textbooks not only caused a dependency upon audition; they exerted pressure upon the lecturer to 'legere ad pennam,' that is, read from his own text slowly and repetitively enough so that his students, able to get down nearly every word, could make books for themselves.[48] The lines quoted above might well have evoked for Langland's contemporaries the image of a master dictating.[49] The Study episode would call attention, I think, not to the fact that students are being taught to write, but to the oral source of instruction. Lecturing 'ad pennam' writes Hajnal, 'ne servait pas seulement à multiplier le nombre des livres, mais ... elle constituait une des methodes par excellence de l'école médiévale ...' By this method were taught not only 'gramer' but that division of rhetoric known as 'pronuntiatio.'

Study's preoccupation with the voice, whether the exiguous cries of the poor or the articulateness of the friars, may relate her intimately to faith, which 'depends on hearing, and hearing on the word of Christ' (Romans 10: 17). Such faith is the 'sothfaste bileue' that Study means by 'Teologie' in the c text (11.132). There 'Teologie' apparently has its older, monastic meaning, equivalent to 'sacra pagina' or 'lectio divina,' the study of the Bible in general accord with Augustine's program in the *De doctrina christiana*.[50] This is faith rooted in a text mediated by the voice. While nothing appears to connect Study with the spiritual comprehension ascribed to this ('The moore I muse þerInne þe mystier it semeþ'), upon her such comprehension would have been thought to depend. This is the sense in which she is 'Cosyn' to Clergy. The latter personifies, as we shall see, the understanding of the law of love essential to all Scripture. Because this allegorical understanding of the sacred page is a digesting of its inner meaning, this understanding was thought to depend on the orality with which the text, in theory, was internalized.

Certain characteristics of Study would follow from a relationship to the 'lectio divina' although none strictly entails it.

1 'Lectio divina' is inseparable from orality. Because even the solitary person, presumably, could not have helped but read the scriptures aloud, the authority of the Bible was in effect an authoritative voice,[51] pre-eminently so in the wisdom books, which Study favours. While Imaginative will tie 'Clergie' to 'bokes' (12.100), the source of these will still have been a voice: the holy spirit has '*seide* what men sholde write' (12.102). As voice, Dame Study was the initial way in which the text, whether heard in the lecture room or meditated as 'sacra pagina,' existed. 'L'éxercise constant et tacite de l'écriture, sans intervention de la lecture du texte à voix haute,' Hajnal observes, 'n'était pas encore possible à l'époque.'[52] Without the habitual knowledge, later made possible by printing, of the written form of words, one had to conserve the auditory memory of the words to be inscribed.

2 The liberal arts, the disciplines where Study reports the least diffi-

culty, found their justification in Augustine, the Victorines, and monastics generally as aids to 'lectio divina.'[53] Further, the manual arts – 'Of alle kynne craftes I contreued tooles' (10.182) – had their place within the monastic tradition of Theophilus Presbyter and Rupert of Deutz as the means of creating an environment for worship through church decoration. Because the Benedictines placed the knowledge of them with 'sapientia,' the image of God, Dame Study makes no drastic leap when she moves from 'leuel and lyne' to 'Theologie' (10.184–5).[54]

3 Study satirizes the conjunction of greed and the 'quaestiones disputatae' of systematic theology. Theology of this kind shifted intellectual leadership from the monastery to the university. If Study embodies a phase of the 'lectio divina,' then pre-eminence shifted from herself. Nevertheless, the fact that 'the "spiritual" interpretation of Scripture was greatly in decline from the end of the twelfth century onwards'[55] does not preclude an appearance by 'lectio divina.' The poet certainly knew at least some of the technique of spiritual reading;[56] and if, in the thirteenth and fourteenth centuries, the ancient Philonic tradition fell into its dotage (to use Beryl Smalley's phrase), much else in the poem also looks back to better times.

4 Increase in charity was consistently held to be the chief purpose of 'lectio divina' – a point to which we must briefly return. Study deplores systematic theology precisely because it leads away from charity.

5 While generosity is praised elsewhere in the poem, it appears to be the only virtue Study knows. Further, in her urging it takes the form traditional in monasteries, hospitality.[57]

6 There is no *prima facie* implausibility in associating a character named Study with some part of the 'lectio divina.' Dorothy Owen long ago found an analogue to Dame Study in Leçon, in Guillaume de Deguileville's *Pèlerinage de la vie humaine.*[58]

The motif of orality by itself in Study's speech does not entail a relationship to the 'lectio divina.' If, however, such a relationship appears possible on such grounds as these, concern with the voice takes on a new depth.

In writing of the 'lectio,' Jean Leclercq, having pointed out that private reading during meditation left 'a muscular memory of the words pronounced,' goes on to describe this process as inscription of 'the sacred text in the body and in the soul. This repeated mastication of the divine words is sometimes described by use of the theme of spiritual nutrition. In this case the vocabulary is borrowed from eating, from digestion, and from the particular form of digestion belonging to ruminants. For this reason, reading and meditation are sometimes described by the very expressive word *ruminatio.*[59] Like a nutriment, the essential meaning is liberated from one text by the juxtaposition of another, as the monk becomes 'une concordance vivante.'

But the 'lectio' supposedly issues not in knowledge alone but in a modification of the will. The allegorical understanding of Scripture (represented by the 'cousin' to whom Study points the way) is above all a perception of that foundation which is Christian doctrine. Such a perception theoretically had the (tropological) effect of building the faith within the individual. This faith would have been both cognitive and conative. Henri de Lubac translates an exegete from the School of St Victor: 'dans toute l'écriture deux objets sont à chercher: la "cognitio veritatis" et la "forma virtutus": à la première concourent l'histoire et l'allégorie; c'est la tropologie qui donne la seconde.' The allegorical meaning edifies, while the tropological reforms the individual's conduct. In tropology itself there is a double sense, as Lubac explains: the first and lesser signifies the 'moralizing' of the Bible, perceiving through the letter the doctrine of right conduct. In this sense, for example, Christ's comfort of the woman taken in adultery (12.81) freed the essence of the seventh commandment. The other, mystical sense 'est au dedans de l'allégorie. Elle fait partie intégrante du mystère. Venant après l'aspect objectif qu'en est l'allégorie, elle en constitue l'aspect subjectif. Elle en est, si l'on peut dire, l'intussusception, l'intériorisation; elle nous l'approprie.' In the 'lectio divina,' after the letter of Scripture has been transposed to Christ and 'cristes loue' (12.71), it should be assimilated to oneself. The temple of Solomon, for instance, allegorically the Mystical Body, is to be understood in both senses of tropology as the human heart: first, a new moral meaning has been perceived within the letter; second, one does not merely perceive the temple; he or she becomes the temple, participates in the Mystical Body; and the allegorical meaning, namely, Christ himself, has been assimilated to the individual believer. 'Le sens de l'écriture, en effet, n'est pas une pensée quelconque, ce n'est pas une vérité impersonnelle: c'est *Lui. Ipse Christi arcanus et reconditus sensus.*'[60]

In the 'lectio divina,' the voice becomes, in several senses, a summons to belief: the reader's own voice incorporates another voice, the voice of authority, the sage; and the object of that voice, 'caritas,' is assimilated to the reader himself or herself. As the voice, able to read the Bible privately as well as the *Analytics* to Oxford probationers, Dame Study denounces the friars and their selfish patrons. For them, knowledge of the letter has produced no integrity with the spirit of Scripture. It is the poor, with Christ in their hearts, who possess the tropological meaning, illiterate though they may be.

Belief in the possibility of such an integrity between scriptural meaning and conduct arises with the experience of a certain integrity within oral communication itself, for a speaker's words have no existence apart from his or her own existence. It arises also with the experience of immediacy – or at least the illusion of immediacy – between speaker and auditor. Oral exchange, bound up with gesture and the exchange of physical tokens, had – or at least from the position of literacy is imagined as having had – ritual and performative power. These experiences and the beliefs and illusions that accompany them are projected backwards by literate culture as part of a better age.

The loss of them, felt everywhere in the poem as an ambivalence to literacy, itself becomes a theme in the episode with Dame Study. Prayers, she regrets, can no longer bring a stop to plagues (10.78). Sermons no longer make people generous or strong in their faith (10.75). But the Study episode is not simply nostalgic, for it recovers for illiteracy a place within the very heart of reading. If Study communicates with her students orally, she is nevertheless reading as she does so, and reading from the same trivial and quadrivial texts that had re-established literate science in the late eleventh and the twelfth centuries. The immediacy of preliterate communication is recovered as the integrity of reader and text within the idea that the tropological level of Scripture becomes fully realized only when the reader internalizes it as a change of life. The orality to which the 'lewed' are condemned becomes, in the Study episode, not an incitement to anxiety, but the oral reading of a text, the first stage of 'lectio divina' and a necessary condition for textual understanding.

4

When, indulged by Dame Study, Will resumes his journey midway through passus 10, he comes 'to Clergie ... as clerkes me saide' (C 11.138).[61] Where Study relies on the imagery of the voice, Clergy, who personifies the corpus of beliefs invoked by Study, draws, by contrast, on the metaphor of vision. 'Clergie' presupposes Latin[62] but goes beyond it – and beyond learning even in a more general sense.[63] Intimate with Scripture (allegorically, they are married), he is something 'done with' it, for the worse or better. For example, in a passage added to C, Dame Study regrets that pieces of Scripture are 'capped wiþ clergie to conspire wronge' (11.80) – perversely construed. 'Clergie' indicates the construction in itself.[64] This interpretive quality Imaginative almost certainly has in mind when, in a c-text revision, he says that 'Kynde-wittede men han a clergie by hemsulue; / Of cloudes and of costumes they contreuede mony thynges' (14.72–3).[65]

These several qualities – none of them is particularly stressed – can be placed alongside the treatment of 'clergie' by Imaginative. In both B and C, Imaginative uses the story of the woman taken in adultery to exalt clergy over kynde wit:

> In þe olde lawe as þe lettre telleþ, þat was þe lawe of Iewes,
> ... What womman were in auoutrye taken, wher riche or poore,
> Wiþ stones men sholde hir strike and stone hire to deþe.
> A womman, as we fynden, was gilty of þat dede,
> Ac crist of his curteisie þoruӡ clergie hir saued.
> For þoruӡ carectes þat crist wroot þe Iewes knewe hemselue
> Giltier as afore god, and gretter in synne,
> Than þe womman þat þere was, and wenten awey for shame.
> Thus Clergie þere conforted þe womman.
> Holy Kirke knoweþ þis þat cristes writyng saued;
> So clergie is confort to creatures þat repenten,
> And to mansede men meschief at hire ende.
> ...
> Forþi I counseille þee for cristes sake clergie þat þow louye.
>
> (12.73–84, 92)

The passage is shortened in c and its beginning revised: 'For Moyses witnesseth þat god wroet and Crist with his fynger; / Lawe of loue oure lorde wroet long ar Crist were' (14.37–8). In both passages Christ himself is an exegete. As earlier commentators had done,[66] the poet juxtaposes the Mosaic law forbidding adultery and the 'signe' (c 14.40) – the mark with an occult meaning that Christ writes at the same time that he enacts the 'lawe of loue.' However, the 'lawe of loue' had existed 'long ar Crist were' as the figurative meaning of the Old Law. Hence it is the Old Law *as something that must be interpreted* that Christ shows with marks that signify exactly so far as they are mysterious. Because his writing and then speaking expose the truth of the Old Law and complete it, they begin and justify the tradition of the gloss.

The perception, then, of the law of love essential to all Scripture is the crucial meaning of 'clergie' in *Piers*.[67] Medieval exegetes knew it as 'allegoria,' the first of the three concentric understandings of the 'sensus' (probably represented by Scripture herself). 'Clergie' is the knowledge ('konnynge') of heaven (12.66) because it results from a certain mode of vision (personified by Imaginative): it 'cometh bote of syhte' (c 14.20). Lubac quotes two sentences from Gregory's *Moralia* explaining this: 'Haec per historium facta credimus, sed per allegoriam jam qualiter sint implenda videamus'; and 'Si vero cuncta haec juxta historiam tractando discurrimus, per allegoriae quoque mysteria perscrutemur ...'[68] Events, not words, are allegorical: human history makes a kind of poem, and the exegete *sees through* the earlier events recorded in Scripture to the oneness of the divine ordonnance. Thus subsumed by a type, the event signifies 'tantôt le Christ, et tantôt l'Eglise, et tantôt l'un et l'autre.'[69] Even when Imaginative, the associated faculty of the mind, is absent, Clergy as object of knowledge still speaks of himself as 'allegoria.' Thus, in a later episode, to keep Conscience from leaving his own dinner party, Clergy says, 'I shal brynge yow a bible, a book of þe olde law, / And lere yow if yow like þe leeste point to knowe' (13.185–6). These exegetical labours require the whole apparatus of the seven arts, refractory though they may sometimes be (13.120–3).[70] This mode of vision requires humility. The ascetic approach to 'clergie' described by Dame Study parallels Augustine's advice that the student should approach Holy Scripture as if anointed with hyssop, 'a meek and humble herb, and yet nothing is stronger or more penetrating than its roots.'[71]

If Will seeks to know Christ, then it is pertinent that through 'allegoria' a divine dispensation is perceived in which a series of singular facts lead 'jusqu'à un autre Fait singulier; un série d'interventions divines, dont la réalité même est significative, achemine à une autre sorte d'intervention divine, également réele, plus profonde et plus decisive. Tout culmine dans un grand Fait ... le *Fait du Christ*.'[72] While 'clergie' 'cometh bote of syhte,' it originates in 'cristes loue' (12.71), not only because Christ is the first cleric, as we have seen, but because Christ's love is what is perceived – literally in the New Testament event, figuratively in the Old Testament one. Priests, connoted by 'clergie,' are Christ's vicars 'to conforte and to cure' (c 14.70) because the loving deeds they must perform continue the series of 'facts' that 'allegoria' sees through, and lead back in their turn to 'un autre Fait singulier, le *Fait du Christ*.'

By understanding Christ as implicit in the Law, 'allegoria' under-stands Christ as divine, in the sense of understanding that his lov-ing acts give a privileged glimpse of the ultimate nature of reality. It is not coincidental, I think, that in teaching 'dowel,' 'dobet,' and 'dobest,' the personification of 'allegoria,' Clergy, dilates for twenty lines or so on not just belief in the Trinity but on a Trinitarian belief resting in a figurative reading of Christ himself – an exegesis of the origin of exegesis (10.238–55a). (Clergy gives only seven lines to 'dobet,' which is an integrity between word and deed, and one line to 'dobest,' correction of the guilty.)[73] Within this dilation, Langland assigns to Clergy the line that ties 'allegoria' itself – here the percep-tion of divinity in Christ's love – to Trinitarian belief: 'And Crist cleped hymself so, þe scripture bereþ witnesse: / *Ego in patre et pater in me est, et qui videt me videt et patrem meum'* (10.252–3). Where the Old Law is understood as figuratively Christ, Christ's own love is understood as a figure for the true nature of the Father. In Imagina-tive's view, the Magi are 'clerkes,' surpassing merely learned peo-ple, because they understand that, in the Son, love has leapt out 'into þis lowe erþe' (12.140).

Will, however, cannot now see God as Augustine did (10.249–51)[74] and concludes from this that he is without grace. At one time exege-sis may have led to contrition;[75] and at the end of the poem, the link is suggested: Friar Flatterer having been so complaisant that Contri-tion ceases to be contrite, Conscience sends for 'Clergie to helpe / And ... Contricion ... to kepe þe yate' (20.375–6). This seems to be the paratactic expression of a causal relationship. Nowhere else does *Piers* propose that 'clergie' actually implies contrition. Will is not unique in his inability to see God through 'clergie.' The theory that a puzzle about 'clergie' caused Langland to break off the A text en-counters some difficulty when, despite the rehabilitation of 'clergie' by Imaginative in passus 12, he suffers such diffident treatment in passus 13. At the banquet at Conscience's house, the sybaritic friar illustrates even to Clergy the indispensability of grace. The friar so far as he is an exegete is a master of 'clergie': Will expects him to show that the expensive dishes, allegorically understood, are 'fode for a penaunt,' and Conscience calls him one of 'ye dyuynours.' His version of 'dowel,' 'dobet,' and 'dobest' condenses Clergy's in pas-sus 10. But his extravagant hypocrisy demonstrates the absence of grace rather than offers the vision of Christ. Clergy himself is abashed, declining to speak in deference to Piers. When the friar wishes to ally with Clergy and Conscience, the latter finds Patience more promising and bids Clergy farewell by saying,

> If Pacience be oure partyng felawe and pryue with vs boþe,
> Ther nys wo in þis world þat we ne sholde amende;
> And conformen kynges to pees; and alle kynnes londes,
> Sarsens and Surre, and so forþ alle þe Iewes,
> Turne into þe trewe feiþ and intil oon bileue. (13.206–10)

This casts Clergy merely as a kind of indoctrinator arriving after the battle. By eliminating the passage altogether, c withholds even this measure of usefulness.[76]

One might suggest historical reasons why 'clergie' does not always offer the vision of God (or perhaps just offers it no longer): in the history of biblical study, the triumph of the letter over the spiritual meaning;[77] in the *Zeitgeist*, the decline of allegory to a parlour game, as the poet shows through the clerical gourmand;[78] or in philosophy, the consequences of Ockhamist epistemology, which justified the possibility of intuiting something that did not exist (as non-existent). Clergie is the appearance of Christ where, in at least one sense, Christ does not exist – in the letter of Scripture or in the phenomenal universe.[79]

But Christ does not appear so to Will. Will is without this inspired body of knowledge. One might better say, he controls a body of knowledge that is no longer inspired. He reacts in two ways. In the more obvious, to certain people evidently damned he attributes 'clergie' in its half-life, no longer the vision of Christ in the Law or of the Father in the Son, but simply a body of communicable doctrine. These include Solomon and Aristotle, wisest in their time, as well as Christian 'clerkes' who are 'witty in feiþ' but faulty in their works (10.395, 402). For critics to claim that Will introduces the virtuous heathen 'in order to dispute the necessity of learning and good deeds'[80] seems to me to get the emphasis wrong (not that this supposed necessity isn't problematic for Langland, as he shows in other places): Aristotle is in hell because he does not believe in Christ. No matter how they talk, neither do many clerics contemporary with the poet. Will also reacts to the failure of 'clergie' for him by concluding that he himself is graceless. When the poet revises Will's last speech in passus 10, he adds a line that makes this explicit: 'me were leuere ...,' he tells Clergy and Scripture, 'a lyppe of goddes grace /

Thenne al þe kynde wyt þat ȝe can bothe and kunnyng of ȝoure bokes' (c 12.227–8). For the rest of passus 10 and during most of passus 11, the poet will react to this sense of preterition. These new reactions will give these passus a number of their puzzling turns.

When Will has expressed his disappointment with Clergy in a 'reductio' ('Thanne is dowel and dobet … *dominus* and knyȝthode?' 10.336) and Scripture rejoins by soberly setting 'pouerte with pacience' in opposition to lordship, Will does not regain his earlier optimism (10.158–61): 'This is a long lesson … and litel am I þe wiser' (10.377). Since he cannot believe and thinks he must therefore lack the grace of God, the poet from here on will dramatize himself more than once as making the case for 'cheap grace':[81] 'That is baptiȝed beþ saaf, be he riche or pouere' (10.351). There is safety in institutions. In answer, Scripture concedes that baptism may suffice for Saracens and Jews who are *in extremis,* but a Christian not at death's door 'sholde louye and lene and þe lawe fulfille' (10.360). This is ethical instruction that resembles Lady Holy Church's. The problem for Will is not that he knows of choices that are ethically superior (where would they be found, if not in Holy Church?) but that the language is ethical at all: Clergy's digression was, of course, the poet's own, from the one thing necessary (the 'optimam partem' chosen by Mary, the sister of Lazarus [11.256a]). And the poet is in the dilemma of rejecting such language ('This is a long lesson … and litel am I þe wiser' 10.377) at the same time as he explores ways he might try to live without belief. He himself will show these to be impossible.[82]

At this point Will says that the upshot of his experience with Scripture is his becoming convinced that he is predestined one way or the other. In c, blame for the message falls, more accurately, perhaps, upon Clergy:

That y man ymaed was and my nam y-entred
In þe legende of lyf longe ar y were.
Predestinaet thei prechen, prechours þat this sheweth,
Or prescient inparfit, pult out of grace,
Vnwriten for som wikkednesse, as holy writ sheweth.
    Nemo ascendit ad celum nisi qui de celo descendit.
And I leue hit wel, by oure lord, and on no lettrure bettere.   (11.206–11)

Those written into the Book of Life have been given the grace to believe, the eyes to see: it is this that indispensably 'de celo descendit.' The great penitents – Dismas, Mary Magdalene, the apostle Paul – had it (10.420–33);[83] illiterate shoemakers and shepherds have it (10.458–71). Will believes he doesn't, just as later, when Scripture preaches that only a few are 'plukked in,' he will fear he is reprobate: 'for tene of hir text trembled myn herte' (11.111–17). As Pamela Gradon has pointed out, fear of reprobation is discussed in *The Chastizing of God's Children* as a temptation to despair.[84] And it is a desperate Will who writhes in vexation when Scripture accuses him of self-ignorant pomposity (11.3).

Will falls at this point into an inner dream, one, as we shall see, that the poet makes predictive of a later crisis in his life.[85] This inner dream is the only one remaining in C. The poet shows himself reckless because desperate; and in fact Langland in his C version reassigns to a character named Recklessness the long speech at the end of passus 10 in which Will had expressed his despair with Clergy and Scripture. 'Rechelesnesse' does not, I think, undergo some peculiar development from his brief appearance in B (11.34–6) to his new role in C, or even during the course of his long substitution for Will in C.[86] A life of pleasure closed out by deathbed repentance, when present misery drowns any memory of pleasure, appears more than once to the poet as the best he can manage. As late as the *Vita de dobe*t, Will will ask the Samaritan,

> I pose I hadde synned ... and sholde nouþe deye,
> And now am sory þat I so þe Seint Spirit agulte,
> Confesse me and crye his grace, crist þat al made,
> And myldeliche his mercy aske; myghte I noȝt be saued?   (17.299–302)

In passus 11, Recklessness, who has not yet literally become Will, advises him, 'Folwe forþ þat Fortune wole; þow hast wel fer til Elde, / A man may stoupe tyme ynoȝ whan he shal tyne þe crowne' (11.35–6). This desperate course is itself the reaction of one who had already, like the merchant of the parable, recklessly invested everything in seeking the one thing needful, giving little thought to status or career ('witlees nerhande, / ... As a freke þat fey were'; 'some lakkede my lif – allowed it fewe'; 'Wolleward and weetshoed wente I forþ after'; 'Heuy chered I yede and elenge in herte'). Surely these distresses are what the narrator means when he thinks back on himself as one who 'hath ychaffared / And ay loste and loste' (C 5.94–5).

He had for a long while been reckless as the friars were supposed to be, not caring too much.[87] His recklessness in the pejorative sense comes from disappointments in that quest. At the start of the inner dream, his desperate recklessness takes the form – a form that he must already know will prove unsatisfactory – of giving himself over hedonistically to the Three Temptations and betting again on cheap grace:

> Coueitise of eiȝes ofte me conforted;
> 'Haue no conscience,' quod she, 'how þow come to goode;
> Go confesse þee to som frere and shewe hym þi synnes.'   (11.52–4)

But only 'costly grace' will do. Langland shows this first in a kind of meiosis, when his confessor withholds absolution until he can find the money to make a cash 'restitution.' Scripture makes the point again by preaching that, while many are called to the feast, only a few are admitted. Will reasserts the sufficiency of cheap grace: 'on holi chirche I þouȝte / That vnderfonged me atte fonte for oon of goddes chosene.' (11.117–18). It is impossible to renounce this 'cristendom,' by which he means, not Christian wisdom, acquiescence to God's 'redeeming impact ... *pro nobis*,'[88] but simply baptism, the assurance that one cannot be fired into hell out of hand. And we hear the narrator asserting the possibility of contrition without faith: in purgatory, temporal punishment for his sins will wring contrition from him at last (11.131–6).[89]

Unprepared to deny the supremacy of God's mercy, Scripture hesitantly grants this unorthodox version of purgatory. But at once the uneasy solution gives way before Trajan, who, ignorant of 'clergie,' has been saved because he satisfied the Law (11.144–5). Will seizes upon Trajan (11.158–63) because Trajan's will is so good that it is *as if* he believed. Trajan declares he was no ordinary believer and received grace 'wiþouten bede biddyng' (he repeats this three lines later) or 'syngynge of masses' (11.150–1). In c, he is explicitly without 'lele bileue' (12.85).

This point Imaginative will contradict. At the end of Imaginative's apology for 'clergie,' Will, who lacks the vision called 'clergie,' attempts to compensate for his lack by an *ad hominem* gesture against the 'grete clerk' Aristotle, who, pagan though he may have been, had been held up by Imaginative as exemplifying a certain poetic gift. While Aristotle may have been 'ymaginatif,' he did not believe in

Christ, says Will, and is therefore lost: 'neiþer Sarsens ne Iewes / Ne no creature of cristes liknesse withouten cristendom worþ saued' (12.278–9). Imaginative responds unpleasantly with Trajan, whom he has mentioned before (12.210–13) and whom Will himself had celebrated, of course, against Clergy and Scripture. Langland has been showing the courses of action open to the person who cannot believe. (The vindictiveness he assigns himself in his attack on the darlings of Imaginative is, unfortunately, one of these.) Through Imaginative, Langland presses again the decisiveness of belief: when he *finishes* talking about Trajan, Imaginative can still say, 'þe worþ of bileue is gret' (12.291). Trajan's relation to this conclusion of Imaginative's is not obvious, however.

Recent interpretation of this Roman emperor in *Piers*, which has been plentiful, has focused on Langland's novel reading of the legend (coincidentally, perhaps, like Dante's), acknowledging at the same time inconsistencies in Langland's treatment. Once Trajan's dramatic function in passus 11 has been distinguished from the function of the references to him in passus 12, then I think that Langland's handling of the legend can be seen as selective rather than untraditional. In passus 11, Will, who cannot believe, makes use of Trajan for his own purposes. Because criticism has not generally taken this view, some readers – especially those who join certain of Will's interlocutors in calling upon him to reform – have even argued that a long speech by Will in passus 11 should be assigned to someone else.[90] Yet it is Will himself who, for perfectly plausible reasons, wants to argue that Trajan receives the grace of God because he did the best he could. At some level Langland knows better than this; and incipient in Trajan's speech is Imaginative's conclusion: 'þe worþ of bileue is gret.'

To see this, we must consider Langland's treatment of Trajan in some detail. In passus 11, Trajan breaks on the scene, 'out of helle,' to declare,

I Troianus, a trewe knyȝt, take witnesse at a pope
How I was ded and dempned to dwellen in pyne
For an vncristene creature; clerkes wite þe soþe
That al þe clergie vnder crist ne myȝte me cracche for helle,
But oonliche loue and leautee and my laweful domes.
Gregorie wiste þis wel, and wilned to my soule
Sauacion for sooþnesse þat he seiȝ in my werkes.

And for he wepte and wilned þat I were saued
Graunted me worþ grace þorȝ his grete wille.
Wiþouten bede biddyng his boone was vnderfongen
And I saued as ye may see, wiþouten syngynge of masses,
By loue and by lernyng of my lyuynge in truþe.   (11.141–52)

The context of this intrusion, again, is the poet's having tested 'clergie' with results that disappointed Will and left him fearing he was reprobate. When Will seizes on *parts* of this speech of Trajan's – when, for instance, he sums it up by saying that 'leel loue and lyuyng in truþe / Pulte out of pyne a paynym of rome' (11.162–3) – he seizes upon exactly that part of Trajan's experience that was manifestly unaccompanied by any special mode of vision. When he says that 'clergie' could not do the job for Trajan ('truþe' saved the 'sarsyn' where 'no clergie ne kouþe' (11.164–6), he is equivocating on 'clergie': Trajan had used it to signify such liturgical practices as intercessory masses (11.150–1), while Will uses it as well to connote his most recent interlocutors in this third vision, Clergy and Scripture. He softens his fruitless experience with them by understanding Trajan to mean that they are dispensable. A truculent Will is not *confronted* by a semi-Pelagian doctrine embodied in Trajan. Rather, that is the doctrine Will adopts; and he is not disinterested in doing so. So far as Will is contentious at the beginning of the inner dream ('Haddestow suffred,' Imaginative will later accuse him, as the outer dream resumes, 'slepynge þo þow were' 11.413), he is resisting 'clergie': 'Thow sholdest haue knowen þat clergie kan' (11.414).

Trajan certainly does not take the position that, by following the best law he knew, he was 'guaranteed ... divine acceptation,' never having needed any conversion on his part to the 'lele bileue' in Christ that in fact he rejected while he was alive (c 12.85).[91] If he had been guaranteed divine acceptation, he would not have been in hell to begin with; but he introduces himself as one who had been 'ded and dampned' (11.142), beyond the reach of baptism.[92] Imaginative also makes clear that Trajan was in hell, although not lodged so deeply there that the Lord couldn't easily get him out (12.210–11). But Pope Gregory knew about his just works, Trajan says, 'wilned þat I were saued; / Graunted me worþ grace þorȝ *his grete wille*' (11.148–9; my emphasis). If God had made a promise from all eternity to accept records like Trajan's as meritorious 'de congruo,' the plea by Gregory would not have been a necessary condition for his salvation.[93]

(Will shrewdly makes Gregory merely a witness to Trajan's salvation [11.157].) While Trajan does not rehearse his whole legend, the portions he gives are consistent with the main tradition, as Gordon Whatley has summarized it: as emphasized particularly by Bonaventure, 'Trajan's salvation was a special case, made possible by his being given a second chance at life itself, so that he might conform himself, however briefly, to the Christian life.'[94] It is only after his first physical death, then, that he is 'ded and dampned.'

Before passus 12, the narrator has already expressed his detachment from that body of figuration called 'clergie.' He expresses this again after Imaginative has celebrated 'clergie,' although Imaginative concedes that a 'grete clerke' like Aristotle may not be saved: 'wheiþer he be saaf or noȝt saaf, þe soþe woot no clergie' (12.270). Will's 'entremetynge' on this occasion takes the form of a contention that Aristotle's salvation is not an open question:

'Alle þise clerkes,' quod I þo, 'þat on crist leuen
Seyen in hir Sermons þat neiþer Sarsens ne Iewes
Ne no creature of cristes liknesse withouten cristendom worþ saued.'

(12.277–9)

Imaginative receives this with ill grace, and returns to the same non-Christian, obedient to the best Law he knew, whom Will himself praised after Scripture had left Will frightened and desperate. Will had found 'clergie' closed to him then; now, in passus 12, these great 'clerkes' (and Imaginative, who personifies, as we shall see, the 'potentia' that they have) once again leave Will 'witlees nerhande' (13.1). A frowning Imaginative defends his 'clerkes' with a '*Contra*!' and goes on to argue towards the conclusion that the question *is* open: 'And wheiþer it worþ of truþe or noȝt, þe worþ of bileue is gret, / And an hope hangynge þerInne' (12.290–1). These difficult lines seem to mean, 'Whether or not obeying the best law that one knows is rewarded by God with salvation, the value of belief (or faith) is great, for it issues in hope.'[95] In arguing towards this conclusion, Imaginative is not easy to follow.

He begins with Trajan, Will's own instance. His argument will then make two turns, each marked by an 'Ac' (12.285, 287).[96] With the first of these he reminds Will that there are actually three kinds of baptism, not simply the one 'in aqua' that Will may have been assuming; indeed, if there were only one, Trajan, Will's own instance, would not now be 'saaf.'[97] With the second 'Ac,' Imaginative turns away, at least initially, from baptism altogether; for the great 'clerkes' in whom he is interested lived before Christ, and therefore baptism with its explicit belief in Christ was not available to them in any form. Yet he argues that a 'trewe god' would not damn them. Imaginative is defending his 'clerkes.' He is not intending to give Will whatever that wanderer might require 'kyndely on crist to bileue.' How could he be, since he is defending righteous men who lived before Christ? No doubt it would be well if a person 'neuere ne trauersed' against the Law. But no such person may exist. Will, in any case, does not think so (15.156–60). And after the birth of Christ that would not be enough. As Anima will observe,

> Iewes lyuen in lele lawe; oure lord wroot it hymselue
> In stoon for it stedfast was and stonde sholde euere.
> *Dilige deum & proximum* is parfit Iewen lawe;
> And took it Moyses to teche men til Messie coome,
> And on þat lawe þei leue and leten it þe beste,
> And ȝit knewe þei crist þat cristendom tauȝte,
> And for a parfit prophete þat muche peple sauede
> Of selkouþe sores ...
> ...
> And studieden to struyen hym and struyden hemselue ...   (15.582–97)

Here are people who act according to the highest law they know and are destroyed. With the first 'Ac,' Imaginative turned away from any simple notion of baptism; he did this as part of a defence that made use of Trajan. With the second 'Ac' he turns to look back before the Christian era (and thus before Trajan), when no more than a 'fides implicita' could be imputed to pagans who made good use of what was naturally at their disposal.[98]

The c text adds to Will's summary of his vision of Imaginative: 'And y merueyled in herte how Ymaginatyf saide / That *iustus* bifore Iesu *in die iudicii* / *Non saluabitur* bote if *vix* helpe' (15.21–2). This does not sound as if God has promised to supply the 'dignitas' to good works, by whomever performed. The case may be (although Imaginative is hardly clear about it) that the means taken by a 'trewe god' to reward the implicit faith of the great pre-Christian 'clerkes' is to give them the opportunity to believe explicitly in the Atonement – the five wounds of Jesus that 'vix' may encode. T.P. Dunning maintained convincingly that in Langland's own time 'the majority of theologians taught that God makes it possible for all men of good will to attain to the degree of faith necessary for salvation.'[99] What is certain is that the value of 'bileue,' 'fides,' is the one thing Imaginative is certain of (12.291, 293). As for the great 'clerkes,' Imaginative may think that 'bileue' follows from something like 'a special inner revelation [post-mortem] of Christ's coming redemption of man.'[100] This 'bileue' would baptize by fire, as legendarily Trajan was so baptized after his first death. Because 'fir' in one sense is the remorse that both constitutes faith and results from it, Aquinas, as Whatley points out, called it the 'baptismus poenitentiae,'[101] '*non comburens set illuminans*' (12.286a). When Imaginative claims that 'þoruȝ fir is fullyng, and þat is ferme bileue' (12.286), the second half-line is ambiguous: one is entitled to 'ferme bileue' in the possibility of Trajan's conversion. Yet 'ferme bileue' itself is a 'fullyng,' in the orthodox view. Imaginative concludes with scriptural quotations taking faith as their subject. By believing in the best law he knew, Trajan was 'super pauca fidelis'; accordingly, he was given the chance to be faithful over much. For it is to the 'fidelibus' that eternal life is given.

We have had to consider Trajan at some length because Will seizes upon him when 'clergie' fails Will. In reaction to this failure to believe in a certain way, the poet had represented Will as giving himself over to a desperate hedonism. The poet also represents Will as avoiding, with certain strategies, the need to believe. Will's emphasis upon the sufficiency of Trajan's 'leute' had been one of these.[102] In passus 11 he has other strategies, which we may briefly consider.

Strategically, Will equates generosity to the poor with 'bileue' in Christ. In the 'liknesse' of the poor 'oure lorde lome haþ ben yknowe' (11.233). Someone treating a poor person well has reason to hope that, like Cleophas, he or she may find that the poor person is actually Christ. Will's strategy of avoidance takes him to a view of poverty resembling his hopeful view of purgatory. When someone has nothing, *then* he or she will be faithful: patient poverty 'Makeþ a man to haue mynde in god and a gret wille / To wepe and to wel bidde, wherof wexeþ Mercy' (11.264–5). To be perfectly destitute means (so the inference seems to go) to be perfect.[103] To be cold and hungry in the winter is to be *as if*, converted by Christ, one had divested oneself for the poor and followed him. By a subtle shift, Will moves from conversion, with which he had begun in justifying poverty,[104] to martyrs and confessors, whose faith is merely assumed; and then contrasts them with the rich, with their many opportunities to sin. When he reverts to the poor, they are hardly the rich young ruler now lacking his things. In a long addition to c on poverty, the poor messenger speeds along simply because he avoids the justice of the Old Law by owning nothing:

> The messager aren this mendenantz þat lyuen by menne almesse,
> Beth nat ybounde as beth ȝe ryche to bowe to þe lawes,
> To lene ne to lerne ne lentones to faste
> And other pryue penaunces þe which þe prest woet wel
> That þe lawe ȝeueth leue such low folk to be excused
> ...
> For if he loueth and byleueth as the lawe techeth–
>> Qui crediderit et baptizatus fuerit, etc.–
> ...
> And knowelecheth hym cristene and of holy kirke byleue,
> Ther is no lawe, as y leue, wol lette hym þe gate ...   (13.78–90)

The letter carried by the messenger matters only because it has no commercial value, and the thieves let him alone (c 13.58–9). It is a naïve affirmation – he 'sheweth þe seel and seth by lettre with what lord he dwelleth / And knowelecheth hym cristene and of holy kirk byleue' (c 13.88–9) – and contrasts ironically with Piers's anguishing pardon and with the costly 'writ' to be borne by *Spes* (17.3–8). On the road to Jericho in the *Vita de dobet*, Everyman will be beaten and robbed, not just the rich.

Uncritical faith, acceptance of the sacraments, sinlessness for want of opportunity, attention to God as the only source of help – this is the alternative with which 'Rechelesnesse in a rage aresenede Clergie / And Scripture scornede' (c 13.128–9). For Recklessness, it is an ersatz faith ('Ac leueth nat ... þat y lacke rychesse'), offering as a relief from his failure to respond to Clergy first the search for God among his humbler creatures and then the compassionate hypostatization, from their point of view, of a kind of belief. The effort, however, to sustain this elaborate structure of assertion, raising in a disguised form the same cheap grace that Scripture once had spoiled, gives way at last when Kynde comes to aid Clergy by making Will scrutinize the 'myrour of Mydelerthe' (c 13.131). The ensuing scene puts the preceding one in an ironic perspective: given the opportunity, people surfeit themselves. Poverty was a piece of good luck. Where

Will's strategy in passus 11 had been to move from scripturally enjoined poverty to poverty imposed by circumstances and enforcing
virtue and belief, the universal human unrighteousness he sees
thereafter presses again the necessity for 'dowel' – and he comes
humbly to Imaginative, as he had earlier moved from Dame Study
to Clergy.

5

Whether the twelfth passus lifts the dreamer to a plateau in his development, as many interpreters believe,[105] cannot be decided apart
from a consideration of the puzzling identity of 'Ymaginatif,' who,
like Reason, Wit, and the others, personifies a 'type' that must be
constantly corrected by what we actually find him doing and saying. Although Frank did not disclose his evidence, he was likely right
that 'The usual explanation of Imaginatif as "memory" is unsatisfactory.'[106] And while Bloomfield's identification of Imaginative as
prophecy[107] left passus 12 largely uninterpreted, it is true that when
Will ponders his vision of Imaginative he hardly speaks as if he has
finished a tour of the past:

> Ymaginatif in dremels me tolde
> Of kynde and of his konnynge, and how curteis he is to bestes,
> And how louynge he is to ech lif on londe and on watre–
> Leneþ he no lif lasse ne moore–
> For alle creatures þat crepen or walken of kynde ben engendred;
> And siþen how ymaginatif seide *'vix saluabitur iustus,'*
> And whan he hadde seid so, how sodeynliche he passed.   (13.14–20)

It is striking that all but the last two lines of this synopsis refer not
to Imaginative's speech but to that last portion of the dream-within-
a-dream beginning,

> and siþen cam kynde
> And nempned me by my name and bad me nymen hede,
> And þoruʒ þe wondres of þis world wit for to take.   (11.321–3)

Imaginative has told Will this 'in dremels' in the sense that Imaginative *produced* the dream. Appropriately, as the faculty responsible
for dreams,[108] Imaginative is tested within the context of Will's quest

for 'kynde knowyng' by being allowed to make, not just a speech, but also a dream. (The dream-within-a-dream attributed to him is the only one remaining in C.)[109] When he confesses to having often moved Will

<blockquote>

to mynne on þyn ende,
And how fele fernyeres are faren and so fewe to come
And of þi wilde wantownesse whiles þow yong were
To amende it in þi myddel age, lest myȝt þe faille
In þyn olde elde, þat yuele kan suffre
Pouerte or penaunce, or preyeres bidde,   (12.4–9)
</blockquote>

he obviously refers to the opening scenes of his recent production, when Will dreamt that youthful self-sufficiency had tempted him to 'acounten Clergie liȝte' until he 'foryede youþe and yarn into Elde' (11.16, 60). Where Imaginative had begun the inner dream with this 'memento mori' for those who contemn 'clergie,' he ends it also with a pageant that, in C at least, is explicitly on Clergy's behalf (13.130). Imaginative's making of this specific inner dream will be hard to understand if we simply think of the large middle section of it as the praise of patient poverty. The inner dream turns out to be prophetic: the 'memento mori' is validated in the final outer dream (passus 20),[110] to which the inner one stands as any 'visio' to ordinary waking life. There the friars will collude with the Seven Sins as earlier they had given Will up to the Three Temptations; the piquant 'foryede youþe and yarn into Elde' will be protracted into a list of geriatric complaints, and so on.

To associate Imaginative with the faculty for making similitudes,[111] however, accounts for not only his ability to prophesy but also the unity of his speech and his special relationship to 'clergie.' For both Aristotle and Augustine, the healthy mind knows, at least during waking hours, that the images presented in imagination are similitudes. Further, since Plato's use of 'phantasma' in the early dialogues,[112] the similitudes of the artist, including metaphor, have been ascribed to imagination. Similitudes became involved in the problem of religious knowledge, first because philosophers like Richard of St Victor sometimes argued that reason could reach the contemplation of invisible things only through the images of visible ones.[113] Second, Scripture was taken to be metaphoric where 'the things meant by the words also themselves mean something.' As Aquinas says in a well-known passage, 'Holy Scripture fittingly delivers divine and spiritual realities under bodily guises. For God provides for all things according to the kind of things they are. Now we are of the kind to reach the world of intelligence through the world of sense, since all our knowledge takes its rise from sensation.'[114]

Although metaphors run all through *Piers*, of course, they proliferate in Imaginative's speech.[115] Because Imaginative, as we have seen, is interested in defending the body of knowledge called 'clergie,' his entire speech will concern metaphor. For example, he promotes 'clergie' by likening the cleric's book to a strong-box (12.109–13). He goes to a metonym for the book, another strong-box, the Ark of the Covenant. The figure is reasonably complex, for the Ark is a chest containing a chest: the Law itself must be unlocked by 'clergie.' The cleric's book is both figuratively the chest and literally within the figurative chest. While characters elsewhere in the poem use metaphor to illustrate, Imaginative uniquely, when he likens clerics to swimmers and kynde-witted men to non-swimmers, attempts to prove a point with a serious, exact analogy.

He draws attention to similitudes, dwelling upon them as related either directly or indirectly to sense impressions – as literal, that is, or metaphoric. Kynde-witted[116] people have learned to be imaginative in their own manner (as C puts it, 'Kynde-wittede men han a clergie by hemsulue' 14.72) – to reflect upon images and interpret them as similitudes of something not present:

> Ac kynde wit comeþ of alle kynnes siȝtes,
> Of briddes and of beestes, by tastes of truþe.
> Dyuyneris toforn vs viseden and markeden
> The selkouþes þat þei seiȝen, hir sones for to teche.   (12.128–31)

'Of cloudes and of costumes they contreuede mony thynges' (C 14.73). Red at morning, for instance, can be read as the image produced by a storm later in the day. As a species of knowledge, 'clergie' is also consciousness of similitudes – (1) Scripture that does not literally proclaim the law of love and (2) the phenomenal world – and their indirect relationship to God's love. The kynde-witted person can be taught to see one state of nature as the sign of another; for 'clergie,' all of nature is a word, metaphoric for God, who alone is 'res.' From Imaginative's viewpoint, therefore, which is a state of grace, the imaginative power is an instrument (metaphorically, a weapon) that the kynde-witted person carries without being able to use it to save himself (12.105–8).

Imaginative had intended in the inner dream to lead Will to understand the view from 'myddelerþe' as similitude. With the failure of that, Imaginative himself demonstrates how the imaginative power, properly guided, can produce 'clergie' out of natural objects:

> Ac of briddes and of beestes men by olde tyme
> Ensamples token and termes, as telleþ þise poetes,
> And þat þe faireste fowel foulest engendreþ,
> And feblest fowel of fliȝt is þat fleeþ or swymmeþ;
> And þat is þe pekok & þe Pehen wiþ hir proude feþeres
> Bitoknep riȝt riche men þat reigne here on erþe.
>
> ...
>
> The larke þat is a lasse fowel is moore louelich of ledene,
> And wel awey of wynge swifter þan þe Pecock,
> And of flessh by fele fold fatter and swetter;
> To lowe lybbynge men þe larke is resembled.
> Swiche tales telleþ Aristotle[117] þe grete clerk;
> Thus he likneþ in his logik þe leeste fowel oute.
> And wheiþer he be saaf or noȝt saaf, þe soþe woot no clergie.
>
> (12.236–41, 264–70)

Precisely because, faithful to the best law they knew, these 'clerkes' made didactic metaphors, Imaginative wishes them well, almost to the point of assimilating them to the contemporary clergy:

> to bidden we ben holden–
> That god for his grace gyue hir soules reste,
> For lettred men were lewed yet ne were loore of hir bokes. (12.274–6)

'Clergie' is no more simple literacy than these tales are ornithology. Because both the poet and the cleric are aware of similitudes, Imaginative identifies them with each other: Aristotle, who 'swiche tales telleþ,' is 'þe grete clerk,' while the good news of the Nativity was manifested to 'poetes,' the magi – 'þe hyeste lettred oute,' anticipating even Christ as exegetes.[118] Only clerics, as Imaginative sees them, are necessarily poets. Kynde-witted people *may* develop a reflexive attitude towards the imagery in their mind, but more often they confine themselves to their delight with 'sensibilia,' exploiting sensory imagery without using it as similitude. The image of Rosamond's beautiful body must be taken as separable from the thing itself and therefore potentially metaphoric, just as (to cite a famous example) the gold in the Pardoner's Tale must be 'read' as no less poisonous than the wine. Otherwise, 'Catel and kynde wit' encumber 'hem alle' (12.45).

Imaginative devotes most if not all of his speech to forwarding 'clergie.' He omits from C an acknowledgment of responsibility for simulacra in dreams (B 12.4–15), perhaps in deference to his power to grasp similitudes in themselves and make and understand them as metaphoric, his more important meaning. In C, he associates 'dowel' and 'dobet' not as in B with virtues present in each of the faithful (12.29–32) but with callings – 'dowel' with material productivity and 'dobet' with clerics. Where 'dowel' merely acquiesces to authority, 'dobet' believes. Imaginative goes on at once in C to denounce 'catel and kynde wit,' which, having made

> loreles to be lordes and lewede men techares
> And holy chirche horen helpe, auerous and coueytous,
> Druyeth vp Dowel and distruyeth Dobest.[119]   (14.20–2)

'Dobet' is not mentioned, perhaps for the reason that, when ignorant people become teachers, 'clergie' itself disappears. This disappearance 'druyeth vp' and 'distruyeth' the other estates: failed teachers cause the damnation of the unlettered labourer (B 12.183–6). As Wit in passus 9 identified himself with the pragmatic person, Imaginative analogously sees himself as the cleric. Thus he says to Will, 'I haue folwed þee, in feiþ, þise fyue and fourty wynter, / And manye tymes haue meued þee to mynne on þyn ende' (12.3–4) – in C, 'wissed the fol ofte what Dowel was to mene.' I have acted towards you, in short, as your priest, the 'ymaginatif' man.

Despite a critical consensus that passus 12 corrects Will on the problem of evil and the question of predestination, Imaginative responds to these largely by denying that anyone should investigate them. Dame Study had promised an answer from him on why God had allowed Adam to fall.[120] But Imaginative says simply: 'Clergie ne kynde wit ne knew neuere þe cause, / Ac kynde knoweþ þe cause hymself ...' and 'Kynde knoweþ whi he dide so, ac no clerk ellis' (12.225–6, 235). If clerics cannot tell you why God made the birds to be good, they can still tell stories about the birds in order to make *you* good. On predestination, Imaginative can only admit that the conversion of one thief rather than another exceeds the clerical competence.

While the origin of grace is a mystery, Imaginative nearly makes grace itself dependent upon the knowledge called 'clergie.' When he opposes 'kynde wit' to grace and then to 'clergie,'[121] he moves towards identifying grace with 'clergie.' The grace to believe bestowed on Dismas is assimilated to the clergy by benefit of which other thieves are physically 'saued' (12.191). Imaginative assumes for 'clergie' the conditions of grace and belief, but cannot say how they may be obtained (12.214–16).

Imaginative leaves Will 'witlees nerhande,' but not necessarily because Langland, like the scholastics, is convinced that poetry is useless for theology.[122] To the contrary, he may face in Imaginative an authorized version of his own vocation.[123] 'Clergie' fails because Imaginative cannot provide first-intentional knowledge of God – the 'kynde knowyng' on which conversion and belief depend. Parallels might include Augustine's preference for the 'visio intellectualis,' an affair of the reason dispensing with imagery altogether. Similarly, Hugh of St Victor sharply distinguished wisdom, informed by the divine presence, from 'scientia,' which is informed by the imagination. Imagination in itself, he thought, casts a shadow.[124]

Imagination as the traditional mediator between sense and reason and passus 12 as supposedly answering all Will's reasonable doubts have led to the notion that Imaginative is 'servant to Reason' in the sense of preparing Will for reason to take charge. But this is not what happens. The plot shows Will eager to dine with Reason – allegorically, no doubt, to become reasonable. Except for his desperate fling with the Three Temptations, however, he seems to want this all along. Further, the idea that Imaginative is 'servant to Reason' may not give sufficient weight to the priority of reason in medieval psychology: imaginative serves it because reason, already established, desires to use it reasonably. This is clear in the *Benjamin Minor*, for instance, and also in a treatise that Horstman attributed to Walter Hilton: 'a saule in *vndirstandynge of gastely thynges* es ofte-sythes touched and kennede thurghe bodyly ymagynacyone, by wyrkynge of aungells.'[125] If intellect – apprehension of the suprasensible, making possible the right use of imagery – was prior even for the mystics, it was more so for someone like Bonaventure, who believed, as Gilson put it, 'that the idea of God cannot be considered as one of the images formed by thought through contact with sensible things.'[126]

These are no more than historical parallels. Imaginative represents the possibility for treating experience in a certain way. On the evidence of the poem alone, it seems clear that he is not the goal of Will's quest to believe 'kyndely on crist.' The usefulness of the power to understand experience as metaphoric depends for Will upon knowledge of another kind. As he awakens from this third vision, he is looking for it still.

The Movement of Conscience I:
From Haukyn towards a
Ground for Patience

The *Vita de dowel* is completed by a second vision, half as long as the first and traditionally less confounding in its turns of action. In this second dream, Langland begins to develop and explore what he personifies as Conscience, who has been absent since the *Visio* and who will disappear again during the *Vita de dobet*, only to re-emerge in a final and crucial development in *Dobest*.

The new vision in *Dowel* makes a new start. Conscience opens it by reacting to the failure of Imaginative. The cynical virtuosity of a gluttonous doctor serves to put 'clergie' and the former vision at a distance. 'Clergie' is present as a personification in the new vision, however; and while Will is eager to meet him again (13.24), Clergy's own reticence during the scene seems something of a projection of the poet's reservations about 'clergie' (and therefore Imaginative too) in the previous dream. Conscience has changed also. The pardon scene had exploded the world of the *Visio*, where Reason and Conscience worked only damnation, first instigating brutal sanctions. In *Dowel*, Reason is unavailable, and when Conscience now reappears, he is uncertain and humbled. Nevertheless, he turns the quest into a new direction; and it will be he, as I shall try to show in the next chapter, who gives Will the vision of God.

Conscience is ambiguous, which is not the same thing, of course, as Langland's having conceived him unclearly. The poet creates the ambiguity by melding several different traditions.[1]

1

While we can discern three sides of Conscience (the moral, the psychological, and what might be called the conative), the psychological will prove crucial in *Piers*. Nevertheless, Conscience personifies first, and in some sense always, the moral conscience, which calculates from the viewpoint of divine law what is obligatory under particular circumstances.[2] Thus, if a villein runs away, Reason 'shal rekene wiþ hym and rebuken hym at þe laste, / And Conscience acounte wiþ hym and casten hym in arerage' (11.131–2). These lines assign the same two functions to both Reason and Conscience, rather than separate out one of these functions and assign it to Reason and take the other and assign it to Conscience. Because the moral sense of 'reson' is the knowledge of rectitude, 'reson' often stands to the moral conscience as cause to effect.[3] When Conscience knows that Reason will reign (3.284), this means, presumably, that Reason will reign over him, too. That is, so far as I, by natural knowledge or revelation, know the obligations of people like me as set by God's conception of us, this knowledge becomes the major premise in an inference about my duty in a specific instance. The moral conscience is the capacity to draw such inferences, the inferring, and the conclusions themselves. In the usual terms of medieval psychology, it is faculty, act, and habit. As determined by 'reson' when it is act and thus habit, conscience is sometimes subordinate to 'reson,'[4] compatible with it,[5] an application of it,[6] or a means of attaining it.[7] Because 'reson' grasps the divine rightness as 'causa causans' and, in turn, governs conscience, conscience is thought to mediate between God and humankind[8] – and is sometimes an intermediary more generally.[9]

Further, because 'reson' as rightness of the will (or justice) connects with natural and positive law, so the moral conscience, informed by 'reson,' is associated with justice,[10] knows equity[11] and canon law,[12] serves the king,[13] designs the material arrangements for society,[14] and holds the line against Meed. Moreover, thus subordinate to 'reson,' the moral conscience implies the same physical distress for those who do not conform with it as 'reson' entailed for the unrighteous,[15] all the while doing nothing, it seems, to relieve mischief.[16] Because Will himself is unrighteous, however, his conscience differs from 'reson': when Piers leaves the banquet that begins the second vision of *Dowel*, 'Resoun ran aftur and riht with hym ȝede; / Saue Concience and Clergie y couthe no mo aspye' (c 15.151–2). Conscience will act here in the absence of righteousness; perhaps he will act in consequence of *un*righteousness.[17] Not everyone may be just, but everyone has a conscience.

If Conscience merely declared one moral course of action or another, it would be the same blind alley for Will that Reason is. But in *Piers* as elsewhere, Conscience is also a sort of record-keeper,[18] knowing the history of one's actual choices and intentions: 'whan I chalange or chalange noȝt,' says Anima, 'chepe or refuse, / Thanne am I Conscience ycalled, goddes clerk and his Notarie' (15.31–2). As judicial officers, notaries recorded the intentions (of contracting parties) rather than interpreted the law.[19] For Augustine, 'conscientia' is this sorry record, open to God's scrutiny: 'Et tibi quidem, domine, cuius oculis nuda est abyssus humanae conscientiae, quid occultum esset in me ...?'[20] Likewise, in confessing his awareness of what he is doing at the moment he covets, Haukyn says, 'Vpon a cruwel coueitise my conscience gan hange' (13.390). The notarial conscience is the psychological one, for it has the acts of the mind itself as object. The psychological conscience, therefore, can grasp simultaneously a judgment of what ought to be done on a particular occasion and also the mind's choice, perhaps, to move towards a very different good. Because mental acts – knowing what is obligatory, choosing something else – are themselves the objects of (the psychological) conscience, they are known intuitively, for such acts are no less present and existing than the mental act that grasps them.[21] Thus, Piers speaks of a place called 'Conscience, þat crist wite þe soþe, / That ye louen oure lord god leuest of all þynges' (5.562–3). Here, consciousness of a choice – namely, that one loves God above all – is itself known by Christ to be 'þe soþe.'

Conscience as psychological accounts for the immediacy that Langland attributes to guilt and shame. The ambiguity that thus arises when Conscience is both moral and psychological appears, for instance, in Will's criticism of the friars for commercializing penance. God, he says, forbids anyone to subsidize splendid friaries lest the donor's

> pride be peynted þere and pomp of þe world;
> For god knoweþ þi conscience and þi kynde wille
> And þi cost and þi coueitise and who þe catel ouȝte.   (3.66–8)

Two things are known – first, the circumstances in which a particular decision is taken (how much the new windows will cost, for instance, or how one came by the money); these, together with the moral law, imply what ought to be done. Such is the work of the moral conscience. Secondly, both the decision actually reached and the appetite accounting for it ('þi kynde wille,' 'þi coueitise') are known. God knows the psychological conscience ('god knoweþ þi conscience'), then, or one's awareness of the discrepancy between the mental act of choice and the conclusion of the rational process that ought to have governed it.[22] Because of the psychological conscience, people know that it was *their* desire that was tested and found wanting by *their* reasoning, and *their* choice to gratify themselves nevertheless. The conscience finds its own certainty a defendant arraigned before itself.[23]

If Conscience were not in this way the accuser in terms of knowing violations of the law,[24] he could not be accusation in that other form, remorseful pangs. But 'conscience' in *Piers* also has this third sense, shame or guilt itself.[25] Thus, for those who covet, conscience does not simply record; it also burdens: 'Lat no conscience acombre þee,' Lady Holy Church warns Will (2.51). When this grief is perfect, the conative conscience is contrition, signified by 'pacience' in at least one of its senses in *Piers*. For instance, as the banquet breaks up, Clergy with a trace of resentment teases Conscience for wishing to go off with Patience. Conscience replies, however, that 'þe wil of þe wye and þe wil of folk here / Haþ meued my mood to moorne for my synnes' (13.190–1). 'A trewe wille' (13.193), begotten by charity, Patience so grieves for having sinned that it feels all temporal adversity as less hateful than ingratitude to a merciful God. Such contrition is already the treasure of eternal life[26] – metaphorically, the Magdalene's 'box of salue' or the widow's 'peire of mytes' (13.194, 196). Because Patience partly means contrition, the conative conscience speaks of himself as choosing or needing Patience;[27] and even Clergy will come to describe Conscience as being tested and perfected by Patience.[28]

Yet the conative conscience differs from Patience, because guilty suffering in itself does not imply faith. Attrition, imperfect repentance, which 'may spring from a sense of the turpitude of sin or from a dread of its consequences here and hereafter,'[29] falls short of contrition. The self-disgust felt by Will and others, whose repentance waxes and wanes as hunger or disease stimulates their imagination, reaches a limit with Haukyn:[30] the movement of Conscience and Haukyn towards Patience (13.181–2, 14.323–6) may be understood as remorse trying to perfect itself. Patience, *from his own point of view*, tends to associate Conscience with contrition:

> And þoru3 feiþ comeþ contricion, conscience woot wel ...
> *Ergo* contricion, feiþ and conscience is kyndeliche dowel,
> And surgiens for dedly synnes whan shrift of mouþe failleþ.   (14.83, 88–9)

But the poet consistently distinguishes conscience from guilt sufficient for justification, and these lines are omitted from the C text. While this omission is part of a larger cut, a much more specific deletion shortly thereafter also keeps Patience from making the same connection.[31]

Because the conative conscience can grieve,[32] human weakness seems to be a *donnée* for Conscience,[33] as it is not for 'reson' or 'liberum-arbitrium.' On the other hand, the sense of shame itself is vulnerable, when, for example, confessors grow complaisant. Thus a friar promises Lady Meed he will 'brynge adoun Conscience' (C 3.43).[34] To keep alive the sense of fear or shame, imperfect though it may be, Conscience towards the very end of the poem sends for Old Age (20.165–6), yet ultimately needs his 'cosyn' Contrition (20.204–8).

To summarize 'conscience' in *Piers*, then, one might stress the psychological conscience – first, because it comprehends the moral conscience (being produced in part when one knows the moral conscience, and knows it to be one's own). Second, the psychological conscience is crucial because it records specific choices in relation to the moral conscience and therefore fills a condition for remorse. Third, being indubitable and immediate itself while deriving in part from a practice informed by God (namely, the act of the moral conscience), the psychological conscience is peculiarly joined to that from which it may most diverge.[35] Finally, the psychological conscience becomes, on specific occasions, an emotion. No longer a perception of the mind's contents, having seen them for what they are, it becomes a grief.[36] Imperfect repentance though it may be, to experience this 'mauvaise conscience' is yet a great good; for not only does it mean that conversion (contrition) is still possible, as Bernard preached;[37] in *Piers* it becomes the knowledge of God.

2

Conscience becomes crucially complicated during the banquet at his house.[38] Possible directions for the poem, represented by the characters there, radiate from the scene, although some are already foreclosed in Will's experience. Conscience nevertheless begins by hospitably deferring to them all (13.27, 31, 58, 112, 119, 134–5). Early in passus 13 he still runs no deeper than the moral conscience, mediating between Will and Reason, wishing to conduct Will to Reason, who is the final human source of direction.[39] After Clergy disqualifies himself, however, Conscience becomes remorse, the conative conscience: 'Ac þe wil of þe wye [that is, Patience] and þe wil of folk here / Haþ meued my mood to moorne for my synnes' (13.190–1). The change parallels the turn in Piers, from the character who undertook to lead the penitent mob in the *Visio* to the one who speaks up suddenly in the C-text version of the banquet, giving there that portion of Patience's speech from B dealing most directly with loving one's enemies.

The change in Piers, to which I shall return in chapter 6, has been a conversion. When in the *Visio* Piers said he would put on 'pilgrymes' clothes and help the penitents search for Truth (6.57–8), he used the phrase figuratively to mean sturdy garments fit for field work. By contrast, Patience in the banquet scene not only looks like Piers but looks like him in the character of a pilgrim ('as he a palmere were'). The *Visio* Piers worked hard, but not for dice players and other rabble, whom Truth had commanded him to avoid. To the contrary, Piers in the C-text version of the banquet scene pleads for unremitting love of one's enemy (15.142–8).[40] As Piers turns from complacency to penance, so Conscience, having witnessed Patience (and witnessed Piers, too, in C), goes off in remorse. Instead of being merely the moral conscience, that is, he becomes remorse.

Under the tuition of Conscience and Patience, Haukyn will turn from Active to Patient also.[41] Despite their confluence, however, these movements by Piers, Conscience, and Haukyn differ significantly. Conscience and Haukyn undergo no conversion in *Dowel*. Conscience does elect to become 'Pilgrym wiþ pacience' (13.182), an element in Piers and likened to him.

Patience thus becomes a choice, like 'dowel,' Christ, and love (which are all formally different from each other but materially the same, since they appear only in the person of Christ). To understand this choice, however, we need to take account of an ambiguity. One kind of 'pacience' may be accessible at this point in the movement of the poem; another may not. In *Piers*, Patience personifies first of all a virtue, presupposing belief, conversion, contrition. Patience also comes to represent, however, not much more than pain itself. ('Patience surely has its name from suffering.')[42] Curiously, this latter meaning comes to dominate passus 14, the last of *Dowel*. As we shall see, after Patience teaches the phases of penance (14.82–97), he wanes as a virtue.

Langland no doubt sometimes intends the virtue – for example, the Patience who says that someone who 'loueþ ... leelly litel ... coueiteþ' (13.149). Charity has this patience, because people who love the good of grace do not fear to lose the goods of earth (13.158–68, 15.177–9).[43] This submission ('*fiat voluntas tua*') is 'lyflode' and 'vitailles' for Patience, the nourishing hope in a *bonté* to come. Whether we can live on such a hope tests not only whether we love, but whether 'oure bileue be trewe' (14.38): patience the virtue, like charity, in its turn presupposes faith.[44] 'Oure sheltrom,' as Patience calls it (14.82), 'leel bileue' sustains us in itself as grass does the beasts (14.39–46a). Faith produces contrition, in his view, and he thinks the two together are enough for salvation (14.85–9).

The longer Patience speaks, however, the less he presents the conventional virtue. It scarcely appears in the 'Distinctio Paupertatis,' where, for example, the immunity of patient poverty to 'ira' has little to do with the virtue:

If wraþe wrastle wiþ þe poore, he haþ þe worse ende
For if þei pleyne þe feblere is þe poore;
And if he chide or chatre hym cheueþ þe worse,
For lowliche he lokeþ, and louelich is his speche
That mete or money of oþere men moot asken.   (14.225–9)

Of all these good reasons for meekness, not one is the virtue that 'veut réellement l'épreuve qui la fait souffrir.'[45] The narrator of the alliterative poem *Patience*, too, thinks of poverty ironically as expedient for avoiding sin: if the poor struggle against their lot, poverty will have made them too weak to succeed. Poverty is thus a natural incentive to patience ('pouerte and pacyence arn nedes play-feres').[46] Just as Patience says that poverty does not worry about thieves (14.304–5), the *Patience* narrator sees poverty grimly as an unlosable possession: 'þer as pouert hir proferes ho nyl be put vtter ...' However, where the *Patience* narrator has yet to be educated through the Jonah story, these are Patience's last speeches in *Piers*. The virtue Patience comes from choices made because pain exists; by contrast, Patience in passus 14 seems to become suffering *per se*.[47]

This latter Patience, then, construes poverty as a help in being good; beyond that, poverty exerts a claim upon heaven, independently of faith. Where Patience in B entertains the possibility of Christ's ultimately helping those among the rich who have taken pity on the poor, C twice eliminates this, substituting merely Patience's hope in the final goodness of a God who appears to damn some with riches and save others with poverty.[48] The assimilation of Patience to pain accounts as well for his version of penance. He sees this attained not by contrition, the love and grief excited by the knowledge of God,[49] but merely by 'alle pouerte'

(C 16.33). Langland's compassion for the destitute exalts Patience to a poignant eloquence.[50] Nevertheless, from the viewpoint of the searcher who will awaken still far from the knowledge of 'dowel,' Patience becomes a kind of spiritual bookkeeper, making present pains or pleasures accounts receivable or payable. William Lynch has noted the 'fascinating principle' that 'sacrifice is more than a negative and ascetical principle of theology; it is also a very positive principle for epistemology ...'[51] Not for Patience, however, who sees physical suffering only in a way that might be called ontological: the gift of poverty is the gift of grace.

Someone forsaking all possessions, says Patience, chooses to suffer – puts 'hym to be pacient' (14.272). As the pain *within* poverty, a priest once assigned it ('pacience and pouere men to fede') to Haukyn as a penance (14.10). Poverty, even though involuntary, may goad one to a kind of conversion; and to be sure, if Christ *were* encountered, he would be found to be poor, too. Thus, in the course of explaining how the poor man escapes the seven sins, Patience says that,

> þou3 Sleuþe suwe pouerte and serue no3t god to paie,
> Meschief is ay a mene and makeþ hym to þynke
> That god is his grettest help and no gome ellis,
> And he his seruaunt, as he seiþ, and of his sute boþe.
> And wheiþer he be or be no3t, he bereþ þe signe of pouerte
> And in þat secte oure saueour saued al mankynde.
> Forþi al poore þat pacient is of pure ri3t may cleymen,
> After hir endynge here, heueneriche blisse.   (14.254–61)

Where the prologue in the alliterative *Patience* carefully keeps poverty and patience distinct, Langland in the present section makes patience primarily the pain in poverty, which turns the poor person towards Christ not in love (indeed, C omits Patience's earlier lines on conversion) but as a last resort. To guard against despair, Patience counsels us to take

> þe Acquitaunce as quyk and to þe queed shewen it:
> *Pateat &c: Per passionem domini,*
> And putten of so þe pouke, and preuen vs vnder borwe.
> Ac þe parchemyn of þis patente of pouerte be moste,
> And of pure pacience and parfit bileue.   (14.190–3)

Patience quibbles with '*Pateat ... passionem ... patente ... pacience*' because he is claiming that salvation depends upon a continuity of pain running between God and human being: the Passion in the instance of Christ, poverty in that of people. This saving continuity makes patience 'payn for pouerte hymselue' (14.317). More than using the familiar trick of religious language that makes 'bread' signify no bread,[52] the poet may be punning on 'payn,' as Judith Anderson suggests:[53] as the pain within poverty, 'pacience' links people with the Passion and therefore with the bread of life.[54] Afflicting the body as it does, however, it makes only an analogy with contrition, which afflicts the soul (14.282–4). It stands to contrition (and Patience the virtue) as the letter to the spirit, or the bread baked by Haukyn to the 'vitailles of grete vertues' (14.37).

Patience, thus equivocating and equivocal, and Conscience, complex in his own way, leave the banquet together, talking about 'dowel.' As it seems to the narrator, who watches from some unidentified point, they meet this Haukyn, whom Will identifies as a 'Mynstral' and who calls himself the same (13.221, 224). Although critics routinely assume that he is one of the flea-bitten, obscene entertainers that the poem elsewhere deplores,[55] it seems likelier that the poet is using 'minstral' in its old-fashioned sense of 'servant' or 'functionary.'[56] This would certainly be accurate, since Haukyn will describe himself as providing bread for every true worker (13.238–40); moreover, it sets up an irony on Haukyn's part, who says he doesn't make much money because he is *not* a minstrel in the usual sense: he can 'telle no gestes, / Farten ne fiþelen at festes ne harpen' (13.230–1).

Industrious Haukyn, who now, with his sense of injured merit, stands opposite Conscience and Patience, is the larval stage of Piers. Where Piers had been confident about his relationship with Truth ('For þouȝ I seye it myself I serue hym to paye'), this baker is immensely insecure. The first survey taken by Conscience of Haukyn's coat dwells on the anxious posing, the boasting, the care for self-presentation of someone 'þat noȝt haþ,' 'pouere of possession in purs and in cofre' (13.302, 300). Moreover, Haukyn's attrition (when misfortune strikes, he grows afraid of crossing God and goes to confession [14.5–11]) reduces Piers's contrite acceptance of the finality of his own failure (7.120–5). Yet the irony is not entirely at Haukyn's expense. And the episode undermines the Piers of the *Visio*, first in subverting him but also in beginning an archaeology of his conversion.

In the best account of Haukyn to have been written, Stella Maguire finds that his 'real counterpart' is 'the good element in the crowd who throng the Field of Folk in the Prologue, and in those of the pilgrims who loyally assist Piers in the ploughing of the half-acre in Passus VI.' These people nevertheless live merely 'a decent, well-intentioned life based on, and judged by, purely temporal conceptions of goodness.' By contrast, Piers lives 'in the light of eternity, directed by the bidding of God.' Thus, he 'includes but transcends Haukyn.'[57] However, Maguire has not allowed for Piers's own self-condemnation, repeated by the figure of Haukyn in the register of parody. Moreover, the baker's sordid shortcomings call into question Piers's notions about Truth, before Piers made 'prieres and ... penaunce' his only plow.[58]

In the *Visio*, the high-minded Piers had entered a convenant with a knight:

> I shal swynke and swete and sowe for vs boþe,
> And ek laboure for þi loue al my lif tyme,
> In couenaunt þat þow kepe holy kirke and myselue
> Fro wastours and wikked men þat wolde me destruye ...   (6.26–9)

Haukyn also has his quid pro quo: he is

> A wafrer, wol ye wite, and serue many lordes,
> Ac fewe robes I fonge or furrede gownes.   (13.226–7)

> Y haue no gode gifts of thise grete lordes
> For no breed þat y betrauaile furste to bryng byfore lordes,
> Nere hit þat þe parsche preyeth for me on Sonendayes.   (C 15.209–11)

Piers and other true labourers in all stations are to be 'pardoned.' Because they succour the poor, Truth promises that

> I shal sende myselue Seint Michel myn angel,
> That no deuel shal yow dere ne in your deying fere yow,
> And witen yow fro wanhope ...   (7.34–6)

This echoes in the reward that Haukyn expects, not merely from other people, but indirectly from God. When it is not forthcoming, he threatens in his own way to 'swynk noȝt so harde' (7.112):

> I fynde payn for þe pope and prouendre for his palfrey,
> And I hadde neuere of hym, haue god my trouþe,
> Neiþer prouendre ne personage yet of þe popes ȝifte,

Saue a pardon wiþ a peis of leed and two polles amyddes.
Hadde ich a clerc þat couþe write I wolde caste hym a bille
That he sent me vnder his seel a salue for þe pestilence,[59]
...
And þanne wolde I be prest to þe peple paast for to make,
And buxom and busy aboute breed and drynke
For hym and for alle hise, founde I þat his pardoun
Miȝte lechen a man as me þynketh it sholde.
For siþ he haþ þe powere þat Peter hadde he haþ þe pot wiþ þe salue.

                                                            (13.243–54)

Piers, too, awaited the 'salue.' Haukyn's disappointing 'pardon wiþ a peis of leed' recalls, of course, the indulgences that the narrator judges inferior to 'dowel.' Yet this judgment reflected Piers's own chagrin when the priest found 'no pardon ... / But do wel,' etc. 'The appalling strangeness' of a pardon expressing itself in the deadly Either-Or of the Athanasian Creed surpasses the plowman's previous understanding of Truth in the same degree that 'dowel' surpasses the indulgences of the narrator's experience. Piers's angry disappointment, not least with himself, is reduced into Haukyn's resentment.

Finally, Haukyn resembles Piers most keenly in his willingness, like the cat in the Prologue, Hunger in the *Visio*, and Kynde in *Dobest*, to coerce sinners. He claims that the pope will not be able to work miracles 'Til pride be pureliche fordo and þat þoruȝ payn defaute.' He sweats and suffers at his baking; therefore, it is just as well that an occasional famine should enforce a just appreciation of him (13.265–70). His 'wafres' fall as short of the bread that Patience makes from his tears, Christ from his body, and Conscience from the grain gathered into Unity as Haukyn's sorrow – whether the pain of rising early or his guilt – falls short of salvific suffering. The latter is represented in *Piers* by Patience as contrition and virtue, by the Passion, and finally by the perfected Conscience itself. Yet there is no knowing their metaphoric bread without real bread – perhaps no knowing poverty of heart without pain of the body. The spirit is rooted in the letter it opposes, just as, for Will, Christ's sorrow may be unavailable in experience without Haukyn's.

Conscience will ultimately unite Active and Patient in contrition. At present, however, Conscience on the one hand comes somewhat too late. Haukyn has been aware for some time of what he ought to have done: he says he has never been able to keep his coat clean for as much as an hour, 'That I ne soiled it wiþ siȝte or som ydel speche' (14.13). On the other hand, Conscience as contrition may be premature. The c text omits references to it here,[60] for Haukyn, like Will, appears to lack the belief presupposed by Patience the virtue and by contrition. While the plowman as Active can be undermined by Haukyn, the plowman as Patient cannot, for his conversion happens with a suddenness and brevity that the narrator himself is left to ponder. There is nothing to be eroded. By contrast with Piers's stroke of self-accusation, Haukyn makes excuses ('I haue but one hool hater … I am þe lasse to blame'). He is helplessly aware of his futile attempts at reform in the past (14.5–15), floundering in self-pity and shame:

> 'Alas,' quod Haukyn þe Actif man þo, 'þat after my cristendom[61]
> I ne hadde be deed and doluen for dowelis sake!
> So hard it is,' quod haukyn, 'to lyue and to do synne.
> Synne seweþ vs euere,' quod he and sory gan wexe,
> And wepte water wiþ his eighen and weyled þe tyme
> That euere he did dede þat dere god displesed;
> Swouned and sobbed and siked ful ofte
> That euere he hadde lond ouþer lordshipe lasse oþer moore,
> Or maistrie ouer any man mo þan of hymselue.
> 'I were noȝt worþi, woot god,' quod haukyn, 'to werien any cloþes,
> Ne neiþer sherte ne shoon, saue for shame one
> To couere my careyne,' quod he, and cride mercy faste
> And wepte and wailede …   (14.323–35)

There are hints of true contrition: he regrets his sin because it has offended 'dere god'; his wishing he had died rather than sinned resembles Alexander of Hales's maxim that the true penitent would prefer the pains of hell to the commission of a single sin.[62] But even more strongly, the swooning and sobbing recall the shame of the drunkard waking bedraggled on the morning after (11.427–34), of Sloth, who obliges Repentance by making yet another vow after forgetting the first forty (5.397), and of the abashed Glutton, who makes a 'gret doel' and vows

> Shal neuere fyssh on þe Fryday defyen in my wombe
> Til Abstinence myn Aunte haue ȝyue me leeue,
> And yet haue I hated hire al my liftyme.   (5.382–4)

Will himself by this point has acknowledged more than once that he has wrecked his life. When Conscience accused him in C, he hurried to church to beat his breast and wail for his sins (5.105–8). Active's imperfect repentance is thus strongly *déjà vu*. C may omit it because the mutual incomprehension of Active and Patient implies it, and because repentance of any kind is potentially part of Conscience.

Because Patience speaks from grace, imbruted Haukyn hears him sceptically and, at least in C, angrily. In a certain respect, however, Patience's point of view does not matter, and unlike other personifications taking the higher end of a vertical dialogue in *Piers*, he is not repudiated. For Patience, as we have seen, is ultimately less virtue than pain; and he inscribes the fact of pain into the poem. Pain unites the grief of Haukyn (grief being essential to attrition, as love to contrition) with hunger and cold and sickness and everything that Haukyn fears. Patience's focus upon this extreme and inalienable part of consciousness closes *Dowel*.[63] While Patience as suffering, unlike the virtue Patience, does not presuppose Conscience, the moral conscience can lead to remorse, whether perfect or imperfect. Like Will, Piers, and Haukyn, it can arrive at suffering. Although Haukyn and the moral conscience, which Piers had relied on, do not reach conversion (hence the Haukyn episode ironizes the confidence of Piers before the 'pardon'), they are part of the movement to conversion. The full development of Conscience will subsume suffering, as I hope that the next chapter will show. Conscience, that is, will finally have a share of Patience, the 'partyng felawe' with whom he chose to travel (13.206).

3

Will awakens with Haukyn's noisy weeping. It will still be a 'wonder longe' time before he can 'kyndely knowe what [is] dowel' (15.1–2); and oblivious to his surroundings, he gets blamed for idleness and for foolishly wounding the pride of his superiors. It is a reprieve when he falls asleep again, this time to dream of Anima.

The long first vision of the *Vita de dobet* – it will include passus 15, 16, and 17 – is inevitably a movement forwards, since the narrator is recalling a succession of events. Yet this vision must be understood to move backwards also. Charity, taken by nearly every critic to be the subject of *Dobet*,[64] is logically prior to Patience, even though Patience appears first.[65] And logically prior to charity is the freedom to make a loving choice. Even freedom has its preconditions. Where *Dowel* ends by unearthing some of the suffering from Piers's 'tene' (7.119), the first vision of *Dobet* moves archaeologically also, towards the conditions for human love. Just as Patience concluded *Dowel* by manifesting itself as pain – not the same as a virtue – so *Dobet* finally reveals something different from charity – a divine love not contingent upon human success or failure.

The conditions for human freedom are crucial to this first vision of *Dobet*, and Langland accordingly expands the role of Liberum Arbitrium in revising B. When Will meets Anima at the beginning of the vision, Anima tells his several names and functions, accuses Will of a gluttony for knowledge, and relates intellectual pride to the clerical avarice that is destroying the Church. Anima contrasts this avarice with 'parfit charite' (15.148), and Will asks, 'What is charite?' Anima then gives examples for more than four hundred lines. For some reason, Will asks again, 'what charite is to mene' (16.3). This time Anima tries a metaphor, allegorizing charity as an apple tree in the charge of Liberum Arbitrium, who acts under Piers. At the plowman's name, Will swoons, and, in an inner dream, Piers shows him the tree, tells of assaults on it by the world, the flesh, and the devil (Piers himself resists the first two, Liberum Arbitrium the third), speaks reticently on the origin of the tree's three symbolic props, describes its apples, and then shakes them down to an unhappy fate. In revising all this, Langland substitutes Liberum Arbitrium for Anima in C 16–18. It is he who comes to have many names and expound charity. In the Tree of Charity scene in C, he shows Will the tree himself and reports defending it against the world and the flesh as well as against the devil. Piers is never mentioned.

This expansion of Liberum Arbitrium's role, presumably because he is vital to the movement of *Dobet*, invites us to pause for several questions. Which of our human powers does he represent? Does he perhaps include all of them and therefore stand simply for the soul itself? Then, what is the 'action' of the episode, in which this personification first seems to explain himself, then describes charity, and finally sustains an evidently unexpected defeat? How does the episode relate to Patience or to the following episodes, when the narrator will glimpse the life of Jesus (C 18.124–78) and then meet Faith, *Spes*, and the Samaritan?

The work of Dom Odon Lottin has made it possible to discern within the context of late-medieval England and France five principal ways of conceiving 'liberum-arbitrium.' One of these may resemble Langland's notion. In two of the traditions, 'liberum-arbitrium' is simply identified with reason on the one hand or will on the other.[66] Because Liberum Arbitrium in *Piers* claims a number of functions, these two traditions do not seem relevant. In the three remaining, 'liberum-arbitrium' was conceived as a separate faculty. In the first of them, a number of late-medieval theologians defined it as altogether apart from reason and will.[67] Because Liberum Arbitrium in *Piers* calls himself 'a will with a resoun' (c 16.176), this tradition does not seem pertinent. A second, represented by the earlier teaching of Thomas Aquinas, also made 'liberum-arbitrium' a distinct faculty, the act of which is choice, but proceeding from the will, just as that faculty in turn had emanated from reason.[68]

Liberum Arbitrium in the poem is even closer to a fifth concept, entertained by such thinkers as Stephen Langton and Robert Kilwardby. This defines 'liberum-arbitrium' as a separate faculty – needed, as Alexander of Hales argued, to account for choice by coming between the reason's judgment of the good and the will's desire for the good – yet one composed of reason and will ('a will with a resoun').[69] That Liberum Arbitrium in *Piers* is the particular power of choice itself is clear: at his 'lykyng,' he says, he may 'chese / To do wel or wykke' (c 16.175–6). His freedom to do 'wykke' is not at odds with an Anselmian description of him elsewhere: *'dum declinat de malo ad bonum, Liberum Arbitrium est'* (c 16.200e–f). As Odon Rigaud (*fl* 1245) pointed out, the Augustinian formulation defines 'liberum-arbitrium' by its object – good or evil – while the Anselmian defines it by its final cause – moral rectitude.[70]

As with other powers of the mind, the poet defines Liberum Arbitrium not just by a conceptual formula at the outset of his appearance, but dramatically, by all that the personification says and does and all that happens to him. Liberum Arbitrium may describe an unlimited number of good choices once made; yet the Tree of Charity scene will press the issue of whether he is presently operable for Will himself – whether, in other words, Langland does not dramatize Liberum Arbitrium as assuming a condition for its operability that in the narrator is not fulfilled.

How Liberum Arbitrium is thus put to the test will not be clear if he is construed as inseparable from love: while Liberum Arbitrium is part of the narrator's own soul, love is hardly a choice that Will makes anywhere in the poem. Moreover, the place of these passus within his whole quest has been partially obscured by the critical opinion, influential now for a number of years, that Liberum Arbitrium is somehow all the powers of the soul lumped together.[71]

Acting upon the hint that the Tree of Charity bears the additional name '*Ymago-dei*' in the c text (18.7), Talbot Donaldson associated Liberum Arbitrium with a Bernardine concept of the will, 'the love-making faculty.' As he understood Bernard, 'liberum-arbitrium' is the image of God in humankind, free from all necessity. While Donaldson was surely right in believing that Liberum Arbitrium personifies a faculty, he was evidently wrong in thinking that Bernard identified 'liberum-arbitrium' with the will ('voluntas').[72] Bernard saw 'liberum-arbitrium' only as 'consensus,' an act, constituted by the concurrent acts of the 'voluntas' and the reason. As a capacity for this kind of act, 'liberum-arbitrium' is also a 'habitus.'[73] In any case, Bernard did not know it as a faculty. As Liberum Arbitrium describes himself, he is not merely volition, as Donaldson thought, and he adapts Anima's catalogue of faculties to include both 'voluntas' ('when y wilne and wolde, *Animus* y hatte' c 16.183)[74] and himself: 'And when y wol do or do nat gode dedes or ille / Thenne am y *Liberum Arbitrium*' (c 16.192–3). Even if a Bernardine 'liberum-arbitrium' might be considered roughly the *Imago Dei*, Langland in c makes Liberum Arbitrium the guardian of 'Trewe-loue' that 'hihte *Ymago-dei*' and not the thing itself.

Liberum Arbitrium represents a separate faculty composed of will and reason; it is neither freedom, love, nor the image of God, and it is not the 'essence' of the soul[75] or the soul in its entirety. George Sanderlin's opinion that Liberum Arbitrium somehow includes all the powers of the soul was based on Liberum Arbitrium's arrogating every name in the Latin catalogue, where they actually apply to *anima*, the soul as the principle of all human activity. Sanderlin related this passage to John Damascene, who, in his view, 'had considered *liberum arbitrium* or free choice a *universal* power of the soul, to be identified with all other powers of the soul ...' Two objections should be made. First, Langland makes Liberum Arbitrium not only 'a *universal* power of the soul,' but a specific one as well (c 16.192–3). This has no counterpart in John Damascene. In fact, so far as I can determine, only Alexander of Hales took a similar view.[76]

The second objection is more serious. 'To be identified with all other powers of the soul' can be wrongly understood to mean, as Odon Rigaud pointed out, that the various powers of the soul are species of the genus 'liberum-arbitrium.'[77] But both John Damascene and Alexander of Hales call 'liberum-arbitrium' a universal power because its act – choice – elicits from the other powers their own activity. Because John is concerned to show that human volition is led by reason, he finds each of the other powers acting in succession so that appetite might be free, rational, and finally satisfied.[78] (The English catalogue in c appears to list the faculties and 'habitūs' in the order in which they occur in any moral decision.) Hugh of St Cher, a few lines above the text quoted by Sanderlin, makes this clear. Following Augustine, he writes that 'liberum arbitrium est penes quod residet supreme auctoritas mouendi membra ...' When, therefore, he claims that 'liberum arbitrium est tres uires anime: rationalis, irascibilis, concupiscibilis, sed habet unum nomen, qua ille tres uires quandoque conueniunt in unum actum,' he means that the three separate powers compose the act of 'liberum-arbitrium' in the sense that they act *because* of 'liberum-arbitrium.'[79] To identify 'liberum-arbitrium' with, say, inquiry is simply to deny what would appear to be a self-evident difference between inquiring and choosing. Inquiring, to the contrary, may exist for the sake of choosing.

Merely a conceptual grasp of Liberum Arbitrium is barren without a sense of the shape of the narrative action in his episode – an episode that is a long moment in the narrator's search for conversion. Conversion may be considered either cause or effect, the compelling experience or its result. In his long speech, extending from the last glimpse of Patience (c 16.163) to the Tree of Charity (c 18.3), Liberum Arbitrium describes himself as the effectual result of conversion: specifically the recognition and choice of Christ as the source of all value and then the various social choices entailed by this that makes us attribute love to a person. The first choice is to believe, for, assuming the knowledge of God that is the *cause* of conversion, Liberum Arbitrium expresses the belief that results: 'hit suffice for oure sauacioun soethfaste byleue' (c 17.119). Christ wrought miracles so that people might see they could be saved only through 'grace / And thorw penaunce and passioun and parfyt bileue,' baptizing with his heart's blood 'Alle þat wilnede and wolde with inwit bileue hit' (c 17.265–6, 269).

The choice of Christ as the unique value implies the choice of hunger and other deprivations if they are the price of keeping the law. Concerning himself with consequences, Liberum Arbitrium anticipates the Tree of Charity by making the Church itself a kind of tree, needing for its health the examples – the specific choices – given by clerics. The failure to believe in Christ results in a failure to love, which then comes full circle in a failure to know other things rightly, even grammar (c 17.87–110). To believe in Christ is to choose the cross of suffering, not the cross stamped in coins. All things being equal, Charity likes to dress handsomely; but in this hard world, to verify the strength of his own belief, he accepts martyrdom and hardship so that English sinners might see the limits of pecuniary power and Saracens might be converted. The structure of passus c 17, then, assimilates clerical hypocrites, who en-

gender no belief, to Mohammed, who inspired a false belief. By contrast, true belief will spread from Christian prelates who choose charity,
linked to the Holy Spirit, Christ's 'coluer' (c 17.246), parallel to the 'mylde
dowue' (c 17.239) with which Mohammed worked his magic. Prelates
must suffer to attest their belief in the inimitable sufferer.

Before Will begs to be taken to charity and we move into the garden
of the heart, Liberum Arbitrium speaks some puzzling lines:

> Iewes lyuen in þe lawe þat oure lord tauhte
> Moises to be maister þerof til Messie come,
> And on þat lawe they leue and leten hit for þe beste.
> And ȝut knewe they Crist þat cristendoem tauhte
> And for a parfit profete that moche peple sauede
> And of selcouthe sores saued men fol ofte.
> ...
> And ȝut they seyen sothly and so doen þe Sarrasynes
> That Iesus was bote a iogelour, a iapare amonges þe commune,
> And a sofistre of soercerie and a *pseudo-propheta*,
> And that his lore was lesynges and lakken hit alle
> And hopen þat he be to come þat shal hem releue.   (c 17.297–313)

If the Jews witnessed Christ's suffering at first hand, how did they fail
to believe? What can prelates, relinquishing their English sinecures for
arduous missions, hope to accomplish by their own *agape* that Christ
did not with his?

These questions press the point that, for many lines, Liberum Arbitrium merely assumes the knowledge that frees 'liberum-arbitrium.' His
ability to enact the works of love that he describes would be the effect.
Who, then, can expect him to doubt the existence of the cause? For him
to understand Will's doubts would be at odds with his status as Will's
hypostatized freedom. When the fruit falls to the devil, Liberum Arbitrium does not alter his viewpoint. He simply disappears. Without the
vision of God, reason and will operate in the damned as in the saved.
Without it, however, 'liberum-arbitrium' ceases to function.[80] This does
not mean it ceases to exist, any more than the power of seeing does in
those who live for a while without light. When Will responds to Liberum
Arbitrium's description of charitable acts by doubting whether a charitable person can be found (c 17.1–3), he questions, in effect, whether
Liberum Arbitrium is free. Since Liberum Arbitrium personifies one of
the possibilities of his own mind, he is probing its utility in relation to

his search. And he continues probing as the next passus begins, indeed with much dubiety: 'Leue *Liberum Arbitrium* ... y leue, as y hope, / Thow couthest telle me and teche me to Charite, as y leue?' (c 18.1–2).

Liberum Arbitrium replies by conducting Will to a garden called 'Cor-hominis,' where he sees an 'ympe' called '*Ymago-dei*,' explained by his guide as 'Trewe-loue ... the trinite hit sette' (c 18.9).[81] The tree is kept alive by 'louely lokynges,' the same subsistent grace imaged later as the 'hete of þe Holi Goest' (c 18.75), which shines most fully on contemplatives. As in B, the tree is braced with three planks,

> thre shides of o lenghe
> And of o kyne colour and kynde, as me thoghte,
> Alle thre yliche long and yliche large. (c 18.20–2)

They 'bytokeneth trewely,' says Liberum Arbitrium, 'the trinite of heuene' (c 18.26). When covetousness threatens the apples growing on the tree, Liberum Arbitrium says that he defends them with the plank called '*Potencia-dei-patris.*' Against lechery he uses 'þe seconde planke, *Sapiencia-dei-patris*, / The which is þe passioun and þe penaunce and þe parfitnesse of Iesus' (c 18.40–1). He wards off the devil with '*Spiritus-sanctus* and sothfaste bileue, / And that is grace of þe Holy Gost' (c 18.51–2). We have only Liberum Arbitrium's account of what he does. Will does not witness any of this. And when the time comes for him to test how well the fruit has been protected, it is found to be in very poor condition.

The meaning of this passage becomes relatively clear if we take the Trinity as a metaphor.[82] Langland himself goes part way towards making this clear in the Latin lines brought together in B from a source not yet known: 'Videatis qui peccat in spiritum sanctum numquam remittetur &c; Hoc est idem qui peccat per liberum arbitrium non repugnat.' (16.47a). The three props 'bytokeneth trewely the trinite of heuene' (c 18.26) because the three mental acts represented by the props are themselves analogous to the Trinity. In the same way that the mental act of 'sothfaste bileue' parallels the act of God associated with the Third Person, so the second, the apprehension of things higher than humanity, reflects God's knowledge of himself ('*Sapiencia-dei-patris*').

The poet is not, of course, the first Christian to use the metaphor. The created trinity of memory, intellect, and will was Augustine's chief ontological basis for knowing the creative Trinity. Alexander of Hales seems to have been the first to include 'liberum-arbitrium' in this inner trinity, and his *Summa theologica* offers a parallel to the poet's three planks. They are metaphoric not just because they are called 'planks,' but because they are called by the names of the Three Persons: 'Quia in anima est imago Trinitatis ex parte cognitivae, scilicet memoria, intelligentia et voluntas; similiter ex parte motivae, liberum arbitrium, ratio et voluntas, ut dicit Augustinus. Voluntas ergo ex ista parte respondet voluntati, ex illa ratio intelligentiae; ergo liberum arbitrium respondent memoriae; ergo sicut mens sive memoria est pars imaginis ex parte cognitivae, ita liberum arbitrium ex parte motivae, et ita videtur quod sit potentia separata a ratione et voluntate.'[83] In *Piers*, however, the powers of the mind signified by the planks and corresponding to the three Persons occur in reverse order. The *'Potencia-dei-patris'* is to be associated with the Father's 'wille' (c 18.121), the human image of which, volition, comes third in the series in Augustine and is called 'Animus' by Liberum Arbitrium (c 16.183). An act of volition is always predicated upon one of cognition, potentially the knowledge of Christ. Hence, the second plank reflects God's knowledge of himself (*'Sapiencia-dei-patris'*). With the knowledge of Christ, choice becomes free, the person becomes free to love. This freedom is figured by the third plank – the only one wielded in B by Liberum Arbitrium. Although Alexander saw it coming first in the Augustinian series, Langland makes it reflect the 'frenesse of *spiritus sancti*' (16.88). And c relates '*Spiritus-sanctus*' to 'sothfaste bileue' (18.51), the indispensable first choice with which, as we have seen, Liberum Arbitrium (and, in B, Anima) concerns himself in the preceding passus. Thus, it seems that as Langland moves from one metaphoric Person of the Trinity to the next, he moves from one act to what that act logically presupposes. Where Liberum Arbitrium in the two preceding passus speaks mostly of loving choices made in accordance with belief, in the Tree of Charity scene he describes metaphorically the psychology of choosing in itself.[84]

So far as Piers has been converted, Liberum Arbitrium belongs to him (B 16.16–17).[85] In B they are both said to deploy the planks, Liberum Arbitrium taking the third, which is himself. Augustine says in his *Confessions* that he has heard there are three kinds of questions: 'an sit, quid sit, quale sit.'[86] Up through the description of the fruit of charity, the questions being answered are the last two. At last the all-important question for Will – 'an sit?' – is answered. The uselessness of choice to unregenerate humanity is dramatized in the loss of the very fruit that Piers has been regarding under an aspect – freedom – that does not exist for Will. The fruit, the works of charity,[87] look very fair, but when they are put to the test of death, even the best begin to cry (16.73–8). Piers has been dealing with the fruit hypothetically: 'Heer now byneþe ... if I nede hadde, / Matrimoyne I may nyme, a moiste fruyt wiþalle' (16.67–8). But the narrator, who has urged on previous occasions the ubiquity of sin, wants the fruit examined. In distinguishing the allegorical from the tropological meaning of the fruit, some critics seem first to ignore that the only apples there are are rotten[88] and consequently not to inquire what the import of this might be – for Liberum Arbitrium, for example. That the fruit is to be snatched away to 'derknesse and drede' makes gallows' humour of Piers's complacent response about the best of the fruit: virginity grows at the top of the Tree, he says; 'sour worþ it neuere' (16.73).

The cause of corruption is hinted by the recurrent use, in C's expanded description of the fruit, of the word 'kynde' in at least two important senses – (1) kind or genus: the fruit is all 'of o kynde' (18.57); and (2) nature as opposed to grace or spirit: we are all 'apples of oen kynde,' having grown on the tree of Adam (18.70, 68). Liberum Arbitrium laces this latter sense with the suggestion of carnality:[89]

Wedewes and wedewares, þat here ownere wil forsaken
And chaste leden here lyf, is lyf of contemplacioun,
And more lykynde to oure lorde then lyue as kynde asketh
And folewe þat the flesche wole and fruyt forth brynge.   (C 18.76–9)

Here, then, we have fruit opposed to fruit – the apples of charity graduated according to the restraint placed upon the body's own fruitfulness. But Reason had taught that 'Man was made of such matere he may nat wel asterte / That some tyme hym bitit to folewen his kynde' (C 13.209–10). This 'matere' is the 'bat of erthe' (C 18.92), and the carnality is common to our kind – as the play on 'kynde' suggests. Liberum Arbitrium, despite himself, takes humanity at its best – Adam, the 'pomo che maturo / solo prodotti fosti'[90] – and then watches the illusion of lives of incessant charity yield to the fact of carnality and imperfection. (In C, explicitly, the charity is not always perfect: we are the fruit of Adam, Liberum Arbitrium says there, 'Somme of vs soethfaste and some variable'; and Will identifies the fruit as 'folk of alle nacion, / Bothe parfit and inparfit' 18.69, 102–3.) Rather than a base metal toughening the gold of charity for secular uses, 'kynde' is the vicious mole itself.

These fruit are the intermittent acts of love. But only belief in Christ makes 'caritas' possible. Only those who 'lyuen in Feiþ' can follow Hope's teaching. Abraham will report that hell is full of people who believed that obedience to the Law in itself was some sort of vade-mecum (17.22–5). This need is clear in Anima's (or Liberum Arbitrium's) hope that the Jews, who love God and their neighbour, might yet come to believe in Christ (15.610); otherwise, their love can never become in-fused with the grace that makes it charity. It will be clear also when the Samaritan will say that no one ever went through the wilderness of this world without succumbing to temptation, 'saue feiþ and my-selue and *Spes* his felawe, / And þiself now and swiche as suwen oure werkes' (17.103–4). Rather than speak of a natural capacity to get through unscathed, owing to God's promise to honour anyone's best efforts, the Samaritan holds, in effect, that none of the apples can meet the test – that all the 'folk,' being sick, need the 'salue' that the Bethlehem child will provide, to 'alle þat lyuen in Feiþ' and follow Hope's teaching. The Tree of Charity scene places the knowledge of Christ morally and psy-chologically. The poem moves from the frustrated stewardship of Piers – the corruption of that love that the virtue Patience would cause us to look for – towards the suppositum for the liberty of 'liberum-arbitrium' itself, the knowledge of God that free choice and, in a fallen world, con-version must have.

4

Sin creates the vacuum into which God's own love advances: '*Libera-Voluntas-Dei* lauhte þe myddel shoriare' (c 18.119).[91] The sequence is not progressive but archaeological, back to the knowledge that Liberum Ar-bitrium needs. From the Incarnation (which is not a sequel to the death of John the Baptist [c 18.114] and his predecessors but a condition for the 'libertas' of choice itself),[92] Will envisions the divine plan just short of the Passion.[93] Will sees the Annunciation first, then Jesus' healing min-istry, his prophetic offer of 'baskettes ful of broke mete' (B 16.126), and the indelible 'enuye and yuel wil' of the Jews. Will's subsequent meet-ing with Faith and Hope does not serve chiefly to follow Christian his-tory from the Fall, for the life of Jesus has just been recounted. Rather, by the succession of ages – the age 'ante legem' with Faith, the one 'sub lege' with Hope – the poet marks his own progress towards an experi-ence of the Passion as present and existing. What is most important about Faith, Hope, and the Samaritan is that they are all acts of the mind, the dynamics of conversion. In *Dobet*, Will learns of them abstractively, from the point of view of doctrine. That is, he learns what faith and hope are, without yet believing or hoping. Similarly, he will learn what *agape* is,[94] which begins with God and manifests itself in the Passion, of which it is both cause and effect. The abstractive, doctrinal knowledge of *agape* will include Christ, the jousting knight of passus 18. *Agape* will not be known intuitively, immediately, compellingly, however, and it will not perfect Will's conversion until the Passion itself is known that way in *Dobest*.

The trio of the theological virtues and the commonplace that the first two are incomplete without the last exist in the action as a kind of anticipated rhythm. Faith and Hope anatomize the act of conversion: Faith assents to the divinity of Christ and consequently to a triune God; Hope, who carries the commandments, represents the fulfilment of the Law in one who has been justified by faith. The Samaritan embodies both the integrity of the act of conversion and, going as he is to Jerusalem to fetch 'salue for alle sike' (17.122), the dependency of conversion upon the vision of Christ.[95] This vision is what the rhythm anticipates. All who lived too early to see Christ are damned: the devil has a lien on the patriarchs and prophets, says Abraham, 'And me þerwiþ' (16.262). Faith's ability to save the man fallen among thieves rests entirely upon the Passion and the knowledge that the Samaritan promises of it. This dependency accounts for the utility of Faith after Christ has been known[96] and metaphorizes the commonplace that faith and hope are futile without love. Faith is not surpassed by the Samaritan. The Samaritan can teach no better than 'lyuen in Feiþ' because he finally represents the *condition* for faith, not a superior option.

In the person of Christ – God disguised 'in Piers armes,' '*humana natura*' (18.22–3) – it is Faith who will recognize divinity.[97] Faith has sought someone he once saw – 'crist is his name' (16.265) – whose banner will bear a device ('Thre leodes in oon lyth') recalling the three men whom Abraham had welcomed in Genesis 18 as one Lord. Thus, the God with his cross coalesces with the God of Abraham. This, after all, is how the Trinity comes to be known: Christ is perceived as the God who satisfies the God who must be satisfied. Abraham appears pre-eminently as the type of one who by choosing the redemptive and therefore triune God continues in himself the work of redemption.[98] Such a generative choice is one of Faith's metaphors for the Trinity:

So god, þat gynnyng hadde neuere but þo hym good þouȝte,
Sente forþ his sone as for seruaunt þat tyme
To ocupie hym here til issue were spronge,
That is children of charite, and holi chirche þe moder.

Patriarkes and prophetes and Apostles were þe children,
And Crist and cristendom and cristene holy chirche.
In menynge þat man moste on o god bileue,
And þere hym lykede and he louede, in þre persones hym shewede.

(15.194–201)[99]

'Children of charite' issue from the 'work' of Christ because they believe 'on o god' whose 'þre persones' express his love. By believing, people create the vehicle of a figure for the Trinity they believe in.

Faith implies a good hope, disclosed not only in contrition, but in the believers' willingness to conform themselves to the justice of a forgiving God by forgiving their own enemies. 'Thus man's righteousness is not the condition, but the consequence of God's action,' Jean Daniélou has written.[100] After Faith, Will meets Hope, who personifies this second phase of conversion. The thousands whom he has saved are saved by faith, being in the lap of Abraham. Yet conversion, or contrition,[101] implies an intention to obey the Law. Beyond stipulating the Law, given by Moses and identified and enjoined by Christ,[102] Hope offers Christ's death as enabling people to obey it and thus to complete their justification (17.5–8). In short, the *agape* of God causes people at last to pay what they owe, to imitate God's mercy towards enemies of their own.[103] On this hang the Law and the prophets – the whole stumbling block of the 'pardon' Truth sent to Piers.

Faith and Hope, however, like such earlier characters as Clergy, are only possibilities for Will, dismissed ('"Go þi gate!" quod I to *Spes*') because unrealized. Although Faith and Hope do not quarrel with each other (17.22), the narrator makes them competitive (17.33–49). By failing to stipulate their interrelationship, he indicates his own unconverted state. Then, however, he meets the polysemous Samaritan. As a teacher, the Samaritan reconciles Faith and Hope, until, as Frank says, 'the two doctrines intertwine like the red rose and the briar.'[104] While conversion is integral in that way, the Samaritan leads, more importantly, to a nexus between God and humanity that Faith and Hope have only presupposed – a necessary recognition between Christ and the rest of humanity.

The imagery used by the Samaritan to show the inseparability of Faith and Hope and to interpret *'redde quod debes'* expresses his basic perception that nature and grace impinge upon each other. The pattern can be contrasted with Faith's imagery earlier. Faith had talked as if grace and nature were self-contained systems or parallel lines. God begets a 'Miȝte, and a mene to se his own myhte, / Of hymsulue and his seruant, and what soffreth hem bothe' (C 18.202–3).[105] 'Crist and cristendom and cristene holy chirche' (B 16.199) make another such procession, entirely within the order of grace. Running analogously with these triads are wedlock, widowhood, and virginity and 'man and his make and mulliere children' (16.221). Neither uncannily different nor overpowering, grace in such language is extrapolated from figures people already know, a matter of 'treys' reflecting 'treys' rather than of intersection and revision.

By contrast, the Samaritan always defines the Trinity through its impact upon humanity. Fingers, taking their power from the fist and guided by the palm,

Bitoknen sooþly þe sone þat sent was til erþe,
That touched and tastede at techynge of þe pawme
Seinte Marie, a mayde, and mankynde lauȝte.   (17.149–51)

Further, humankind touches the Trinity; for although the fingers have been extended to draw people to God, people can hurt God in 'þe pawme,' frustrating the power of the whole 'hand.' God intercepts the fallen world to evoke 'loue and bileue' (17.213). He penetrates it by the example of his own *agape*, which the Samaritan sees entering experience as unmistakably as the heat and light of a torch. The warmth deployed by God and required of humanity signifies 'kyndenesse,' which, in the Samaritan's view, unites not only God with humanity but humanity with its own 'kynde.' It is 'Good wille, good word boþe,' wishing for 'Alle manere men mercy and forȝifnesse' (17.352–3). So far as forgiveness is possible, it is thus univocal, not analogous, with grace, 'goddes owene kynde' (17.25), offered by God to his own enemies. Like Liberum Arbitrium, the Samaritan plays upon 'kynde,' but he thinks of it as humanity's hope for fulfilling the Law rather than as the carnal trap.[106] He reaches backwards and forwards to Piers, who eventually took and will take the part of enemies of his own.

Historically, the Samaritan, like Reason and Conscience, merely exacerbates in Will 'the suffering of being unable to love.' Will's question to him, who has taught that God does not forgive the uncharitable, gives it away: 'I pose I hadde synned so and sholde nouþe deye, / And now am sory þat I so þe Seint Spirit agulte' (17.299–300). This is the old question of what might happen between the stirrup and the ground; and on awakening from this fifth of the outer dreams, Will describes himself as a careless fellow, spending time 'like a lorel.' Nevertheless, that the moment of Will's conversion – for which the pending joust at Jerusalem is only metaphoric – has still to occur does not cancel the psychological progress achieved when the Samaritan focuses all the doctrine of salvation on the point where God and humanity meet. Although he teaches that this point is forgiving one's enemies, requiring a conversion not yet Will's,[107] it is an analogue none the less to the vision of God.

There is more to the Incarnation, however, than 'kyndenesse.' The Samaritan rushes along to fetch 'the blood of a barn,' the suffering of Christ. Suffering is where God and Will will meet. For this reason, the Samaritan stands to the success of *Dobest* as his counterpart, Anima,[108] does to the failure of the Tree of Charity.[109]

5

The Movement of Conscience II: Suffering and Knowledge

Will finds the converting knowledge of God in Conscience, who brings the meaning of the poem to its climax in the *Vita de dobest*. The Harrowing of Hell, in which legality is flooded over by God's unquenchable love and darkness and wrangling give way to the Light of Life and Easter bells, is sublime; but it no more consummates *Piers Plowman* than the 'Inexplicable splendour of Ionian white and gold' draws together the meaning of *The Waste Land*. In the Harrowing, which occupies the second of the outer dreams of *Dobet*, Will sees God's love answer human treason by putting on the 'gaye garnementȝ' of 'pacience' (18.175, 168). Nevertheless, as the dream dissolves on Easter morning, Will yet, perhaps, has no 'kynde knowyng' of Christ: the cross, which he calls his wife and daughter to revere, is a relic that presently stands in for Christ, a talisman that can frighten the devil (18.427–31).[1] The cross does not yet belong to Will, only to Christ, and Will goes to church without any real sign of contrition: 'In myddes of þe masse þo men yede to offryng / I fel eftsoones aslepe' (19.4–5). Christ is a description from the gospels, canonical and apocryphal, a pageant figure evoking momentary awe, known abstractively rather than intuitively. Malcolm Godden has discerned the difference between the 'kind of man-centered debate,' on the one hand, that had dominated the colloquy with Anima and the several passus immediately preceding and, on the other, the Messianic figure of the Harrowing who may gratify an 'intense, almost mystical yearning' in Langland.[2] But in passus 18, Christ, not the poem, 'consummatum est.' One need only remember the intervention by the 'lewed vicory' in the first dream of *Dobest* or the irruption of *Nede* in the waking interval between that dream and the last to realize that 'man-centered' debates will return. The Harrowing of Hell does not give Will the object of his quest.

The dream that begins when Will falls asleep during the offertory opens in a fashion curiously similar to the previous one. There, during Lent, Will dreamt that 'Oon semblable to þe Samaritan and somdeel to Piers þe Plowman / Barefoot on an Asse bak bootles cam prikye' (18.10–11). Obviously Will does not recognize the historical Jesus. When Will asks Faith about the meaning of the commotion, and Faith replies that Jesus and the devil will duel for possession of the fruit of 'Piers ... þe Plowman' (18.20), Will asks whether Piers is present 'in þis place.' He had always recognized Piers, and now discovers that Faith is using the name to mean the vulnerable human body in which Christ will be duelling. Subsequently, during the offertory, at the start of the first dream of *Dobest*, Will dreams

> That Piers þe Plowman was peynted al blody
> And com in wiþ a cros bifore þe comune peple,
> And riȝt lik in alle lymes to oure lord Iesu. (19.6–8)

This time Will recognizes Piers at once. Still, since Piers has been beaten and is carrying a cross, Will wants to know whether the person might not be Jesus. Earlier, the unknown figure was somewhat like Piers (18.10). Now, Will sees Piers, but in all his limbs Piers resembles Jesus (19.8). Like Faith, Conscience identifies Jesus and reveals that Piers is his vulnerable flesh (19.12–14).

The one certain change in the figure witnessed by Will is that Jesus has gone from looking 'spakliche,' 'lively' (18.12), to having been badly beaten. Thus, Faith's metaphor has become literalized: he had signified by certain figurative partial coverings of the body – 'Piers armes,' 'his helm and ... his haubergeoun' (18.22–3) – the human nature of the stranger who wore these coverings. These being the 'gay garments' of 'pacience,' they offer no physical protection. The metaphor becomes literalized because the vehicle becomes the referent: as if by the dream work that Freud described, Jesus *qua* wounded becomes literally Piers. Or at least someone mistaken for Piers. Conscience metaphorizes Piers again, but by then the poem has hypostatized Christ's suffering as a separate character. Conscience teaches Will to see Christ *through this plowman*. Jesus comes to be discerned through human suffering. This motif will govern both Conscience's ensuing speech, which draws together the two great previous movements of the *Vita*, and the action of the rest of *Dobest*.

Conscience in this speech organizes the doctrine surrounding the Incarnation by dividing Christ's career into three phases. The first two enfold the *Vita de dowel* and *Dobet* respectively, and the third unfolds into *Dobest*. Where the first two phases of Christ's life convert Mary and then Thomas (19.119–21, 163–81a), the third will convert Will. The phases correlate with the three acts of Conscience – the conative, the moral, and the psychological conscience – and become, as we shall see, analogous to the stages of the recovery of the knowledge of God. The historical cause of conversion, towards which *Dobet* had pulsed, was not in itself a psychological cause. Conscience will discover (by re-enacting) Piers's own conversion, where the abortive attrition of Haukyn had not discovered it. When Conscience – a faculty, not a person – begins the last stage of the poem by discerning Christ within Piers, this may be a clue that Piers at the end of the *Visio* had changed his course of life because he had somehow discerned Christ within himself.

Conscience explains the life of Christ three times, twice using 'knyght, kyng, conquerour' and once using 'dowel,' 'dobet,' and 'dobest.'[3] While Conscience makes these the phases of the life of Christ, which correlate with phases in the movement of the poem, I do not mean to imply that Conscience's exposition is particularly straightforward. For example, Jesus as knight and 'dowel,' behaving lawfully (19.86–90), echoes some earlier explanations of 'dowel' – as being true with one's tongue and two hands, for instance (8.81); Jesus as king and 'dobet,' who has 'lustified and tauȝte' the Jews the law of life (19.44), echoes Patience's definition of 'dobet' as 'doce' (13.137, 138). Further, the three phases anatomize the Atonement. Because Jesus, knight and 'dowel,' has lived justly, his death repairs the effects of original sin. These effects include the lameness, hunger, and the like that, as king, he remedies (19.124–39). Because these effects also include the slavery of the will, his Atonement as king includes a restoration of the freedom of choice, figured, I think, by the way in which 'þo þat bicome cristene bi counseil of þe baptiste / Aren frankeleyns, free men' (19.38–9). Christ as conqueror supposes that freedom has been restored. Coming with the cross of his passion, he teaches us 'þat whan we ben tempted,' we should fight with the cross and 'fenden vs from fallynge into synne' (19.64–5). That this anatomizes a single act on Christ's part is part of the meaning of how knight, king, and conqueror can be 'o persone' (19.27). Conscience also complicates his explanation by taking up Christ as conqueror (19.31–41) and king (19.42–9), not only in reverse order, but before he takes up Jesus as knight in detail.

Nevertheless, interwoven with these complexities is a strong thread that ties repeated meanings within the passage to the movement of *Piers*. In the first moment of his career, Jesus is just.[4] Only the wholly good person can redeem the sins of her or his sisters and brothers:

> In his Iuuentee þis Iesus at Iewene feeste
> Water into wyn turnede, as holy writ telleþ.
> And þere bigan god of his grace to do wel:
> For wyn is likned to lawe and lifholynesse,
> And lawe lakkede þo for men louede noȝt hir enemys.
> ...
> So at þat feeste first as I bifore tolde
> Bigan god of his grace and goodnesse to dowel,
> And þanne was he cleped and called noȝt oonly crist but Iesu,
> A fauntekyn ful of wit, *filius Marie*.
> For bifor his moder Marie made he þat wonder
> That she first and formest ferme sholde bileue
> That he þoruȝ grace was gete and of no gome ellis.
> He wroȝte þat by no wit but þoruȝ word one,
> After þe kynde that he cam of; þere comsede he do wel.   (19.108–23)

As water turns into wine, so human nature, in the person of Jesus, recovers its lost righteousness. Out of his 'grace and goodnesse' God becomes flesh so that people, beginning with himself, might live righteously.[5] Even at his birth, the magi's gifts show that the Law ('Reson couered vnder sense' and 'Rightwisnesse vnder reed gold') is obeyed in Jesus' love ('pitee apperynge by Mirrhe'). The notion of fulfilling the Law by loving one's enemies (19.112–14) reaches back to Haukyn, whose willingness for others to suffer so that he might be esteemed reticulates into all the sins. Closer at hand, the notion reaches to the Samaritan. He pointed forwards to Christ the king and conqueror, the saviour from original sin and the cause of contrition;[6] and yet his ethical teaching – the forgiveness of enemies that alone reconciles Faith and Hope and satisfies '*redde quod debes*' – anticipated Jesus the knight, the righteous paradigm evoking remorse like Haukyn's from a fallen world. Conscience's preaching thus recapitulates the action of the *Vita de dowel* and *Dobet* up to the sixth outer dream (18.4).

Conscience enfolds the rest of the *Vita de dobet* in teaching about Jesus the king. As 'king,' God becomes reconciled with humanity by descending to meet it on its own level and by revealing his nature – love – through his suffering. Thus, 'he Iustified and tauȝte ... / The lawe of life' (19.44–5). Preferring the good of others, he protects and defends them (19.42, 46–67). Jesus the king is God as *agape*. Because Jesus the 'knight' is the just man, Jesus the 'kyng is fairer, for he may knyghtes make' (19.29) – by presenting the lost knowledge of God, the condition of faith. The phase of Jesus' life called 'dobet' by Conscience coincides with this kingship, for it is marked by healing and helping until the Jews first call him 'fili Dauid,' believing no one as worthy 'To be kaiser or kyng of þe kyngdom of Iuda' (19.138), and then enviously kill him. In the Harrowing of Hell, which traced God's suffering to insatiable 'loue' (18.365), Jesus called himself 'Rex glorie' (18.317a), 'kyng of kynges,' and 'þe kynges sone of heuene' (48, 55, 320, 384), said that his second coming would be 'as a kyng, crouned' (371), explained that the redemption stations him to the wicked like a 'kyng' in his 'kyngdom' (381), and described his own *agape* as regal: 'For I were an vnkynde kyng but I my kynde helpe' (398).

The *agape* that makes Jesus unlike other people may be distinguished from what is represented at some earlier points in Will's search, which seem to bear what Nygren would have called the contaminating trace of *eros*, egocentric love, the human 'longing and questing for the eternal,' and a turning 'from this transitory and corruptible life … to the higher world from which the soul originates.'[7] *Eros* ascends to the God who will satisfy all the needs of the ego, which comes to rest by knowing how it participates in his totality. Similarly, the love taught by Lady Holy Church is as good as possessing God himself, makes a person 'a god by þe gospel, a grounde and o lofte,' descends to earth only in order that a person might ascend, teaches, 'Date et dabitur vobis,' and expresses itself in law.[8] There is perhaps less trace of *eros* in the speech of Anima, who nevertheless believes that love prefers to be dressed in 'riche robes,' is the merit that might deliver a person from purgatory, and must be governed by law;[9] and despite an emphasis on proselytic suffering, Anima does not escape the dilemma of egocentricity – especially clear in the c text – in the command to love God: 'þat is charite, leue child, to be cher ouer thy soule' (17.148).[10] To define 'love' cannot fall to humanity, which, given the chance, will 'aske after his' (15.159). The self-enclosed trinities of Faith also betray *eros*, it would seem: 'Divine love is for Bonaventure, as for Augustine and Pseudo-Dionysius, primarily the Divine self-love: it is the love within the Trinity, in virtue of which the Divine being – amans, quod amatur, amor – eternally circles about itself and is bent upon itself.'[11]

Nygren's contention that *eros* infects Augustinian 'caritas' has been disputed, of course. Even if there were no dispute, any suggestion that the emphasis of *Piers* shifted from *eros* to *agape* would be, in the absence of a full study, quite conjectural. Furthermore, were the speeches of Lady Holy Church and others laced with *eros*, that would not prove that they leave Will uneasy for that reason. It seems clear, nevertheless, that the *Vita de dobet* consummates in *agape* much as Nygren described it. First, Will dreams of the New Covenant, the revaluation of the Law accomplished when God, rather than drag humanity before the bar at his level, satisfies the death sentence he himself has imposed by descending to the level of humankind: 'þat was tynt þoruȝ tree,' Mercy tells Truth, 'tree shal it wynne' (18.140). Second, the fruits of the New Covenant are acquired, not through 'fides caritate formata,' a belief in God that is essentially the desire for him,[12] but rather by the experience of God's love for humanity. Christ will deliver, not those who love him, but rather 'Tho ledes þat I loue, and leued in my comynge' (18.401). Finally, Nygren insists that only the cross defines Christian love.[13] After the Harrowing of Hell, Will bids his wife and daughter approach the cross on their knees. At the start of the next passus, falling asleep when the mass begins, he dreams that the wounded Piers enters carrying a cross; and the cross inspires the long speech of Conscience, as the narrator himself sums it up: 'Thus Conscience of crist and of þe cros carpede / And counseiled me to knele þerto' (19.199–200).[14]

While the logic of the Harrowing of Hell implied the centrality of God's death, in Langland's text it was not the centre but the periphery that came into focus. First, Mercy described the juridical consequences of the Passion; then Christ described its cause, his own love for humanity. His love solved the quarrel among the Four Daughters, it broke like light into Lucifer's stronghold, and it completed God's knowledge: having known eternity, God came to experience fallen nature (18.212–25). In this way, the Harrowing of Hell took us all around the Passion, which entered Will's experience only '*secunda scripturas*,' to adapt his own expression (18.112). He saw its doctrinal meaning.[15] But he did not yet know the Passion as God's presence and existence. The apostle Thomas, by contrast, finds this simply in his sensory evidence of the resurrection of the crucified.

Where the 'dobet' phase of Christ's life, which Conscience describes as terminating Christ's earthly career,[16] includes the conversion of Thomas, Will himself finds the knowledge of God in the *Vita de dobest*, where the Passion becomes realized in his own suffering. In suffering, God knows and is known by guilty humanity. From the viewpoint of the psychological movement towards conversion, the *Vita de dobet* comes to a climax in the old evocative concretion, Piers the plowman (19.6), who stands with his cross, wounded, as an objective correlative for the knowledge of God at the place where the *Vita de dobet* and the *Vita de dobest* meet. The quarrel of the Four Daughters precedes his appearance as an explication. In the source for late-medieval versions of the story of the Four Daughters[17] and in most of the versions themselves, the quarrel occurs within an allegory made from the parable of the man fallen among thieves. Humankind having been stripped of the four virtues, the virtues dispute his fate until the Son declares that 'he will have pity on the servant, will take his vesture upon himself, sustain his judgment, and end discord.'[18] The story of the Four Daughters begins in *Piers* analogously to the way it is begun in the other versions, with the loss of the patriarchs and prophets to the thieving devil (passus 16), and continues with the priest, Levite, and Samaritan, and then with the argument. Although in *Piers* the Passion seems to be placed before the quarrel (18.47–59),[19] it occurs as part of Will's conversion only at the end of *Dobet*, after the quarrel, analogously with its position in the other versions. Where Piers before the Harrowing of Hell appears eager ('spakliche') and well protected in steel helmet and hauberk, at the beginning of passus 19 he comes in bleeding; and the 'vesture' of this suffering 'thral' that Christ takes upon himself is only bloody cloth ('hise colours and his cote Armure').

In the *Vita de dobest*, the reader confronts certain puzzles:[20] its frequent parallels with the *Visio*, the strange gifts of the Holy Spirit, the importance given to the cardinal virtues, the virtual absence of any mention of Christ, the disappointingly slight progress apparently made towards reform, the advice of Need, the fall of Unity. The reader must come to grips especially with the central role and disastrous complaisance of Conscience; with his appeals for grace, Piers, and a 'fyndyng' for friars; and finally with his own departure from Unity as a pilgrim.

These difficult facts unavoidably raise the question of whether the poem ends by representing a success or a failure.[21] The speed with which grace and virtue come under attack, first by the familiar sins, then by fearful shapes pitting libido against the rest of the cosmos, undoubtedly registers as a sickening, staggering defeat after the sunshine and hymnody of the Resurrection. Yet this reappearance of evil is an accelerating reprise of old themes prior to a final resolution; and that, in this rigorist poem, is not the reconciliation of Mercy and Truth at the end of the Harrowing of Hell, but the agony at the end of *Dobest*. The rubble in *Dobest* of broken institutions and human failures fulfils, for Langland in his particular moment, the very condition for the vision of God. Because the poet, like Jesus (at least in Bultmann's view), never thought of God's kingdom 'as something embryonically present in human nature and society, to be brought to realization by steady progression from strength to strength,'[22] the return to the ravages of the Field does not mean that we are finally left with a 'frustrated sense of seeking without finding.'[23]

My interpretation of *Dobest* proceeds from two assumptions. First, the road to salvation that the *Visio* offers the narrator abruptly terminates with Piers's decision to follow no plow but penance. Second, the similarities between *Dobest* and the *Visio* serve both to return the reader to the road that had come to such a puzzling stop and to throw the changes into relief. These differences – principally, the new and ambiguous roles of Piers, his pardon, and Conscience – result from the long, often unsuccessful explorations in the *Vita* and illuminate the ending of the *Visio*. To describe the movement as if it were a static arrangement: *Dobest* brings *Dowel* and *Dobet* to bear upon the *Visio*. While Jesus as knight and 'dowel' reaches back to *Dowel* and the remorse of humanity unable to love, and Jesus as king and 'dobet' embraces the divine love of *Dobet*, Christ as conqueror and 'dobest' makes the changes in *Visio* events that the poet now reintroduces into the outcome of *Dowel* and *Dobet*. Only when, in *Dobest*, the *Visio*-world is looked at through the two lenses of *Dowel* and *Dobet* does Christ reveal himself in it.

In Conscience's recounting, Christ's brief work as 'dobest' picks up from the *Visio* a pardon for Piers:

          do best he þouȝte
And yaf Piers pardon, and power he grauntede hym,
To alle manere men mercy and forȝyfnes,
Myght men to assoille of alle manere synnes,
To alle maner men mercy and forȝifnesse
In couenaunt þat þei come and kneweliche to paie
To Piers pardon þe Plowman *redde quod debes.*
Thus haþ Piers power, be his pardon paied,
To bynde and vnbynde boþe here and ellis,
And assoille men of alle synnes saue of dette one.
Anoon after an heigh vp into heuene
He wente, and wonyeþ þere, and wol come at þe laste
And rewarde hym right wel þat *reddit quod debet,*

Paieþ parfitly as pur truþe wolde.
And what persone paieþ it nouȝt punysshen he þenkeþ,
And demen hem at domesdaye, boþe quyke and dede,
The goode to godhede and to grete Ioye,
And wikkede to wonye in wo wiþouten ende.   (19.182–98)

While the Law and its sanctions ('do yuel and haue yuel,' 'wikkede to
wonye in wo wiþouten ende') have not changed since the *Visio*, the nature of the price paid for Piers's pardon undergoes a shift in emphasis.
In the *Visio*, there are two purchasers of the pardon, although only one
is emphasized. On the one hand, Truth 'purchaced' Piers 'a pardoun *a
pena & a culpa*' (7.3). On the other, the extent of pardon in passus 7 appears to be calibrated to the lawfulness of the recipients' behaviour ('Men
of lawe leest pardon hadde, … / For þe Sauter saueþ hem noȝt, swiche
as take ȝiftes' 7.40–1), because good behaviour is the purchase price:
merchants praised 'Piers þe Plowman þat purchased þis bulle' (7.39).
The price reappears in *Dobest* as the injunction '*redde quod debes*,' which
Conscience understands in alternative ways. These are not, as in the
Visio, alternative purchasers (Truth or Piers) but alternative modes of
purchase. And where the *Visio* had merely glanced at Truth as purchaser,
the emphasis in *Dobest* is differently distributed:

'How?' quod al þe comune; 'þow conseillest vs to yelde
Al þat we owen any wight er we go to housel?'
'That is my conseil,' quod Conscience, 'and Cardinale vertues;
Or ech man forȝyue ooþer, and þat wole þe Paternoster.'   (19.391–4)

On the one hand, you are entitled to the Eucharist if you have paid
every debt. (How, for example, does the woman taken in adultery lay
hold of this alternative?) On the other, if you cannot claim (in the *Pearl*-
poet's words) that you are the 'ryȝtwys man,' 'Hondelyngez harme þat
dyt not ille, / þat is of hert boþe clene and lyȝt,' then, believing that
your own debts have already been forgiven, you had better try to forget what is owing to you. Critics of *Piers* for the most part have given
little weight to the fact that '*redde quod debes*' is the fateful demand of a
servant in one of the parables of the kingdom who has conveniently for-
gotten that his own debts have been forgiven. Conscience, taking the
point of the parable, identifies '*redde quod debes*' with 'ech man forȝyue
ooþer' (19.394). Some may see, and think they need, no pardon but law.
Piers may once have thought this. But for those who think otherwise,

paying 'Piers pardon ... *redde quod debes,*' cannot mean material satisfaction for every offence, because 'redde' then would simply reinsert the infinite demand of the Law as an infinite condition for forgiveness. To the contrary, those who believe that they stood, and will stand, in need of forgiveness and that they have been forgiven pay Piers's pardon.

In the pre-Reformation world, perhaps the poet can describe belief that pays the pardon only as 'fides caritate formata'; and indeed the payment is associated with love, as in Kynde's counsel ('Lerne to loue' 20.208).[24] Similarly, Unity personified, Lady Holy Church, had taught Will that love opens into heaven. This ability to love God, merely assumed by the Franciscans in passus 8, is assumed also of the apostles – with better reason, since Unity/Holy Church/love is founded (in the long passage quoted a little earlier) by the historical Christ. Thus, in Langland's view, the Paraclete simply strengthens charity that arises in the primitive church with a contemporaneous knowledge of Christ. This *assumption* of charity explains the emphasis upon the cardinal virtues. It is an assumption not clear at first. Just as the pardon is retained from the *Visio* within Conscience's interpretation of it, so the immense corporate effort of the *Visio* to extract the mustard seed of salvation appears to return in Will's vision of Pentecost (19.200–344), when Conscience figures love as something that must be produced. Oxen and bullocks, plow and harrow, horses, cart, and barn, all draw attention to the spot where love at last, it would seem, is to be grown.

> Thise foure sedes Piers sewe, and siþþe he dide hem harewe
> Wiþ olde lawe and newe lawe þat loue myȝte wexe
> Among þe foure vertues and vices destruye.   (19.309–11)[25]

Something like a method for getting to heaven thus appears to be retrieved from the *Visio*, a version of the route given to the penitents by Piers. None the less, the words 'loue myȝte wexe / Among þe foure vertues' mean that the infused moral virtues are connected by charity. That is, so far as they are true and perfect (that is, infused), they result from charity;[26] for 'Spiritus temperancie' here is already the Augustinian 'uti' of created goods, 'Spiritus fortitudinis' is Christian patience, and 'Spiritus Iusticie' the decision to pay all, including God, what is due them.[27] The virtues here are forms in which love expresses itself by abounding, not a step towards bringing it into existence.

Beyond *presupposing* conversion and love, the cardinal virtues direct people's attention to society and the claims of that 'earthly house of [their] tabernacle,' the body.[28] As 'seeds,' they form part of an agricultural allegory for the success of the primitive church. The allegory includes fortifying the 'barn' with a 'moat,' dug by repentance (19.367–9). The primitive church must be fortified against the church of the latter day – must (an ironic wish) be prevented from becoming the church of Langland's world, in which the pope is governed by pride and his cardinals by covetousness and unkindness (19.223–4). Yet the allegory of the founding of the primitive church follows the division of the gifts of the Holy Spirit, which are sometimes agricultural in a literal way because they have a singular character here.

In their source (1 Corinthians 12) they are the various ways of proclaiming 'Jesus is the Lord.' Here, predicated of the state of grace, they simply remove that mental disorder brought in by sin, restoring the talents of astrologers, grammarians, merchants, and other workers.[29] Like God's bestowal of 'cræftas' in Cynewulf's Christ II,[30] this is less the division of grace than the division of labour, a conflation plausible enough if indeed the poem shows 'that the virtues which gain us salvation are the same ones which will improve earthly life.'[31] Undoubtedly, Grace, assuming that people already love, acting as if there were to be no failure in love, unites with nature in shaping the just life: Grace directs Piers and his fellows to make Conscience their king and Craft their steward (19.256); the agricultural metaphors for Piers's work with the gospels, doctors, and virtues (the work of the moral conscience) blend with Craft's literal agricultural 'conseil' to till, dig, and thatch. Craft relates closely to kynde wit, the faculty for self-preservation and the guarantor of bodily life, used as a metaphor by Conscience in Dobest for efficiency in spiritual affairs (19.360, 372). This conjunction of Conscience and Craft, which means bringing the moral conscience to bear upon the supplying of physical necessities, recalls from the Visio the 'Conscience and kynde wit' that Piers said gave him a knowledge of Truth (5.539). As if possessed of the homely gifts of the Spirit, Piers had delved, tailored, threshed, and tinkered; and he initiated his metaphorical pilgrimage by first forbidding the penitents to argue with 'conscience' and then pulling on 'his cokeres and his coffes, as Kynde Wit hym tauhte' (c 8.59).[32] 'One of the major features' of Dobest, Malcolm Godden has observed, 'is the insistent concern with the necessities of physical existence.'[33] Instituting conscience and craft in the primitive church obviously reintroduces, in a compressed form, Piers's having organized the folk into 'alle kynne crafty men þat konne lyuen in truþe' (6.68).[34] In fact, it also reintroduces Truth's conditions for his pardon.[35]

Not only do the virtues and gifts direct attention to social claims and the needs of the body; they immediately become normative. And at once their tenuous and primitive connection with an anterior faith and the experience of Christ dwindles,[36] and similarities to the *Visio* multiply. The virtues and gifts become the foundation of a code: people each receive a grace lest idleness, envy, or pride encumber them. Each 'craft' must love each other. Temperance prohibits drunkenness, irritability, extravagance in clothing; fortitude, the sulks; justice, guile and cowardice. These norms draw a line (a moat, as Conscience has it), and on the wrong side of it are 'comune wommen,' 'a sisour and a sumonour' (19.367, 369) – the prostitutes and collectors, in short, once sought out by Jesus. On 'formalism,' which in *Dobest* thus supplants the apostolic vision of God, Kenneth Kirk has this to say:

codification of principles goes hand in hand with corporate discipline: and even corporate discipline is an agency for good as long as it is exercised for pastoral and remedial purposes – to strengthen, that is to say, and to co-operate with, the personal self-discipline of the individual. But corporate discipline can have a very different side.

If it is employed not *pastorally* but *penally* – not to strengthen the weak and restore the falling, but to exclude them – the moral code, however carefully and truthfully expressed, becomes an instrument of tyranny which dragoons the many into purely outward observance, and breaks the heart of the spiritual genius who needs freedom from restraint to realize the gifts which God has given him. And because the Church soon began to forget that its charter was simply and solely to help men to be pure in heart that they might see God, it sowed for itself in its exercise of discipline a harvest of evils of almost inconceivable gravity.[37]

Those excluded in *Dobest*, plainly sinners (the brewer, the 'lewed vicory,' the chiselling magnate, the minatory king), doubtless recall the wastrels and 'shrewes' of the *Visio* too fond of their own ways to measure up to Piers's code. Conscience's subsequent appeal to Kynde for defence and wish that 'Coueitise were cristene' (20.141) parallel the recourse Piers had to Hunger, as all the miseries deposited by Kynde and Need's unbending advice about the friars ('siþen þei chosen chele and cheitiftee / Lat hem chewe as þei chose') parallel Hunger's stern sanctions and counsel (the sluggard 'shal go begge and bidde and no man bete his hunger' 6.237). Where Piers had withheld bread pure and simple, Conscience withholds the Eucharist.

The many similarities between the *Visio* and *Dobest*, however, increase the significance of the differences. Piers is now more complex. If, in tilling the cardinal virtues, he resembles the servant of the Truth known by Conscience and Kynde Wit, he no longer proudly coerces loafers into becoming useful (6.171–98). Rather, the Piers familiar to the 'lewed vicory' 'peyneþ hym to tilye'

> As wel for a wastour and wenches of þe stewes
> As for hymself and hise seruauntʒ, saue he is first yserued.[38]
> So blessed be Piers þe Plowman þat peyneþ hym to tilye,
> And trauailleþ and tilieþ for a tretour also soore
> As for a trewe tidy man alle tymes ylike.   (19.434–9)

Because the vicar describes Piers as using both an old plow and a new one, the vicar adopts the agricultural metaphors that had ended in the bread of the Eucharist, where referent and vehicle come back together. Nevertheless, he puts himself at odds with Conscience. In one sense the vicar completes the string of parallels with the *Visio*, because he makes the point that Piers may have made in tearing the pardon: you may find yourself standing on the wrong side of the moat once you have finished digging it. Once conformity to the moral conscience and possession of the virtues are preconditions for pardon, 'Thanne,' he says, 'is many a lif lost.'

> I am a Curatour of holy kirke, and cam neuere in my tyme
> Man to me þat me kouþe telle of Cardinale vertues,
> Or þat acountede Conscience at a cokkes feþere.
> ...
> For þe comune ... counten ful litel
> The counseil of Conscience or Cardinale vertues
> But it soune, as by sighte, somwhat to wynnyng.
> Of gile ne of gabbyng gyue þei neuere tale.
> For *Spiritus prudencie* amonge þe peple is gyle,
> And alle þo faire vertues as vices þei semeþ.
> Ech man subtileþ a sleiʒte synne to hide
> And coloureþ it for a konnynge and a clene lyuynge.   (19.410–58)

Robert Adams, for one, has contested the vicar's reliability.[39] But 'lewed' is not decisive. (Adams, of course, does not claim that it is.) A 'lunatik' in the Prologue had urged the king to rule righteously (125–7). Long

Will, lean like the lunatic, is first and last accused of ignorance; yet he, something of a clerical odd-jobsman also (c 5.45–7), shares certain opinions with the vicar that must be authorial – on cardinals, for example (Prol 107–11; 19.413–23), or on the propensity of 'Ech man' to look out for Number One (15.158–60; 19.457–8). The vicar's view of Piers, countering the formalism of (the moral) Conscience, actually connects with Conscience's own double understanding of Piers's pardon. After all, a brewer, who understood the pardon in only one way, had grown angry with Conscience, who grew angry in return (19.403–8). Even personifications are not always up to their own best insights.

As 'dobest' and conqueror Christ is the source of the felicity that the Atonement has opened to humankind (19.52–3, 58–62). But the redemption from sin presupposes acts by which human beings make the freedom operative. The freedom that Conscience metaphorizes as juridical freedom (19.34–40) is, in the idiom of medieval psychology, a habit, and it presupposes free acts. At the point when Christ as conqueror does 'best,' he

> yaf Piers pardon, and power he grauntede hym,
> Myght men to assoille of alle manere synnes,
> To alle maner men mercy and for3ifnesse
> In couenaunt þat þei come and kneweliche to paie
> To Piers pardon þe Plowman *redde quod debes.* (19.182–7)

Within the anatomy of Atonement, the establishment of the primitive church is itself figurative for the human act that appropriates the Atonement. '*Redde*' names this act.

From one point of view, the pardon in *Dobest* that will send 'The goode to godhede and to grete Ioye' is exactly the 'two lynes' Truth had furnished Piers. The code inaugurated by the virtues and gifts, like the marginalia on the *Visio* pardon and the letter Truth sent privately to merchants, glosses 'goode' and 'wikkede,' embracing 'alle libbynge laborers þat ... lyuen in loue and in lawe' and excluding 'beggeres' and 'bidderes' (7.62, 63, 66). The pardon from this viewpoint asks restitution and tries to rectify all injuries under the code. This view was articulated by Repentance in passus 5. There, a Welshman and Robert the Robber attempted in their repentance to satisfy the Law by making good what they had wrongfully obtained, and they understood God's mercy as underwriting what they could not work hard enough or live long enough to pay back.[40] Unconverted people see such a 'pardon' (as indeed Paul did) as setting them a job of heroic proportions – see it in fact as the iron rod with which God rules the damned (18.396–7) – and remain unconverted, convinced they are lost. *'Redde quod debes'* looks like this to the 'shrewes' on the wrong side of the moat:

'How?' quod al þe comune; 'þow conseillest vs to yelde
Al þat we owen any wight er we go to housel?'
...
'Ye? baw!' quod a Brewere, 'I wol noȝt be ruled,
By Iesu! for al youre Ianglynge, wiþ *Spiritus Iusticie*,
Ne after Conscience, by criste! while I kan selle
Boþe dregges and draf and drawe at oon hole
Thikke ale and þynne ale; þat is my kynde,
And noȝt hakke after holynesse ...'   (19.391–2, 396–401)

The second view of the pardon – from what one might call the 'inside' – has been described in part by Robert Worth Frank: 'Love of God and neighbor, expressed in the forgiveness of others, is an essential part of penance.'[41] The burden of restitution appears to have been reduced to good wishes, a mere token repayment:

For þer nys sik ne sory, ne noon so muche wrecche
That he ne may louye, and hym like, and lene of his herte
Good wille, good word boþe, wisshen and willen
Alle manere men mercy and forȝifnesse,
And louye hem lik hymself, and his lif amende.   (17.350–4)[42]

But unkindness, the opposite of what appears to be this mere gesture, is really the denial that we are all in the same boat.[43] Christians forgive their enemies because, as Anima explained, though Christians 'suffrede al þis, god suffrede for vs moore' (15.260). Having become the 'hole breþeren' of Christ through 'baptisme' (18.377), people go on within themselves, under that New Covenant of belief in God's forgiveness,[44] to fulfil the Law by forgiving their own debtors: before Christ, 'lawe lakkede ... for men louede noȝt hir enemys' (19.112). *'Redde quod debes'* is drawn from the parable of the kingdom in which a servant owed his master a vast sum. Threatened with the sale of himself, his wife, and his children, so that the debt might be paid, the servant pleaded for more time. The master 'released him, and forgave all the debt. But as that servant went out, he met one of his fellow-servants who owed him a hundred denarii, and he laid hold of him and throttled him, saying, "Pay what thou owest." His fellow-servant therefore fell down and began to entreat him, saying, "Have patience with me and I will pay thee all." But he would not; but went away and cast him into prison until he should pay what was due.' The master, upon hearing of this, takes a low view of the man whose debt he had forgiven.[45] The forgiveness of others, far from being a low hurdle set up for those who cannot clear the high ones, issues from belief. The Conscience of *Dobest*, if not the Conscience of the *Visio*, uses '*redde*' to mean this, at least at points, thus posing the third and final difference between *Dobest* and the *Visio*, the prominence and complication of Conscience.[46]

Because Will represents the desire for God, Unity is not only grace for him as an individual, but that collective state of grace, the Church. Its latter sense matters more in the breach. Standing not so much for individual Christians who keep their mutual love as they severally deepen their knowledge of God,[47] Unity seems rather an institution expected to suffice in the absence of belief.[48] Contrition's sickness (20.357, 369–70, 377) suggests this, as do the description of the founding and defence of the Church as procedures (19.321–34, 372–80) and Conscience's final abandonment of it. Piers drops out of sight. While the Church as a cultural and political institution may be perpetuated, belief can look elsewhere – 'Till,' in Robert Lowell's phrase, 'Christ again turn wanderer and child.' At the end, the simonists are left to their shell. The decision by Conscience to forsake its palliatives can be understood (and explain, in turn, much of the meaning of Conscience, *Dobest*, and, perhaps, the poem) if we turn to those puzzling termini of the last vision, the appearance of Need and Conscience's curiously narrow and concrete wish that the friars had a 'fyndyng.'[49] These are alternatives for the narrator.

The ultimate target of the attack in the last vision of the poem is suffering in general and specifically remorse. Contrition, which hypostatizes synderesis in the Franciscan sense of that term (conscience as remorseful), dramatizes as well in the last vision the fate of remorse in the hands of illiterate and hypocritical priests (20.218–27, 300–3) and glozing friars (20.362–7). The voluntary poverty of friars – their institutionalized neediness – becomes a metonymy in *Dobest* for an attenuation of remorse. This attenuation is allegorized, further, as the propagation and success of Sloth and Wanhope (20.156–66, 217). They succeed when Contrition wants an easier confessor than the 'leche' still faithful to Conscience (20.316–17), gets one in Friar Flatterer, consequently forgets 'to crye and to wepe,' and finally falls asleep (20.369, 377). Contrition thus parts company with itself: 'Contricion' has 'lafte' 'Contricion' (20.371). Having observed this victory, Sloth emboldens himself to attack Conscience, the sense of remorse itself (as distinct from Contrition, who personifies remorse as the product of an institutional procedure). Conscience's leaving Unity to keep a sense of remorse coincides with his wish that 'freres hadde a fyndyng' (20.382), a guarantee of their physical necessities and thus a protection of the sacrament that solicits remorse.

The struggle to keep remorse alive begins with Langland's satire on 'nede.' When the previous vision (the first of *Dobest*) had ended, Will awoke dispirited from the recrudescence of intractable unbelief. In this waking interval he meets Need,[50] who stands to him (and his Conscience) as Hunger stood to Piers near the end of the *Visio*. Robert Adams rightly suggests that Need personifies 'an ethically neutral condition'[51] (except, of course, as any attempt to delete morality as a perspective cannot be morally neutral). Need tempts Will to reduce all suffering to hunger, 'þurst,' and 'chele' (20.19, 236), to see these as merely physical suffering, and to conclude that nothing about them might conduce to good. If nothing does, then (Need's argument goes) the law, not to speak of scruples about trickery (20.14), must be suspended so that this physical suffering might end. Penn Szittya has pointed out that Need also suspends such 'central ideas' in the poem as 'patience, *ne soliciti sitis, fiat voluntas tua,*'[52] including the idea, inscribed by Kynde in passus 20 itself, that Will will never lack clothing or food for the duration of his life if he faithfully loves (20.210–11). By contrast, Need upbraids Will for not feeding himself straight away. 'Nede haþ no lawe ne neuere shal falle in dette' (20.10). No worry here about paying what one owes. 'Nede at gret nede may nymen as for his owene / Wiþouten conseil of Conscience or Cardynale vertues' (20.20–1). Because the Son of Man sees a kingdom not of this world, he, unlike the foxes and birds, has nowhere to lay his head. With the scriptural reference, however, Need urges Will to help himself to 'cloþes and to sustenaunce' (20.7). He adduces the cross – the 'Sicio' – to encourage Will to slake his thirst 'at ech dych.' Need turns 'nede' into something that, by definition, must be removed. And he would clear away remorse, as if scraping for a cancer, by making a travesty of temperance.

True to Pride's threat to confuse all the world, the previous vision ended with a splurge of figures in whom Conscience and Contrition had indeed been 'coloured ... queyntely.' Representatives of the three estates – a brewer, a vicar, a lord, and a king[53] – transmogrified three of the cardinal virtues.[54] 'Justice' was the king's word for taking from the commonwealth whatever he lacked (19.468, 473–4). The vicar lamented that the commons want to use their intelligence ('*Spiritus prudencie*') only on 'gyle' (19.455). The lord called this '*Spiritus Intellectus*' (19.463), the ingenuity spent by his officers in making their demands on his tenants. '*Spiritus fortitudinis*' for him is the political strength he can muster should a tenant protest. Thereafter it falls to Need to redefine temperance by making it the unique guide to appropriation, superior to the other virtues only because Need defines fortitude and justice much as the lord and king had just done and makes prudence simply the prediction of physical events (20.25–33a).[55] Need is sophistical, not in making temperance supreme (there he is simply unconventional, justice being the usual choice), but in conceiving all the virtues in isolation from reason, asking Will, in effect, to consult only his own sense of when he has consumed enough, ignoring any objective character he might have as a creature of God.

What is this temperance that is intended to supersede Conscience? Need offers little by way of ostensive definition, but there are two hints, one fairly remote, one less so. The temperance that is to govern in appropriating food, clothing, and drink is evidently an internal judgment about how much is healthful. Thus, Need says a good word for 'mesure' (20.26). 'Arys vp,' Hunger too had advised, 'er Appetit haue eten his fille' (6.264). Although Hunger urges such temperance in detail (6.257–67), he is last seen frenziedly stuffing his face and asking 'after moore' (6.296). Consequently, while Need's proposal to exclude friars from Unity may be good for Conscience, as Hunger's advice to treat the wasters like hogs could have meant a profit for Piers (6.181), Need may want the friars to go hungry (20.234–41) so that he might not. (He had given fair warning, after all, that he is capable of 'sleightes.') Need never lets on that the meal in Unity is sacramental. He simply perceives – one is tempted to say 'projects' – the friars' greediness.

That Need reintroduces the voraciousness of Hunger, and not just a claim to subsistence, is clear from a passage closer to Need than the Hunger episode. The friars, voluntarily poor, 'for nede flateren,' as Conscience knows (20.383). In one respect the following dream is an 'insomnium' that carries Need's doctrine from the waking world into sleep, for Antichrist is seen there to upturn 'þe crop of truþe' by causing 'mennes nedes' to 'spede' (20.53, 55).[56] Where there is 'nede' (as a justification) in the 'insomnium,' so friars abound to exploit it.[57] The friars sophistically equate owning nothing with being *in extremis*, as, conversely, Need had equated Christ's extremity with the *voluntary* poverty of 'philosophres' (20.38). Hence, no quantity of 'copes' or 'siluer' (20.58, 367) can ever be impugned, since these are begged, by definition, merely to sustain life. As Pamela Gradon has pointed out, the bull 'exiit qui seminat' linked necessity to temperance.[58] Consequently, whatever was taken by the voluntarily poor was susceptible of being understood, *by definition*, as consumed in moderate amounts. In this fashion, Need invites Will to ignore the moral conscience and the Law, thereby never to know guilt.

The 'fyndyng' Conscience wishes for friars correlates with his understanding of Need, for it is the sense of remorse that must be kept alive. Folk hold within Unity so far as they repent (19.368). Unity is secured when the moat fills up with 'water for wikkede werkes, / Egreliche ernynge out of mennes eighen' (19.377–8). In the final dream, attack comes almost exclusively against remorse, the latter represented both by 'Contricion' and by Unity, the (collective) state of grace consequent upon contrition. 'Contricion' (not less the acknowledgment of sin than of sinful humanity's indebtedness to God, the payment of 'redde')[59] saves a person all by itself (14.85). Accordingly, Conscience resists the personified refuges from remorse. One of these, 'a lord þat lyueþ after likyng of body' (20.71), holds memory in abeyance with present pleasure. This refuge reappears in Lechery 'wiþ laughynge chiere,' *Lyf* with his erotic clothes, and Revel, called the 'compaignye of confort.' There are other havens: possibly the debilitation of civil law, certainly the numbness of 'Sleuþe' and the appliances of 'phisik.' Conscience fights these by using the fear of death to drive the memory of sin into consciousness.

Fear by itself does not pay the pardon. Payment of that comes after Contrition and Confession, and there – in the sacrament of penance – Conscience is in danger from 'inparfite preestes and prelates of holy chirche' (20.229). Imaginative had pointed out how a 'lewed' person has 'no contricion er he come to shrifte; & þanne kan he litel telle'

But as his loresman lereþ hym bileueþ and troweþ,
And þat is after person or parissh preest, and parauenture vnkonnynge

To lere lewed men as luc bereþ witnesse:
  Dum cecus ducit cecum &c.   (12.180–5)

Handicapped by a dissolute secular clergy (20.218–27), Conscience calls for help. 'Freres herden hym crye' and offer aid (20.230), as in the thirteenth century the new fraternal orders had specialized in developing the penitential system. Warned by Need that these contemporary friars deal easily with those who seek absolution, being 'pouere' and looking to donations (20.235, 234), Conscience promises to fill their material needs – in order, or so the context suggests, that they might face no conflict of interest in the confessional.[60] He makes this 'breed and cloþes' conditional upon the friars' limiting their numbers, perhaps so they do not become needy all over again. In the event, they remain outside Unity, declining Conscience's condition, and go to school, perhaps to learn how they might refute his reasons for restraining their growth.

Conscience finally admits the friars, not because they ever mount an argument against him, but because he now shows an ambivalence towards penitential rigour. After he has actually found 'a leche' who knows how to shrive with 'sharp salue' (20.306), some of the communicants complain, asking Conscience by letter whether there might be a 'surgien' in the besieging army who can 'softer ... plastre' (20.310). When a lecher recommends Friar Flatterer, Conscience denies there is any real need for him (20.318), but defers to the request: 'I may wel suffre ... syn ye desiren, / That frere flaterere be fet and phisike yow sike' (20.322–3). Like Piers *vis-à-vis* the loafers, Conscience is reluctant to impose sanctions: he would be less remorseful, less conscious of everyone's common indebtedness, were he not.[61] So, on the one hand, he admits even the friars. On the other, once, predictably enough, the friars condone the sins of their donors and 'Contricion hadde clene foryeten to crye and to wepe' (20.369), Conscience reverts to his earlier plan, wishing 'þat freres hadde a fyndyng þat for nede flateren' (20.383).

The action ends, however, not with Conscience's shoring up the corrupted institution, but, as every reader will remember, with his going forth to

                    bicome a pilgrym,
And wenden as wide as þe worlde renneþ
To seken Piers þe Plowman ...   (20.380–2)

The departure from Unity is not just the surrender of a decayed institutional prop. Unity being associated with Satisfaction, the mystical body, and the state of grace, Conscience's departure acknowledges sin; it dramatizes the remorse he has fought to sustain. He relinquishes as well the attempt to direct the religious consciousness to the needs of the body and to society: as with Piers ('Grace gaf hym þe cros' 19.321),[62] there is little he can do to save others except with the example of his own suffering.

Of all the perspectives tried by Will on the continuing facts of the existence of a just God and of his own sin, Conscience is the last. Among its verifiable senses, Conscience means, as we have seen, the psychological conscience: primary consciousness, the indubitability and first-intentionality with which thoughts themselves are known. Conscience has named not only this certainty but specific objects of it. The first of these are the judgments of the moral conscience, the agent of Reason in the *Visio*, called by the king for counsel in making society just and orderly – the Conscience directed by the Paraclete to rule the Christianized 'mundus,' to bring humanity's quotidian activity into a moral light. As a form of cognition, moreover, Conscience knows violations of the law as well as the Law itself; knows – as we have seen in his sermon prefacing *Dobest* – not only the righteousness that leaves humanity helpless like Haukyn but the divine *agape* that stooped to the withered tree of life.

Conscience, then, as the psychological and moral conscience, is the condition for people's knowledge of their own sin; but as the conative conscience, or remorse, it responds to this knowledge. Conscience is suffering, not merely for the discrepancy between the Law and human action, but also for the inadequacy of human response to the divine love that removed the discrepancy for ever. Conscience pays the pardon that Conscience knows.

We may go a little farther. Conscience is a person's knowledge both of God's suffering (*agape*) and of the human suffering ('*redde quod debes,*' contrition) that the knowledge of God's suffering can call into being. 'Conscience,' then, names exactly the point where the divine suffering and human suffering meet in human consciousness; and the meeting is as certain as consciousness itself. God is seen when his great analogical qualities that can be learned or inferred, such as his justness and his love (all, in short, that set him apart from humanity), issue from a point he shares with humanity.[63] That would seem to be an indispensable condition for faith; and it is met in *Piers* when the narrator's Conscience perceives the divine love through the suffering Christ, and sees the suffering Christ through himself. Conscience obtains this vision of God simultaneously with organizing Christ's life into phases correlated with these great stages of conversion: Christ is just (knight), is *agape* (king), and raises humanity from death into paradise (conqueror). So conquest (*Dobest*, contrition, entry into the kingdom) occurs from knowing remorse (*Dowel*, the fact of human *in*justice) and Christ's Passion (*Dobet*) together. To see *Dowel* and *Dobet* thus is to see God, and contrition becomes possible with the vision of God.

As I shall try to show in the last chapter, Piers himself possesses such knowledge at the moment when he tears his pardon. Suffering itself has become cognitive: because of God's love, God chooses to suffer as the means of knowing human sin (18.210–17, 222–5). Because of human sin, humanity suffers as the means of knowing God's love. Suffering itself is a kind of hypostatic union,[64] approached in *Dowel* from nature and in *Dobet* from grace. In preaching Jesus as knight, king, and conqueror, 'dowel,' 'dobet,' and 'dobest,' Conscience reaches back to the helplessness of human sin (Haukyn and the Conscience who left with Patience), back to the theophany of the cross (*Dobet*), and then forward to *Dobest* and the contrition that has seen them together. In doing so, Conscience both unravels the mysterious ending of the *Visio* (Piers's conversion)[65] and becomes the conversion of Will himself.[66]

6

Piers and His Pardon

Because there is no good reason to divide Will from the poet (except so far as no 'I' in the text is identical with what narratologists call the subject of the 'énonciation') Langland may very well be left as pensive as Will when Piers tears his 'pardoun' (7.151). When Will starts out to hear 'wondres' (Prol 4), we cannot be sure that Langland already knows that a desire to believe 'kyndely on crist' lies behind this restlessness, much less that Langland is already planning to test the moral conscience and 'kynde wit' against this desire. Nevertheless, I shall move towards a conclusion by interpreting the pardon scene as partly a collapse, the end of such an exploration, foreseen or not. Like some other readers of the poem, I shall be assuming that this collapse probably sets the poet himself a puzzle that the whole of the *Vita* is needed to work out.[1] But I shall also want to assume the provisional accuracy of the description I have offered up to now of the action of the *Vita*. And thus I shall want to suggest what is eventually discernible in the tearing of the 'pardoun.' This discovery, at whatever point it is made, is consistent, I think, with changes that come over Piers. These, however, like the pardon scene itself, are best seen in light of the whole action of the *Vita*.

Considering Piers in such a light will not exhaust the possibilities for interpreting him. When, for instance, we hear that Grace has empowered him to make 'breed ... and goddes body' (19.385), no doubt we are to think of an ideal prelacy that was to have been introduced into the world by labour and love.[2] While different contexts allegorize Piers in ways like these,[3] the action of the poem as a whole may give him a continuing core of meaning.[4] Piers after the pardon scene is in certain respects a negative figure. He reappears in the poem only rarely. His attributes when he does appear have the character of isolated thrusts towards a knowledge of the relation between Christ and contemporary humanity – sketches towards a final view that itself will remain largely immanent in the structure of the poem. Langland is clear only about what does not work. I do not believe that the vision of God attained by Piers in the pardon scene yet had any positive content for Langland. If it did, then Will's experience of search thereafter would be largely factitious and contrived, for Langland, despite all he shares with his wanderer, would be holding back from him what Will requires, as if the poet were intending to manipulate the wanderer into some sort of deserving moral improvement that he himself had already achieved. To the contrary, Will is the poet looking.

If Piers, at the moment he hears his 'pardoun,' comes to see God for the first time – makes a discovery that only the action of the whole poem will construct for Will – then the representations of Piers at all later points will be consistent with Piers's experience in the pardon scene, however tentative and cryptic these representations may be, as the poet himself gropes towards an understanding. In epitomizing the *Visio*,[5] the 'pardoun' may move Piers to the very point of suffering at which God and humanity meet,[6] and therefore to a possibility of the knowledge of God and to conversion. In any case, from the time Piers wrathfully destroys his 'pardoun' he serves as the type of the converted person.[7] The structure of the whole poem will show this to mean that he comprehends his guilt under the Law but sees God in the suffering that results. This vision of God he then manifests in the forgiveness of his own enemies. In fact, changed from the man willing to use Hunger to extract from wasters their debt of labour, Piers will love his 'enemye' unconditionally; the physical beating he once administered (Hunger 'buffetted þe Bretoner aboute þe chekes' and 'bette hem so boþe he brast ner hire mawes' 6.176, 178) becomes metaphoric: Patience's advice to lay into your enemy with love ('And but he bowe for þis betyng, blynd mote he worþe' 13.147) is assigned in c to Piers. Where Piers had foreseen that loafers and beggars would be excluded from the benefits of Truth's 'pardoun' (7.65–99), later he will labour as hard for wasters and prostitutes as 'for hymself and hise seruauntʒ' (19.434–6), his example being the God who 'sent þe sonne' to shine on good and bad alike.

After the pardon scene, suffering – in *Piers*, the cause of conversion on the one hand and, on the other, the contrition that follows – always characterizes the plowman. Like Conscience in *Dobest* trying to preserve remorse, Piers vows to concentrate on penitential prayers (7.124–5). Contrition is guilt. Hence, Piers walks 'in medio vmbre mortis.' If, like Conscience, he finds in this guilty suffering the knowledge of God, then contrition becomes also a confession of faith: 'non timebo mala.'[8]

Suffering as such a condition for the knowledge of God and as such a consequence of it can help to explicate some of the plowman's baffling appearances. Patience personifies sometimes pain and sometimes contrition. For these reasons, he resembles 'Peres the ploghman' (c 15.33–4), so much that a portion of a speech by Patience in B (13.136–47) can constitute virtually the entirety of an appearance by the plowman in c (15.138–48). Suffering as a condition for the knowledge of God would account for Piers's wounds making him look like Jesus to the narrator. On the one hand, because the death of God, who will conquer through the better fortitude of patience, is impossible 'in deitate patris,' the Son must have human flesh like Piers, who can suffer: 'This Iesus of his gentries wol Iuste in Piers armes, / In his helm and in his habergeon, *humana natura* ' (18.22–3). On the other, this tormented flesh is also necessary to Conscience, for without it he could not see God:

> þise arn Piers armes,
> Hise colours and his cote Armure; ac he þat comeþ so blody
> Is crist wiþ his cros ...   (19.12–14)

While God and humanity meet at suffering, God suffers principally, at least in this poem, the pain of flesh. Piers represents this. Humanity suffers psychologically from knowledge of the broken Law. The unity of God and humanity in suffering is signified by Piers's embodiment of this, the suffering of contrition, as well.

Christ may be seen through Piers because Piers himself may have seen Christ through his own suffering, as Conscience eventually does. Whether or not Christ is glimpsed through the anguished heart, it is Christlike to glimpse the suffering heart, the contrite will. Piers surely becomes identified with Christ in penetrating to it:

> Ac Piers þe Plowman parceyueþ moore depper
> What is þe wille and wherfore þat many wight suffreþ:
> *Et vidit deus cogitaciones eorum.*
>
> ...
>
> Therefore by colour ne by clergie knowe shaltow hym [Charity] neuere,
> Neiþer þoru3 wordes ne werkes, but þoru3 wil oone,[9]
> And þat knoweþ no clerk ne creature on erþe
> But Piers þe Plowman, *Petrus id est christus.*   (15.199–200a, 209–12)

As suffering, Piers is both subject and object. That is, not only does Piers unite with Christ as a knowledge of the reason for human suffering; as if to complete the possible transformations, Piers signifies the suffering that Christ himself comes to know. This is clear when Jesus jousts in Piers's arms. It may also account for the otherwise enigmatic passage in which Piers is said to teach Jesus leechcraft:

> Piers þe Plowman parceyued plener tyme
> And lered hym lechecraft his lif for to saue
> That, þouȝ he were wounded with his enemy, to warisshen hymselue
> And dide hym assaie his surgenrie on hem þat sike were
> Til he was parfit praktisour if any peril fille.
> And souȝte out þe sike ...   (16.103–8)[10]

What could a plowman teach Christ? If Piers represents the experience of suffering, then Langland here recalls Christ much as Bernard of Clairvaux did, in the *De gradibus humilitatis et superbiae*:

In order to have a miserable heart because of another's misery, you must first know your own; so that you may find your neighbor's mind in your own and know from yourself how to help him, by the example of our Savior, who willed his passion in order to learn compassion; his misery, to learn commiseration. For, just as it is written of him, *Yet learned he obedience by the things which he suffered*, so also he learned mercy in the same way. Not that he did not know how to be merciful before, he whose mercy is from everlasting to everlasting; he knew it by nature from eternity, but learned it in time by experience ... 'For in that he himself hath suffered being tempted, he is able to succour them that are tempted.' I do not see what can better be understood from these words, than that he wished to partake of the same suffering and temptation and all human miseries except sin (which is being made like unto his brethren), in order to learn by his own experience how to commiserate and sympathize with those who are similarly suffering and tempted.[11]

Christ's compassion constitutes in part his sinlessness. Possible within time and history only because he learns from his own human nature the temptations to which other people are subject, his compassion – his 'curing himself' – flows from his Passion, his knowledge of Piers. The more he learns from Piers, the more merciful he becomes. A shameful death merely increases his desire for the objects of his love:

I fauȝt so me þursteþ ȝit for mannes soule sake;
May no drynke me moiste ne my þurst slake,
Til þe vendage falle in þe vale of Iosaphat ...   (18.367–9)

Christ's suffering – his intuitive knowledge of human sin, of which it is the effect – results in mercy, in the same way that Piers's guilt, an effect of God's love and the only human intuitive knowledge of it, becomes contrition.

The Piers who stepped forward in the *Visio* implicitly to practise the doctrine of Holy Church, opposing Meed and abiding by Reason, thought he knew God in a different way. His God, who is Truth, he knows by conscience and kynde wit – inferences from a knowledge of one's own creatureliness about obligations to the Creator and (so far as kynde wit goes) an eye for the transformability of the material world (through tailoring, threshing, and the like) and for the benefit from such labour. Anyone working like that will have something to show 'at euen' (5.552); and it is not entirely clear why it is Truth rather than Piers who needs Piers to ditch and dig. By acting with conscience and kynde wit, Piers puts the second vision into motion just as Meed, the gifts of fortune[12] when they are given or enjoyed without regard to justice,[13] motivates the first one. Piers prides himself on squeezing the less scrupulous into his own mould (6.196); if he is proud of anything else, it would have to be his clean conscience, for his testament balances like a ledger (6.83–97), instantly examinable.

The contrast between Piers and Meed – country and town, innocence and experience – runs at right angles to the line between the hill and the pit. Indeed, the fair field resembles an electrical field. Unknown to those 'bisie ... aboute þe maȝe,' lines of force run through it. Piers feels them and tries to arrange the folk like iron filings, facing towards heaven. The amorality of Meed would hide the lines by substituting for True and False the simple opposition between pleasure and pain. Piers has attained a sense of the Law, unlike the bejewelled lady, but has got no further. Informed by love the Law may be;[14] yet mostly its normative side appears in the *Visio*, where disobedience is endemic. Hence the need for coercion in the absence of a faith that might lead to love. A need to coerce obedience appears in the Prologue in the angel's address to the king ('Nudum ius a te vestiri vult pietate') and in the fable of the rat parliament, which reveals, in Anna Baldwin's view, Langland's 'preference for absolutism.'[15] The same need immediately reappears in the speech of Holy Church: kings and knights keep 'treuþe' by taking 'transgressores' into custody, as archangels exert an analogous 'myȝt' over the other divine companions ('meynee') (1.94–7, 105–8). The opposition between justice and mercy – mirrored by a dichotomy in Holy Church's speech[16] – enters the *Visio* chiefly as evidence that the Law will not be obeyed. Knowledge of the Law brings the knowledge of sin. Ironically, by conceiving God as the Truth which has informed his conscience, Piers designs the pardon he will get.

The pardon calls into question this conception and the powers of the mind responsible for it. While Will, having witnessed the pardon scene, will concur with the priest that salvation depends upon 'dowel,'[17] he will not hunt 'dowel' in the *Vita* with simply the moral conscience and kynde wit. In order to understand why he will not, as well as to see the place in Piers's conversion of the 'pardoun' they sponsor, we should consider the force of these two modalities of knowledge within the action of the *Visio*.

The moral conscience is formalistic, kynde wit egoistic. The two together know God as the architect of society, the legislator and judge of human conduct, the ultimate enjoyment. God is known thus in the natural knowledge forming the major premises of our judgments of right conduct. As we have seen, such natural knowledge was called 'synderesis' in the Dominican tradition. The moral conscience and kynde wit attempt to relate to the divine rightness every scrap of human existence. Conceiving social reform in terms of justice and satisfaction only, these powers distribute work according to social degree and apportion enjoyment according to social function. Thus, with eyes for equity only,

> Conscience and Kynde Wit and knyghthed togedres[18]
> Caste þat þe comunes sholde here comunes fynde.
> Kynde Wytt and þe comune contreued alle craftes
> And for most profitable a plogh gonne þei make,
> With lele labour to lyue while lif on londe lasteth.   (c Prol 142–6)

Far from being marred by cupidity,[19] this vision of an ideal society cannot satisfy Will in itself, although it is charitable (since love shapes the Law, as Holy Church says) and just. From the outset, the program of conscience and kynde wit serves to identify rather than transform inveterate sinners, not least the narrator himself, 'vnholy of werkes' (Prol 3). Aside from the lunatic, goliard, and angel, the next folk on the field are sergeants-at-law who will not practise without payment. And the meed-grubbers of the Prologue proliferate into Meed's retinue – all who would consolidate the goods of fortune with injustice. If the moral conscience and kynde wit succeeded in regulating human conduct, they would adjust human relations to provide for the general welfare, the 'comune profit.' But they do not. The second dream of the *Visio* no less than the first will show 'oscillations between the dynamic of reform and the richly naturalistic pictures of the unchanging, irredeemable, and at times comic incapacity of man to be other than he is ...'[20] The general welfare in practice means unconditional personal enjoyment. In the allegorical fable of the rat parliament – a kind of dumb show presaging the *Visio*'s complex revelation that the moral conscience and kynde wit save no one – the rodents would plunder like the cat if they were not physically contained:

> And many mannes malt we mees wolde destruye,
> And also ye route of Ratons rende mennes cloþes
> Nere þe cat of þe court þat kan yow ouerlepe;
> For hadde ye rattes youre raik ye kouþe noȝt rule yowselue. (Prol 198–201)[21]

The cat, whose vicious caprice serves to keep the vermin within their own walls, foreshadows the crowned predator of *Dobest*. The social order glimpsed in the Prologue flickers with possibilities: the goliard, the 'gloton of wordes,' opens the way to the cat and beyond by arguing that the very title 'rex' implies unlimited power. As the allegorical name of Piers's son claims (6.80–1), it is folly to stand against these political and economic realities, immoral or amoral though they may be.

Because the moral conscience, informed by such acquired knowledge as Scripture as well as by the natural law, knows God to be love, it teaches that positive law must effectuate mercy. While no law could seem less burdensome, if people do not wish to obey it the moral conscience can move them only by the prospect of reward or punishment. Truth's 'pardoun' is explicit in the *Visio* almost from the beginning, for Holy Church says that all who

> werchen with wrong wende þei shulle
> After hir deþ day and dwelle with þat sherewe.
> Ac þo þat werche wel as holy writ telleþ,
> And enden, as I er seide, in truþe þat is þe beste,
> Mowe be siker þat hire soule shal wende to heuene ...   (1.128–32)

Reason's sermon has the same gist: God will disown those who antagonize Truth, but save those who seek him (4.143–4, 5.54–7). While in theory the 'pardoun,' like all positive law, elaborates the two commandments to love, those who would enforce the law shortly find themselves implicated in violent coercion. The angel's warning to mingle zeal with pity darkly foretells the starvation to be inflicted for the sake of justice.[22] In driving Lucifer from heaven, the angelic militia set the pattern for all Christian knights (declares Holy Church), for the knightly function is not to fast but to fasten – that is, to 'tyen' transgressors (1.96). Piers has this permissible punishment in mind when he cautions a knight to 'tene no tenaunt but truþe wole assente' (6.38).[23] And the knight covenants to protect Holy Church and Piers, because idlers and wasters drain the food supply and ought to be punished.

The division of Holy Church's instruction into two parts, in effect, exhibits the tension created by the moral conscience on the one hand and, on the other, the knowledge that people already break the Law and will probably continue to do so. Her strategy in explaining the Tower of Truth by first teaching temperance makes sense if the reader bears in mind that she brings to Will's question the same moral point of view, with its limitations, that had been determined by conscience and kynde wit in the Prologue. Between them, they treat the goods of earth justly; and Holy Church begins there. Because she makes only a moral use of the Law, however, some of her teaching on love in the second half of her speech strikes a minatory note: love is first of all a commandment – 'to louen þi lord leuere þan þiselue. / No dedly synne to do' (1.143–4). Love will penalize humanity for its misdeeds (1.161–2), and she knows it first of all as the *sine qua non* for escaping hell (1.176–205). She of course represents more than the moral conscience and kynde wit, for the redemptive love she speaks of, penetrating with this grace the last obstacle raised by human callousness (1.153–8, 167–71), already presupposes the moral conscience – and presupposes it as having been ignored. Nevertheless, she adduces this redemptive love primarily as a binding example. She uses it in a moral, not a psychological, structure, although Will had asked her a psychological, not a moral, question (1.81–2); and the chief cause she leaves Will for imitating it is fear of the dark pit. The split between justice and redemptive love periodically reopens throughout the whole poem, but in Holy Church's teaching, as elsewhere in the *Visio*, the split merely underscores the likelihood that the Law will not be obeyed; that the Law by itself cannot procure obedience.

'Religion,' Whitehead once observed, '... runs through three stages, if it evolves to its final satisfaction. It is the transition from God the void to God the enemy, and from God the enemy to God the companion.'[24] The *Visio* moves from God the void to God the enemy; from Truth standing above the world in his tower, invoked as formal and final causes, to the apocalyptic and wrathful God who has sent 'þise pestilences' (5.13). As Reason and Conscience probe Will's conscience in the waking interval between the first two visions of the c text, so the requirements of rectitude come down hard in both texts on all the followers of Meed. 'Mercede' is to be enforced on persons so obscure as idle 'Beton.' The final sanction for 'mercede' being damnation, everyone must quit the seven sins. Allegorically, the sins personified look for a guide to righteous action. Piers kindly offers himself: 'Hadde I eryed þis half acre and sowen it after / I wolde wende wiþ yow and þe wey teche' (6.5). In arriving here after the menaces of Reason, have we moved from the agent of God the enemy to a type for God the companion?

Our answer will depend on two other questions: how good is the repentance of the multitudes envisioned by Will? How good is the guide?

Although individuals such as weavers and monks confess the sins in passus 5, Repentance is not individualized. It is true he may have a surrogate. Robert the robber, bitterly weeping, confesses his thefts to Christ in order to keep remorse alive – 'that *penitencia* his pik he sholde polshe newe / And lepe wiþ hym ouer lond al his lif tyme' (474–5). But Robert has already identified himself with his fellow thief Dismas, who had the grace to believe in the divinity of the man crucified next to him (5.464–6). This juxtaposition of the vision of Christ and repentance anticipates the action of the whole poem, which discovers God through guilty suffering. Langland, however, in revising B, moves Robert from his climactic position at the *end* of the confessions and relocates him within the confession of Covetousness, where he inscribes an incapacity to repay an illicit gain (responding, in effect, to 'ʒeuan-ʒelde-aʒen,' who personifies this very urge to restore [c 6.310]). In short, Langland makes it doubtful that Repentance actually characterizes any of the thousands who, having confessed, bluster forth 'as beestes' (5.514). Repentance, the voice of contrition ('Sorwe for synne is sauacion of soules' 5.127) and conversion,[25] knows, as Dismas did, God the companion, who died 'in oure sute ... / On good fryday for mannes sake' (5.487–8). When Repentance speaks of the human likeness to God, B cites texts about God's having made people in his own image and about the charitable person's dwelling in God. At the same place in c, however, Christ teaches that one who sees him sees the Father. Those who witness God's Passion, that is, see the conquest of wrath by patient love. The 'qui me videt' (c 7.129a) sounds the theme of the poem, the vision available only indeed to sinners, who can find themselves still 'ad ymaginem et similitudinem' of God. Repentance thus leans towards the *Vita*.

Yet his confession of faith remains largely a hypostasis. The folk know what Repentance must be, although the condition for it – the knowledge of God – for most of them remains unmet.[26] Thus, in passus 5 their repentance is strikingly imperfect. Envy, for example, begs for forgiveness, 'corsynge alle his enemyes' (c 6.64). Robin Hood and the Earl of Chester come to life in the imagination of Sloth, who nevertheless knows nothing of 'oure lord.' He begins with 'Benedicite' and ends by snoring. Where the sins have been shriven before (although perhaps only, as in Sloth's case, when moved by fear [5.513–14]),[27] now they accuse themselves again. No one would expect from a personification called Coveteousness more than a promise to stop swindling, since genuine contrition would delete the existence of Covetousness himself. The essential point, however, is the motive for the promise – the question of *why* he might stop. The 'pattern,' as Anne Middleton has written, is precisely one 'of repetition rather than revelation.'[28] Because the moral conscience and kynde wit still preside in the mentality of the *Visio* the sins can describe and affirm a sinlessness that they have no way of attaining.

As John Burrow has shown, the second vision of *Piers* follows a pattern that begins with Reason's sermon and the resulting confessions and concludes with pilgrimage. Just as the first two of these phases do not give Will what he needs, so Piers's pilgrimage also presents difficulties. Piers, cherishing the Truth of Holy Church and undertaking all Reason's duties, doubts neither that he knows God ('He is þe presteste paiere þat pouere men knowe') nor that he can describe the way to 'his place,' as 'conscience and kynde wit' taught him (5.539). This reliance on the moral conscience and kynde wit forms the context in which Piers promises to lead the penitents on pilgrimage. Kynde wit enables one to identify others' intentions towards her or him as helpful or not; it classifies material substances by their potential benefits. Because God is just, obeying must be ultimately beneficial. Moreover, since God has never commanded people to starve or ignore the labour shortages, kynde wit can effect social reforms that are compatible with Truth.[29] Just as 'The commune contreued of kynde wit craftes' (Prol 118), so Piers's knowledge of the way to Truth leaves him free to conceive such social measures as setting ladies to work at useful sewing. One may object that he assigns these as *preliminary* to leading a pilgrimage:[30]

> I haue an half acre to erie by þe heiȝe weye;
> Hadde I eryed þis half acre and sowen it after
> I wolde wende wiþ yow and þe wey teche. (6.4–6)

But we probably have here some benevolent dissembling. After the folk have learned by doing, they will see that work makes the only legitimate pilgrimage that conscience and kynde wit can discern. From Piers's point of view, his promise is the one inducement presently intelligible to the folk that can cause them to arrive at their ultimate object. The two other pilgrimages he mentions are explicitly metaphorical; this one is implicitly so.[31]

In the first of these other two, Piers gives the route to Truth as mapped by the moral conscience. Some readers may so regret the stiffness of the allegory[32] that they neglect a curious feature of its plot. The pilgrim begins by submitting to the moral conscience: 'Ye moten go þoruȝ mekenesse, boþe men and wyues, / Til ye come into Conscience' (5.561–2). Once pilgrims have submitted themselves to it, they learn to travel through the Ten Commandments:

> Two stokkes þer stondeþ, ac stynte þow noȝt þere;
> Thei hiȝte Stele-noȝt-ne-Sle-noȝt; strik forþ by boþe;
> Leue hem on þi lift half and loke noȝt þerafter. (5.576–8)

Having withstood these temptations, the pilgrim will reach 'a courte cler as þe sonne. / The moot is of mercy' (5.585–6). Penance and prayers for intercession support the bridge. What, however, is being expiated? The Ten Commandments have been obeyed. Mercy seems no more necessary than 'Grace … þe gateward' and his helper Amend-yourself. To have disobeyed one dictate of the moral conscience would be to have turned aside from the road and never have got to Truth.[33] Grace at Truth's court is sanctifying, not prevenient.[34] And Mercy and Faith ('bileef-so-or-þow-beest-nouȝt-saued'), rather than make the pilgrimage possible, come out to welcome the survivors.

If it coincided less with the limitations of the moral conscience, this incongruity between allegory and Augustinian theology might scarcely matter. It prefigures, however, the 'pardoun' Truth will send to Piers.

Once all the stipulations of the 'pardoun' have been met and one has 'done well,' what remains to be forgiven?

Before starting to plow with the others, Piers promises to raise food for all who will help him by fulfilling their functions, excepting jugglers, gamblers, storytellers, and bawds. Going on to make his will, he prefaces it by mentioning still another pilgrimage:

> For now I am old and hoor and haue of myn owene
> To penaunce and to pilgrimage I wol passe wiþ oþere;
> Forþi I wole er I wende do write my biqueste.　　　　　　　　(6.83–5)

Piers testifies that he has paid God, church, and his fellows equitably; with his remaining income, he says, 'I wol worshipe þerwiþ truþe by my lyue, / And ben his pilgrym atte plow for pouere mennes sake' (6.101–2). Scrupulous to the end, Piers makes the pilgrimage metaphoric: he will spend his superfluous income on the worthy poor rather than on seeing foreign places. The 'pardoun' will direct merchants to dispose of their own surplus in a similar way.

This charity, useful and obligatory, yet involves no cost.[35] Cost – pain – begins, for instance, when one loves enough to overcome one's justifiable wrath. The character Hunger throws this into relief, for he is the weapon unleashed by a lawful fury: the labour inflicted on Adam means we can starve wasters until they work (6.231–7).[36] For himself, Hunger wants simply to consume; he would not be Hunger if he left without being fed: 'I bihote god … hennes nil I wende / Er I haue dyned by þis day and ydronke boþe' (6.278–9). When he urges Piers to eat moderately ('Arys vp er Appetit haue eten his fille' 6.264) and to feed idlers as little as possible without killing them (6.212–17),[37] Hunger keeps himself viable as a personification. If he were simply a person, we would suspect him of making sure that there will be plenty of food left for him. Morally neutral like any force, Hunger lends himself to coercion.[38] The compliance he obtains has been foreshadowed in the Prologue by the rodents' truculent acceptance of the cat.

Most important, immersed in the vegetable world, tending to reduce all value into feast or famine, Hunger reveals one of the poles of Piers's own thought: for whatever the plowman assumes about the nature of God he uses either to vindicate or constrain his consumption of food. In setting society straight, there is no alternative, so far as Piers (or Langland, perhaps) can see, to the use of force. Righteous anger impels him to it. Yet Malcolm Godden, for one, believes that the poet gradually discovers 'the active life' to mean a 'corrupting engagement with the world' – that religious language, in Piers's use of it, is 'only a validating metaphor for a fundamentally secular activity.'[39] It is true that Piers mentions (being uneasy, perhaps, over the *élan* with which he has scoured the field) the deepest sense of *'redde quod debes'*: these folk, he says, 'are my blody breþeren ... / Truþe tauȝte me ones to louen hem ech one' (6.207–8). God having atoned for all people, it behooves one person to forgive another. Yet Piers still thinks mostly of 'Truþe,' the unmoved mover of his own self-righteous, conscientious bustle; and rather than pay for the wasters, he asks Hunger 'how I myȝte amaistren hem and make hem to werche' (6.211).[40]

The delinquents of the half-acre recall the jokers and jugglers who never even qualified for the social contract, the waferer, cutpurse, and apeward appalled by the sheer ascent to Truth, and those who so felt the weight of their own flesh – the 'wife' who clung to them – that they demurred from the virtues Piers had heaped on top of the commandments. In the B text, no one at all hastens to go with Piers on his pilgrimage, and in C the sole enthusiast is Contemplation, whose carelessness of 'famyne and defaute' (7.306) is not so much the remnant of Piers's penance in passus 7 of B as it is a hint of the somewhat disembodied nature of anyone hoping to complete this pilgrimage. So help me God, says the wafer-seller to Piers, if I thought you were telling me the truth, I wouldn't go with you a foot. Here for the first time, Piers thinks of Christ:

> Mercy is a maiden þere haþ myȝt ouer hem alle;
> And she is sib to alle synfulle and hire sone also,
> And þoruȝ þe help of hem two, hope þow noon ooþer,
> Thow myȝt gete grace þere so þow go bityme. (5.635–8)

There is a pardoner present, who, apparently at this mention of mercy,[41] cannot keep silent: to make sure Mercy recognizes him, he says, 'I wol go fecche my box wiþ my breuettes & a bulle with bisshopes lettres' (5.640). The pardoner may be someone ludicrously ignorant about the visa to heaven. No doubt, like the apeward and cutpurse, he is a confirmed rogue, and, like them and the carnal folk occupying the corresponding place in C, he finds the price of righteousness too dear. Nevertheless he not only quits the pilgrimage, but does so with a sad and dirty joke. Believing little in Piers's last-minute gesture towards mercy, he mocks it by assimilating it to his own degraded version. He mocks

Piers as well by offering this incredible excuse. The vision of all people as the 'blody breþeren' of Christ lies a world away; a 'comune womman' tells the pardoner, 'Thow shalt seye I am þi Suster'; and they head off ('I ne woot where þei bicome') like a pair out of Villon, tersely dropped by the poet with pity and scorn.

The pardoner is crucially ironic. While the forms of forgiveness he sells may be (like the indulgences familiar to the priest in passus 7) utterly invalid, nevertheless he, in a sense, is a student of mercy. Damned or not, like the 'lewed vicory' in *Dobest*, who will also head for home (19.480), he can tell a hawk from a handsaw. And the burden of the Law, the means offered by Piers for seeing God 'sitte in þyn herte,' is cold comfort.

Of the pardon scene itself, 'the climax' of the *Visio*, as Frank rightly observed, and 'the gateway' to the *Vita*,[42] I wish chiefly to emphasize an interpretation already maintained by certain critics, recast this from a psychological point of view, and apply to it the argument worked out in the preceding chapters.

The plowman's inconclusive struggle with the wasters fades into a prediction of ineluctable famine unless 'god of his goodnesse graunte vs a trewe' (6.331). The next passus begins by picking up the very word:

Treuþe herde telle herof, and to Piers sente
To taken his teme and tilien þe erþe,
And purchaced hym a pardoun *a pena & a culpa*
For hym and for hise heires eueremoore after.
And bad hym holde hym at home and erien hise leyes,
And alle þat holpen to erye or to sowe,
Or any maner mestier þat myȝte Piers helpe,
Pardon wiþ Piers Plowman truþe haþ ygraunted.   (7.1–8)

But where 'a trewe' would relieve misery, 'Treuþe' presses obligation again, with its tacit threat. Exactly as Dunning held, the 'pardoun' – the two lines introduced by a sort of covering letter from Truth or, it may be, by an improvised gloss from Piers[43] – 'constitutes a perfect epitome of the principles laid down in passus [A] i, of which the intervening six passus have been simply the allegorical and, as it were, concrete presentation.'[44] The 'pardoun' and its introduction proffer, 'not the *mede* which God grants in mercy, out of all proportion to human deserving, but the *mercede* which is our due.'[45] In the opinion of numerous critics, this is all that Piers needs. The 'pardoun' justifies his course of life.[46]

In the face of sin's devastating consequences, a 'pardoun' comes from a mentality still informed only by the moral conscience, bringing to bear the immutable tenets of righteousness. The answer to how such a document came to be called a 'pardoun' (7.3) is simply that it is the idea of one that 'Treuþe' has.[47] This does not make it truly a pardon, for 'Treuþe' has the special meaning we considered in relation to 'reson.' Thus, only bishops are in the 'pardoun' who enforce 'boþe lawes' (7.14). Merchants get a full indulgence only if they use their profits on hospitals, bridges, and other merciful works. Lawyers are excluded who impose a charge on the poor for pleading for them (7.40–59). Poor people are excluded who have enough bread to sustain life but beg for more (7.84–90). A generous sentiment from Gregory counselling indiscriminate charity disappears from C,[48] where the note of obedience rings like a threnody, touching everyone from monks and lords (C 9.219–36) to poor men who might try, by becoming beggars and hermits, to get away from hungry children, hard work, and 'litte wynnynge' (C 9.207). This 'pardoun' surely saves from '*pena & ... culpa*.' Those who purchase it by obeying the Law as Piers seems to do would obviously incur no guilt and therefore no penalty. Is the 'pardoun' valid? While gathering up the Law stated by Holy Church, Conscience, and Piers, it yet forgives nothing and is clearly no pardon. It makes forgiveness contingent upon righteousness and voids the meaning of 'pardoun' altogether.[49]

If the two lines bring to a point everything promoted by this upright and diligent plowman, why, in the A and B texts at least, does he try to destroy them?

'Peter!' quod þe preest þoo, 'I kan no pardon fynde
But do wel and haue wel, and god shal haue þi soule,
And do yuel and haue yuel, and hope þow noon ooþer
That after þi deeþ day þe deuel shal haue þi soule.'
And Piers for pure tene pulled it asonder
And seide, '*Si ambulauero in medio vmbre mortis*
Non timebo mala quoniam tu mecum es.
I shal cessen of my sowyng,' quod Piers, '& swynke noȝt so harde,
Ne aboute my bilyue so bisy be na moore;
Of preieres and of penaunce my plouȝ shal be herafter,
And wepen whan I sholde werche þouȝ whete breed me faille.'   (7.115–25)

Anne Middleton's eloquent answer seems to me to go to the core: 'The belief that one may win heaven by works alone is everywhere for Lang-

land the original and final delusion of mankind, yet it is so very tena-
cious, and so very reasonable – especially to those who care as deeply
as Langland does about civil virtue – that it always in this poem requires a violent shock to dislodge.'[50] The priest's impugning of the pardon 'is the moment of Piers' total defeat,' and yet (as A.C. Hamilton
went on to say) the tearing of the 'pardoun' marks the irruption of
grace, 'through which man may be freed from the bondage of the Law
to live under the covenant of Mercy.'[51] The 'do wel' of the 'pardoun'
expresses not only the Law, but, as Coghill pointed out, its fulfilment
by the Passion;[52] and Howard Meroney proceeded to consider the Piers
of the *Visio* 'a ridiculous Adam-Moses,' bearing 'the Do-Well of an Old
Testament Haukyn ... the tiresome righteousness of a model laborer ...
Then a priest, apparently going astray like Aaron, but one whose fore-
sight can be hindsight, scoffed the Pardon down,' and Piers tore it up
as Moses had smashed the tablets of the Law.[53]

I wish to revise such earlier criticism only by giving it a somewhat
new context. The rigour and brevity of the 'pardoun' evidently amaze
the priest. In that purity of 'do wel' Piers himself may find no allowance
for two of the phenomena arising, evidently, whenever the moral conscience and kynde wit try to regulate human life: the coercion involved
in rectifying the mob and the loss of the sight of God in deducing from
assumptions about him a code for the use of material things.[54] Even if
Piers is not mortified, he is at any event disappointed, for he has been
expecting something that the priest tells him he does not get. Truth, who
has sent this 'pardoun,' is, Piers thinks, an open book for him. He uses
the cliché himself (5.538). His intimate acquaintance ('I haue ben his fol-
were al þis fourty wynter') has led him to look forward to prompt payment: 'He is þe presteste paiere þat pouere men knowe; / He wiþhalt
noon hewe his hire þat he ne haþ it at euen' (5.551–2). Piers Plowman's
'pardoun' is his due-bill, and with a certain pathetic innocence he submits it to the cleric. When Guile, earlier in the *Visio*, enfeoffed Meed and
False Fickle-tongue with various metaphorical estates, the canon lawyers,
already bribed, were prompt to authorize the charter (2.69–114). The
priest in the pardon scene finds that the bull from Truth gives nothing.
If he had been looking for money, he finds none to be made: 'Peter! ... I
kan no pardon fynde ...' Will later takes him to mean that the 'pardoun'
is no indulgence. He does. But for Piers the 'no pardon' says that 'þe
presteste paiere' has not paid. Although the 'Treuþe' known by Piers is
rooted fully in the moral teaching of the Church, Piers has known it
chiefly as a set of socially and personally convenient premises given by

his own honest heart.[55] Uneasy about the 'meschief' he had inflicted on the wasters, Piers realized that 'god bouʒte vs alle,' a reason to 'louen hem ech one' (6.207–8). But an impulse towards love of neighbour is neither unnatural nor particularly Christian: Love the unfortunate, Hunger had counselled, 'for so lawe of kynde wolde' (6.221). What Piers has not done is to think what it could mean for God to have 'bouʒte' him too. Not so much the temple or the Old Law as this projection of a certain kind of God is cloven with a stroke;[56] and standing before us disconsolate is the *Vita* Piers, devoted to 'penaunce and ... sorwe.'

A modality of knowledge, not just a course of action,[57] momentarily disappears. The moral conscience, sponsor of 'mercede,' can constrain but not convert. Piers, who could depict a pilgrimage when he meant the relief of man's estate, could also describe as intimacy with 'Treupe' only his lifelong familiarity with good order and hard work. Not simply because he has been too 'bisy' has his life not been Christocentric, but also because, having never really seen God, he, like Will, must learn 'on crist to bileue.' With faith, all things – including the redemption of whores and lawyers – are possible; without it, a lifetime of labour is not enough, temporal order becomes a trap, and 'mercede' is Midas' touch, turning heaven and earth into an infinity of stipulations. The *Visio* takes ethical thinking as far as it can go and finds it wanting. Piers, by conceiving God as Truth, cannot receive any other 'pardoun' than the one he gets.

Between the time Piers holds out his 'pardoun' and then destroys it, God the void becomes for him God the enemy. His 'tene,' surely ambiguous, is likely some resentment at Truth who has not paid. Piers walks 'in medio vmbre mortis.' But his 'tene' may also be sorrow and anger with himself,[58] for the priest's 'no pardon' may give voice to much doubt suspended in Piers's mind ('Miʒte I synnelees do as þow seist?' he had asked Hunger). Congar recalls that William James, in *The Varieties of Religious Experience*, 'saw conversion as the end of an unconscious incubation of feelings and of ideas which finally appear, or rather explode, upon the level of clear consciousness under the pressure of our desire to replace the decrepit and dispersed elements of our mental synthesis by a stronger and more unifying principle, either through an emotional shock, a new perception, or a combination of circumstances which throw light upon the wear, the disorganization, and the lack of cohesion in our previous system.'[59] Because the vision of God attained by the *Vita* subtends the moral conscience, Piers's tearing the 'pardoun' may mislead, and the c text omits it.[60] Nevertheless, the 'no pardon' catalyses a conversion,[61] and the tearing shows with a kind of explosion that it has registered upon Piers. Instantly, he moves from knowledge of God the enemy to God the companion, from the valley of death to 'non timebo mala.' Like the 'sudden blow' marking for Yeats a great reversal in the history of human temperament, with the 'tene' and tearing one mentality replaces another.

Apart from accusing himself of having worried too much about getting food, Piers gives no reason for what he does. His action sets the narrator musing, and no criticism, after all, should dispel its puzzling effect. The unconverted Will, seeing no less in 'do wel' than had the unconverted Piers, has only that to guide the search for salvation.[62] Remembering what he has seen, nevertheless, he will suspect any person's claim to do well; and the quest for 'dowel' will turn into the quest for Piers.

The notion even that a conversion is signified in the tearing of the 'pardoun' may seem gratuitous. All the while we are rightly insisting on an absence of explanation in the scene itself, however, we may remember that it opens into the *Vita*, precisely 'The poem of the mind in the act of finding / What will suffice.' This poem within a poem bores through the dimensionless point of our non-information about Piers's behaviour to a vision of Christ – enthroned, not in 'a cheyne of charite,' but in 'the foul rag-and-bone shop of the heart.'

NOTES AND INDEX

Notes

ELH   ELH: *English Literary History*
OFB   Omitted from the B text
OFC   Omitted from the C text
Patrologia   *Patrologiae Cursus Completus ... Series Latina*   ed J.P. Migne,
Latina   221 vols (Paris 1844–90)
PMLA   PMLA: *Publications of the Modern Language Association of America*

CHAPTER ONE

1   George Kane writes, in effect, of this connection between a search for a context for the moral law and obedience to the law itself. He remarks that Langland 'is always ready to renew the act of faith. What is significant of him is the recurrence of the need for renewal.' Kane evidently sees that Langland needs this because he 'senses unmistakably that he is living within and writing about a major crisis of ethics': 'The Perplexities of William Langland' in Larry D. Benson and Siegfried Wenzel eds *The Wisdom of Poetry: Essays in Early English Literature in Honor of Morton W. Bloomfield* (Kalamazoo: Medieval Institute Publications 1982) 89. Kane does not take up the possibility that Langland is anxious over his own inability to believe. To the contrary, 'The poem clearly and repeatedly affirms the great articles of the faith' (74).

2   On the one hand, Philippa Tristram compares *Piers Plowman* with the *Divina Commedia* in its 'exigence and intensity of search' – a search that Piero Boitani has called 'tormented.' Describing *Piers* as 'truly an existen-

tial poem,' Morton Bloomfield suggested that it is the 'the first poem in English (and perhaps in any European language) that ... raises questions rather than answers them.' Will, Anne Middleton has observed, 'declares himself a writer for whom the business of writing is *finding things out*' (her emphasis). On the other hand, George Kane speaks for many other critics in arguing that, in *Piers*, 'for all its quest motif, there is no real search ...' Elizabeth Salter strikes something of a balance: Langland, she believes, ultimately undervalues 'anything except the search for the heart of the matter'; nevertheless, for long stretches, he 'seems to be doing no more – and no less – than the *compilatores*: the manipulation and rearrangement of large quantities of traditional material, with an eye to their greater accessibility to varied classes of readers.' Seriatim: Philippa Tristram *Figures of Life and Death in Medieval English Literature* (London: Paul Elek 1976) 94; Piero Boitani *English Medieval Narrative in the Thirteenth and Fourteenth Centuries* (1980) tr J.K. Hall (Cambridge: Cambridge University Press 1982) 83; Morton W. Bloomfield 'The Allegories of *Dobest* (*Piers Plowman* B XIX–XX)' *Medium Aevum* 50 (1981) 37; Anne Middleton 'Narration and the Invention of Experience: Episodic Form in *Piers Plowman*' in Benson and Wenzel eds *Wisdom of Poetry* 120; George Kane 'Langland and Chaucer: An Obligatory Conjunction' in Donald M. Rose ed *New Perspectives in Chaucer Criticism* (Norman, Okla: Pilgrim Books 1981) 13; and Elizabeth Salter 'Langland and the Contexts of *Piers Plowman*' *Essays and Studies* ns 32 (1979) 21

3 Anne Middleton 'The Audience and Public of *Piers Plowman*' in David Lawton ed *Middle English Alliterative Poetry and Its Literary Background* (Cambridge: D.S. Brewer 1982) 109

4 'John Ball's Letter to the Essex Commons' in R.B. Dobson ed *The Peasants' Revolt of 1381* (London: Macmillan 1970) 381

5 Middleton 'Audience and Public' 123

6 For example, Stephen Barney has likened Will to St Augustine, 'who knew Christianity at the outset but whose *Confessions* reveal the long struggle to comprehend and make vital what he knew': *Allegories of History, Allegories of Love* (Hamden, Conn: Archon 1979) 83

7 Augustine *Enchiridion ad Laurentium de fide et spe et caritate* 1.5, 2.7 ed E. Evans, *Corpus Christianorum Series Latina* 46 (Turnhout, Belg: Brepols 1969) 50–1

8 Bernard of Clairvaux *De gratia et libero arbitrio* 4.11, 6.16, 7.21 in *Opera* ed J. Leclercq and H.M. Rochais, 8 vols to date (Rome: Editiones Cistercienses 1957–) 3: 173–4, 177, 182

9 M.M. Adams *William Ockham*, 2 vols (Notre Dame, Ind: University of

Notre Dame Press 1987) 2: 1259. The debate within *Piers* criticism has focused, for instance, on the pardon scene. For an Augustinian interpretation, see Denise Baker 'From Plowing to Penitence: *Piers Plowman* and Fourteenth-Century Theology' *Speculum* 55 (1980) 715–25. For a semi-Pelagian reading of the same scene, see Robert Adams 'Piers's Pardon and Langland's Semi-Pelagianism' *Traditio* 39 (1983) esp 406, 411, 417. Philomena O'Driscoll sees Langland conducting a debate throughout *Dowel* between the two positions (with Thought and Wit, 'natural faculties,' on the semi-Pelagian side, for instance, and the friars, Clergy, and Scripture on the Augustinian). See her 'The *Dowel* Debate in *Piers Plowman* B' *Medium Aevum* 50 (1981) 18–29.

10 See M.M. Adams *William Ockham* 2: 1278, 1286; Graham White 'Pelagianisms' *Viator* 20 (1989) 246.

11 See M.M. Adams *William Ockham* 2: 1278.

12 Fyodor Dostoevsky *The Brothers Karamazov* tr Constance Garnett, rev R.E. Matlaw (New York: Norton 1976) 48

13 Flannery O'Connor 'A Good Man Is Hard to Find' *The Complete Stories* (New York: Farrar, Straus and Giroux 1972, 1975) 132. Beginning to emerge in passus 16 of *Piers*, Malcolm Godden proposes, 'is the belief that what is urgently necessary for man is the divine, numinous, Messianic force from outside man ...': *The Making of 'Piers Plowman'* (London and New York: Longman 1990) 123. I think, to the contrary, that this belief motivates the poem from the beginning.

14 M.-D. Chenu 'La psychologie de la foi dans la théologie du xiiie siècle' *Etudes d'histoire littéraire et doctrinale du xiiie siècle* 2 (1932) 163

15 Walter Ong 'Voice as Summons for Belief' in M.H. Abrams ed *Literature and Belief: English Institute Essays, 1957* (New York: Columbia University Press 1958) 88–90

16 Rudolf Bultmann 'Bultmann Replies to His Critics' in his *Kerygma and Myth: A Theological Debate* rev ed, ed H.W. Bartsch, tr R.H. Fuller (New York: Harper Torchbook 1961) 198

17 Rudolf Bultmann 'New Testament and Mythology' in *Kerygma and Myth* 31

18 See eg, Plato's *Timaeus* 34–6, 41, 43; and Aristotle's *De anima* 404b, 429b.

19 See Augustine *The Soliloquies* 1.2 tr T.F. Gilligan in The Fathers of the Church, A New Translation 5 (New York: Cima 1948) 350.

20 Thomas Aquinas *Summa contra gentiles* bk 4, ch 72 tr English Dominican Fathers 4 vols (London: Burns, Oates 1929) 4: 249; Gordon Leff *Gregory of Rimini: Tradition and Innovation in Fourteenth Century Thought* (Manchester: Manchester University Press 1961) 176

21 William of Ockham *Scriptum in librum primum sententiarum ordinatio* prol, q 7 ed Gedeon Gál, S. Brown, and G.I. Etzkorn, 3 vols (St Bonaventure NY: Franciscan Institute 1967–77) 1: 199. Because it was revised and complete, Ockham's commentary on the first book of the *Sentences* is usually referred to as the *Ordinatio*.

22 Gordon Leff *William of Ockham: The Metamorphosis of Scholastic Discourse* (Manchester: Manchester University Press 1975) 537. I need to make explicit that the problem that I find to be Langland's I am not imputing to Ockham, his predecessors, or his followers.

23 For a particularly useful explanation of what it means for a proposition to be evident, see T.K. Scott 'Ockham on Evidence, Necessity, and Intuition' *Journal of the History of Philosophy* 7 (1969) 40–3.

24 Cf E.A. Moody 'Ockham, Buridan, and Nicholas of Autrecourt: The Parisian Statutes of 1339 and 1340' *Franciscan Studies* 7 (1947) 140; Leff, *William of Ockham* 21–4; and M.M. Adams *William Ockham* 1: 501.

25 Ockham *Ordinatio* prol, q 1 (ed Gál, Brown and Etzkorn 1:31) and *Philosophical Writings of William of Ockham* tr Philotheus Boehner (London: Nelson 1957) 23

26 See Duns Scotus *Ordinatio* prol 3, q 3, articulus i in *Opera Omnia* ed Scotistic Commission, 9 vols to date (Vatican City 1950–) 1: 95–6.

27 See Ockham *Ordinatio* prol, q 1 (ed Gál, Brown, and Etzkorn 1: 61).

28 Leff *William of Ockham* 529; cf 532. Hence the natural impossibility of knowing that one knows 'as an *imago Dei*.' But contrast J.S. Wittig 'The Dramatic and Rhetorical Development of Long Will's Pilgrimage' *Neuphilologische Mitteilungen* 76 (1975) 66.

29 Ockham *Ordinatio* prol, q 1 (ed Gál, Brown, and Etzkorn 1: 33)

30 Mary Clemente Davlin understands 'kynde knowyng' sometimes to mean 'a knowledge which grasps the *nature* of the person known through *connaturality* between knower and known.' While I believe that this is the 'kynde knowyng' that Langland finally works through to (see ch 5), the action of the poem might be described as a search for the 'kynde' of this 'connaturality.' Love, and therefore any knowledge that might result from it, does not seem a possibility, since the narrator finds himself unable to love. Even close to the end of the poem, Kynde must still tell him, 'Lerne to loue ...' (20.208). See Davlin '*Kynde Knowyng* as Middle English Equivalent for "Wisdom" in *Piers Plowman* B' *Medium Aevum* 50 (1981) 5–17; quotation from p 11. Apart from Davlin's, there has been only one fairly specific identification of 'kynde knowyng.' Willi Erzgräber (who assimilates 'kynde knowyng' to 'kynde wit') calls it the divine light of 'ratio naturalis': *William Langlands 'Piers Plowman': Eine In-*

terpretation des C-Textes (Heidelberg: Carl Winter 1957) 45. Lady Holy Church, as I discuss below, surely uses it in this sense. But if this is what the narrator means by 'kynde knowyng,' it is hard to see how he might think that he lacks it. Several later critics substantially repeat Erzgräber's definition: see, for instance, Elizabeth D. Kirk *The Dream Thought of 'Piers Plowman'* (New Haven: Yale University Press 1972) 38; Janet Coleman *'Piers Plowman' and the 'Moderni'* (Rome: Edizioni di Storia e Letteratura 1981) 55; and Hugh White *Nature and Salvation in 'Piers Plowman'* (Cambridge: D.S. Brewer 1988) 56–7. A number of non-technical definitions of 'kynde knowyng' can be readily admitted. I summarize these in 'Langland's *Kynde Knowyng* and the Quest for Christ' *Modern Philology* 80 (1983) 246n25.

31 Better in part, perhaps, because preliterate. I have suggested some of Langland's reasons for ambivalence towards literacy itself in my 'Dame Study and the Place of Orality in *Piers Plowman*' ELH 57 (1990) 2–6.

32 Coleman *'Piers Plowman' and the 'Moderni'* 188

33 See Daniel Murtaugh *'Piers Plowman' and the Image of God* (Gainesville: University Presses of Florida 1978) 78–80. Some of Murtaugh's discussion seems to me weakened by his neglect of the 'potentia dei ordinata': eg 'God's absolute freedom meant that he could choose at random those acts and those men who would be pleasing to Him. The resulting indeterminism was at once exhilarating and terrifying' (79). The distinction between the absolute and ordered powers is implicit in any claim that Langland is semi-Pelagian in his thinking.

34 Cf Philotheus Boehner 'The Notitia Intuitiva of Non-Existents According to William Ockham ...' *Traditio* 1 (1943) 223.

35 Camille Berube 'La connaissance intellectuelle du singulier matériel au XIIIe siècle' *Franciscan Studies* 12 (1952) 193–4

36 See Nicholas of Lyre *Textus Biblie cum Glosa Ordinaria, Nicholai de Lyra Postilla, Moralitatibus Eiusdem ...* ed Sebastian Brant, 6 vols (Basel 1506–8) 2: 275v as quoted by Robert Adams 'Some Versions of Apocalypse: Learned and Popular Eschatology in *Piers Plowman*' in T.J. Heffernan ed *The Popular Literature of Medieval England* (Knoxville: University of Tennessee Press 1985) 214.

37 See Sebastian Day *Intuitive Cognition: A Key to the Significance of the Later Scholastics* (St Bonaventure NY: Franciscan Institute 1947) 91–2; cf 67–8.

38 J.F. Boler 'Scotus and Intuition: Some Remarks' *Monist* 49 (1965) 566–7

39 Ockham *Ordinatio* prol, q 1 (ed Gál, Brown, and Etzkorn 1: 63); cf distinctio 3, q 6 (ibid 2: 492).

40 See Moody 'Ockham, Buridan, and Nicholas of Autrecourt' 131–44.

41 See eg, John Wyclif's *Tractatus de trinitate* ed A. duP. Breck (Boulder, Col: University of Colorado Press 1962) 12.

42 W.J. Courtenay 'Nominalism and Late Medieval Religion' in Charles Trinkaus and Heiko A. Oberman eds *The Pursuit of Holiness in Late Medieval and Renaissance Religion* (Leiden: E.J. Brill 1974) 51

43 Heiko A. Oberman 'Some Notes on the Theology of Nominalism, with Attention to Its Relation to the Renaissance' *Harvard Theological Review* 53 (1960) 62

44 'Holy Church does not directly answer Will's naive question "Who does all the treasure in the world belong to?"': Margaret E. Goldsmith *The Figure of Piers Plowman* (Cambrige: D.S. Brewer 1981) 25. In one of his last published comments on the poem, J.A.W. Bennett remarked that, after a brief passage on the Passion (1.148–72), the 'social context' of Holy Church's discourse leads her back to didacticism: 'The Passion in *Piers Plowman*' in his *Poetry of the Passion: Studies in Twelve Centuries of English Verse* (Oxford: Clarendon 1982) 88

45 William of Ockham *Theory of Terms: Part I of the 'Summa Logicae'* tr Michael J. Loux (Notre Dame, Ind: University of Notre Dame Press 1974) 105

46 Ibid 107

47 Leff *William of Ockham* 141

48 Ibid

49 Ockham *Theory of Terms* 74

50 John of Damascus *Dialectica* ed O.A. Colligan from the version of Robert Grosseteste (St Bonaventure NY: Franciscan Institute 1953) ch 14; quoted by Ockham *Theory of Terms* 108

51 Cf Courtenay 'Nominalism and Late Medieval Religion' 57.

52 See eg, M.M. Adams *William Ockham* 1: 507–8.

53 When Imaginative makes 'kynde knowyng' synonymous with 'kynde wit,' he touches upon the sensitive intuitive cognition that is the condition for the intellective: 'Alle hir kynde knowyng com but of diuerse si3tes' (12.135). Later, Will wonders in the presence of Anima whether 'names an heep' (15.43) define real things. Anima taxes him with intellectual gluttony, believing Will seeks a diversity of objects. To the contrary, interested in the intuitive (and therefore concomitantly sensitive) test of any object, Will wishes that even the subtlest 'craft' be 'kouþe kyndely' in his 'herte.'

54 Robert W. Frank *'Piers Plowman' and the Scheme of Salvation: An Interpretation of 'Dowel, Dobet, and Dobest'* (New Haven: Yale University Press 1957) 46; cf P.M. Kean 'Langland on the Incarnation' *Review of English Studies* ns 16 (1965) 360–1.

55   Cf Thomas Aquinas *Summa theologica* 2–2.47.6 and *ad* 1. Cf Greta Hort
     'Piers Plowman' and Contemporary Religious Thought (London: Society for
     the Propagation of Christian Knowledge [1938]) 69–82.
56   Francis Carnegy *The Relations between the Social and Divine Order in
     William Langland's 'Vision of William Concerning Piers the Plowman'* (Bres-
     lau: Priebatsch 1934) 4, 7. John Alford and Gerald Morgan have recently
     offered the same view: J.A. Alford 'The Design of the Poem' in J.A. Al-
     ford ed *A Companion to 'Piers Plowman'* (Berkeley: University of Califor-
     nia Press 1988) 35; and Gerald Morgan 'The Status and Meaning of
     Meed in the First Vision of *Piers Plowman' Neophilologus* 72 (1988) 455.
57   Judith H. Anderson has observed that 'the centre of Christianity for
     Langland ... is the realization of a person in every sense' and that
     'Mankind needs not a second coming but in the present to realize the
     first': *The Growth of a Personal Voice: 'Piers Plowman' and 'The Faerie
     Queene'* (New Haven: Yale University Press 1976) 134, 75. Guy Bourquin
     describes the poem as at least beginning 'comme pélerinage de l'âme
     humaine à la recherche de Dieu': *'Piers Plowman': Etudes sur la génèse lit-
     téraire des trois versions*, 2 vols (Paris: Honore Champion 1978) 2: 692.
     Anne Middleton identifies Christ as 'the goal of all [Will's] longing':
     'William Langland's "Kynde Name": Authorial Signature and Social
     Identity in Late Fourteenth-Century England' in Lee Patterson ed *Liter-
     ary Practice and Social Change in Britain, 1380–1530* (Berkeley, Los Angeles,
     and Oxford: University of California Press 1990) 46.
58   Cf 11.335–44, 369–72, 402–4.
59   When the narrator changes 'Do Well' from a verb to a noun, he abuses
     language, in Maureen Quilligan's view, just as Lady Meed had: *The Lan-
     guage of Allegory: Defining the Genre* (Ithaca and London: Cornell Univer-
     sity Press 1979) 70. John Norton-Smith, however, writes of 'the firm
     identification of Dowel [at 7.199] with Christ': *William Langland* (Leiden:
     E.J. Brill 1983) 65.
60   See Leff *William of Ockham* 148.
61   Ibid 166
62   In such predicate positions, 'what' is used for 'who' from OE down to
     the end of the seventeenth century: see Tauno Mustanoja *A Middle En-
     glish Syntax* (Helsinki: Société néophilologique 1960) pt 1: 182.
63   Ockham *Ordinatio* d 3, q 2 (ed Gál, Brown, and Etzkorn 2: 404–5)
64   Ibid prol, q 1 (1:28)
65   Its one appearance is in a speech by Peace, where the Fall is considered
     happy in part for allowing Adam 'sorwe to feele, / To wite what wele
     was, kyndeliche to knowe it' (18.220–1). This 'kynde knowyng' is equiv-

alent to 'imperfect intuitive cognition,' the knowledge of a particular previously known intuitively when that is no longer present. Cf M.M. Adams *William Ockham* 1: 517. By an act of will, something may be recalled in an imperfect intuition ('kyndelich to knowe it') even though it was undervalued when present.

66 John Lawlor is one who, long ago, put the matter succinctly: 'we must not identify poet and Dreamer, lest we miss the nature of the Dreamer's progress' (*'Piers Plowman': An Essay in Criticism* [London: Edward Arnold 1962] 319). Lawlor offers this caution having discerned 'the defensive blindness of the Dreamer' (302). Among recent critics, Godden seems still to take basically this position, writing of 'the I-figure' as really 'a complex of different identities and voices rather than a single personality' (*Making of 'Piers Plowman'* 23). Within this complex, the 'dreamer' is usually separated out on the basis of intellectual or moral limitations 'the stupidity of a straw man,' for instance (Godden *Making of 'Piers Plowman'* 23). Margaret Jennings believes that 'Holychurch's advanced reflections on the purposes of human life ... are quite beyond the province of a spiritually dull-witted Dreamer': 'Piers Plowman and Holychurch' *Viator* 9 (1978) 368, 369. Margaret Goldsmith writes of the dreamer's 'comic and endearing obtuseness' (*Figure of Piers Plowman* 2). Marie Collins taxes him with 'wrongheaded doctrinal pugnacity,' and James Weldon with 'inherent defects of character' and 'waywardness': Collins 'Will and the Penitents: *Piers Plowman* B x 420–35' *Leeds Studies in English* ns 16 (1985) 304; Weldon 'The Structure of Dream Visions in *Piers Plowman*' *Medieval Studies* 49 (1987) 265, 276. John Bowers believes that 'Langland has arranged [for the dreamer] a concatenation of vices leading from idleness and somnolence to sorrow and finally madness ...': *The Crisis of Will in 'Piers Plowman'* (Washington: Catholic University of America Press 1986) 152. Related to idleness is a 'lust for knowledge,' instead of which, in A.V.C. Schmidt's view, the dreamer needs 'spiritual understanding': *The Vision of Piers Plowman: A Critical Edition of the B-Text* (London: Dent; New York: Dutton 1978) xx. The dreamer begins by seeking 'theoretical' knowledge but must rather begin to love: M.C. Davlin *'Kynde Knowyng* as a Major Theme in *Piers Plowman* B' *Review of English Studies* ns 22 (1971) 2. He must discover his sinful condition: Wittig 'The Dramatic and Rhetorical Development' 52, 75. By these defects, Langland modelled Will upon himself, Bowers suggests, 'though without steady interest in mirroring his own image in any literal manner ... The most profitable approach ... must lie in considering Will as a *stylized* reflection of Langland himself, bent and molded into an image better

suited to the poem's didactic ends' (Bowers *Crisis of Will* 183–6). Qualifications like that of Bowers upon the idea of the dreamer as a separable character attend to the dream convention that does in fact identify dreamer and poet, not to mention the conditions of oral performance and the conventions arising with them: see R.W. Chambers 'Robert or William Langland?' *London Mediaeval Studies* 1.3 (London 1948) 437–62; P.M. Kean 'The Pearl,' An Interpretation (New York: Barnes and Noble 1967) 134–5; and George Kane *The Autobiographical Fallacy in Chaucer and Langland* (London: H.K. Lewis 1965).

67 See Brian Stock *The Implications of Literacy: Written Language and Models of Interpretation in the Eleventh and Twelfth Centuries* (Princeton: Princeton University Press 1983) 506.

68 He is available only as the subject of the statement (*énoncé*), not of the enunciation: see Jacques Lacan 'Analysis and Truth or the Closure of the Unconscious' (1964) *The Four Fundamental Concepts of Psycho-Analysis* ed J.-A. Miller, tr Alan Sheridan (New York and London: Norton 1978) 138.

69 Stock *Implications of Literacy* 350

70 Eric A. Havelock *Preface to Plato* (1963; New York: Grosset and Dunlap 1967) 224

71 See Bruno Snell *The Discovery of the Mind: The Greek Origins of European Thought* 2nd ed tr T.G. Rosenmeyer (1948; New York: Torchbook-Harper 1960) 8–17. This is not to imply that Greek ever lost the sense that the physical organ meant the resultant function.

72 Stock *Implications of Literacy* 79

73 See Havelock *Preface to Plato* 228.

74 Stock *Implications of Literacy* 523

75 Ibid 363

76 Havelock *Preface to Plato* 229

77 See Kenneth Burke *The Rhetoric of Religion* (Boston: Beacon 1961) 20–1, 151.

78 See G.H. Russell 'The Poet as Reviser: The Metamorphosis of the Confession of the Seven Deadly Sins in *Piers Plowman*' in Mary J. Carruthers and Elizabeth D. Kirk eds *Acts of Interpretation: The Text in Its Contexts, 700–1600: Essays on Medieval and Renaissance Literature in Honor of E. Talbot Donaldson* (Norman, Okla: Pilgrim 1982) 53–65.

79 M.M. Bakhtin 'Discourse in the Novel' (1934–5) in his *The Dialogic Imagination: Four Essays* ed Michael Holquist, tr Caryl Emerson and Michael Holquist (Austin: University of Texas Press 1981) 261–2. See also David Lawton 'The Subject of *Piers Plowman*' *Yearbook of Langland Studies* 1 (1987) 1–30.

80 See, eg, Middleton 'Audience and Public' 117; 'Narration and the Invention of Experience' 103, 105–6, 110–11, 115–16; 'William Langland's "Kynde Name"' 29. Wendy Scase has also recently emphasized the problem of authority faced by Langland. She claims that, at the beginning of passus 12, Will describes himself as a non-professional: 'The concept which brings together the notion of reading and writing for private amusement, the rejection of association with those whose clerical vocation is their living, and the language of the gyrovague is the concept of the "nonprofessional."' Earlier clerical authors of anti-clerical satire had used the habit of the extra-regular as their cover. But what is the authority of this new writer who 'had usurped the clergy's literary lordship? ... No way had yet been established of distinguishing between the new anticlerical writer and the cleric': 'Piers Plowman' and the New Anticlericalism (Cambridge, New York, New Rochelle, Melbourne, Sydney: Cambridge University Press 1989) 169–70, 173; see also 138–45.
81 Kane suggests of the 'autobiographical' passage that begins C 5 that 'the poet seems to be registering an insight of awful clarity into the nature of his own zealous anger against the abuses of religion: this not merely is irrelevant to his salvation but relates to his own moral inadequacy' ('Langland and Chaucer' 17).
82 See esp Middleton 'William Langland's "Kynde Name"' 58.
83 Ibid 45–6
84 Middleton 'Audience and Public' 117. Passages where Will is clearly appetite – 'movement towards' an object, a quester – include 5.4–5, 7.148, 8.13, 9.25, 10.148–51, 160, 12.25–8, 15.149–51, 16.18–19, 53–9, 17.86–8, 18.21, 111, 20.213.
85 Leo Spitzer 'Note on the Poetic and Empirical "I" in Medieval Authors' Traditio 4 (1946) 416–18
86 The word 'wille' seems to name the rational appetite at C 9.111, B 8.95, C 13.94, C 14.24, 26, B 13.140, 192, 193, B 14.20, B 15.150, B 16.88, and B 18.212.
87 A.J. Minnis 'Langland's Ymaginatif and Late-Medieval Theories of Imagination' Comparative Criticism: A Yearbook 3 (1981) 87
88 Geoffrey Chaucer Boece bk 5, pr 4, in Larry D. Benson et al eds The Riverside Chaucer 3rd ed (Boston: Houghton Mifflin 1987) 463. Cf White Nature and Salvation 70, 74–5; but contrast Norton-Smith William Langland 119.
89 Cf esp Mary-Jo Arn 'Langland's Characterization of Will in the B-Text' Dutch Quarterly Review of Anglo-American Letters 11 (1981) 297, 299.
90 The dreamer consults thought, wit, study, scripture, receiving from

each a partial answer to his questions ... but it is his job as a complex human being to synthesize the different accounts': David Mills 'The Dreams of Bunyan and Langland' in Vincent Newey ed '*The Pilgrim's Progress': Critical and Historical Views* (Totowa: Barnes and Noble 1980) 171.

91 Quilligan *Language of Allegory* 61; Norton-Smith *William Langland* 102, 78, 126; and White *Nature and Salvation* 2

92 Elizabeth Salter 'Langland and the Contexts of *Piers Plowman' Essays and Studies* 32 (1979) 19–21

93 Morton W. Bloomfield '*Piers Plowman' as a Fourteenth-Century Apocalypse* (New Brunswick: Rutgers University Press [1961]) 8–34. Among others proposing genres contributory to the poem, Middleton suggests that Langland extended the form of the 'chanson d'avanture' ('from a short enigmatic report of a brief encounter to a lyric history'): 'Audience and Public' 114–16; quotation from 115. M.C. Davlin situates *Piers* in the tradition of the biblical wisdom books, especially Job, with their 'mixed and overlapping genres, elliptical and aphoristic discourse, changes in point of view, and ... various kinds of disjuncture': ('*Piers Plowman* and the Books of Wisdom' *Yearbook of Langland Studies* 2 (1988) 23–33; quotation from 33. Steven Justice has interpreted the *Visio* as a sequence 'not of narrated actions, but of narrative genres,' which the poet tests in search of a genre 'that will accommodate an authority neither abusive nor idiosyncratic.' This sequence includes the 'internal dialogue,' satire, the confession manual, and 'the action of the Mosaic books.' Langland progressively abandons 'authorial control in favor of control by the biblical text': 'The Genres of *Piers Plowman' Viator* 19 (1988) 292, 291, 295–301, 303.

94 See Lawrence M. Clopper 'Langland's Markings for the Structure of *Piers Plowman' Modern Philology* 85 (1988) 245–55.

95 See R.W. Frank 'The Number of Visions in *Piers Plowman' Modern Language Notes* 66 (1951) 309–12.

96 The first to argue for an arrangement among the four sections was H.W. Wells, who held that the *Visio* concerns the virtues proper to the ordinary communicant and the *Vitae* the three mental attitudes exemplified in clerical life: altruistic service in *Dowel*, contemplation in *Dobet*, and, in *Dobest*, the active mode in which the corporate church guides all of society. See 'The Construction of *Piers Plowman'* PMLA 44 (1929) 123–40; 'The Philosophy of *Piers Plowman'* PMLA 53 (1938) 339–49. Conrad Pepler attempted to co-ordinate the three *Vitae* with three stages of mystical progress, the purgative, illuminative,

and unitive ways: *The English Religious Heritage* (St Louis: Herder 1958) 44. Taking a suggestion of Wells's, R.W. Frank related the *Vitae* to three helps, each associated with a person of the Trinity, provided by God for humanity in seeking salvation: *'Piers Plowman' and the Scheme of Salvation* 16–17. Thereafter, Barbara Raw compared the movement through the *Vitae* with the three phases of the Augustinian version of the image of God – memory, intellect, and will: 'Piers and the Image of God in Man' in S.S. Hussey ed *'Piers Plowman': Critical Approaches* (London: Methuen 1969) 173–5. More recently, Lawrence Clopper has proposed that the *Visio*, *Dowel*, and *Dobet* are related respectively to the image of the Father and instruction in the Faith, the Son and the attainment of Wisdom, and 'the Holy Spirit by whose grace Will is instructed in Charity.' In *Dobest* Will sees God in his unity: 'Langland's Trinitarian Analogies as Key to Meaning and Structure' *Mediaevalia et Humanistica* ns 9 (1979) 102.

97 Northrop Frye *Anatomy of Criticism: Four Essays* (Princeton: Princeton University Press 1975) 318, 317. Barney implicitly shares Frye's view of the poem: see his *Allegories of History, Allegories of Love* 88–9.

98 Frye *Anatomy of Criticism* 52, 77, 83

99 See my 'The Plot of *Piers Plowman* and the Contradictions of Feudalism' in Allen J. Frantzen ed *Speaking Two Languages: Traditional Disciplines and Contemporary Theory in Medieval Studies* (Albany: State University of New York Press 1991) 112–13.

100 See esp Middleton on the way in which the episode in *Piers* characteristically has the form of a dispute: 'Narration and the Invention of Experience' 95–7.

101 Clopper is the most recent critic to assign basically consistent meanings to the three 'Dos' regardless of which character uses them. See 'Langland's Trinitarian Analogies' 96, 99–100.

102 Piero Boitani and Denise Baker have each proposed the metaphor of the spiral, to which I return in ch 5. See Boitani *English Medieval Narrative* 81; and Baker 'Dialectic Form in *Pearl* and *Piers Plowman' Viator* 15 (1984) 471–2.

103 James Druff 'Genre and Mode: The Formal Dynamics of Doubt' *Genre* 14 (1981) 299

104 See B.F. Huppé 'The Translation of Technical Terms in the Middle English *Romaunt of the Rose' Journal of English and Germanic Philology* 47 (1948) 338–9; Paul Molinari *Julian of Norwich* (London: Longmans, Green 1958) 62; and Bloomfield *'Piers Plowman' as a Fourteenth-Century Apocalypse* 37–8.

CHAPTER TWO

1   H.W. Wells 'The Construction of *Piers Plowman*' PMLA 44 (1929) 128
2   T.P. Dunning *'Piers Plowman': An Interpretation of the A Text* 2nd ed, ed
    T.P. Dolan (Oxford: Clarendon 1980) 25. D.W. Robertson and B.F.
    Huppé (*'Piers Plowman' and Scriptural Tradition* [Princeton: Princeton
    University Press 1951] 28–9, 70–1, 73, 97) qualified and elaborated
    Dunning's definition. Cf also P.M. Kean 'Love, Law and *Lewte* in
    Piers Plowman' *Review of English Studies* ns 15 (1964) 243n; Greta Hort
    'Piers Plowman' and Contemporary Religious Thought (London: Society
    for the Propagation of Christian Knowledge 1938) 84; J.A. Burrow
    'The Action of Langland's Second Vision' *Essays in Criticism* 15 (1965)
    251; Dorothea Siegmund-Schultze 'The Idea of "Reason" in 14th Cen-
    tury English Literature' *Wissenschaftliche Zeitschrift der Martin-Luther-
    Universität, Halle-Wittenberg, Gesellschaft- und Sprachwissenschaftliche
    Reihe* 8 (1959) 757–62; R.C. Goffin 'Chaucer and "Reason"' *Modern
    Language Review* 21 (1926) 13–18; and Myra Stokes *Justice and Mercy
    in 'Piers Plowman'* (London and Canberra: Croom Helm 1984) 28. J.A.
    Alford defines 'reson' in one sense as the 'partial image' of the eter-
    nal law imprinted in the human mind, applicable by conscience in
    particular circumstances: 'The Idea of Reason in *Piers Plowman*' in
    E.D. Kennedy, R.A. Waldron, and Joseph Wittig eds *Medieval English
    Studies Presented to George Kane* (Cambridge: D.S. Brewer 1988) 204.
    This 'imprint' is the meaning of 'synderesis' in the Dominican sense
    and the meaning of 'kynde knowyng' in Lady Holy Church's usage
    (see p 14 above) and 'inwit' in Wit's usage: see B.J. Harwood and
    R.F. Smith 'Inwit and the Castle of *Caro* in *Piers Plowman*' *Neuphilolo-
    gische Mitteilungen* 71 (1970) 648–54.
3   Cf Alford 'Idea of Reason' 213. If 8.53 appears to assign intellect ('wit
    and free wil') to the brute creation, the next line but one attributes it
    pre-eminently to man – which would contradict passus 11 if 'wit and
    free wil' were actually equivalent to 'reson.'
4   Barbara Palmer 'The Guide Convention in *Piers Plowman*' *Leeds Stud-
    ies in English* ns 5 (1971) 17
5   Geoffrey Chaucer *Boece* bk 4 pr 6 in Larry D. Benson et al eds *The
    Riverside Chaucer* 3rd ed (Boston: Houghton Mifflin 1987) 451. Cf OED
    sv 'Reason' sb 6.
6   Geoffrey Chaucer *Canterbury Tales* G 1199–200 in Benson et al eds
    Riverside Chaucer 278
7   Cf 17.257–9: here Reason ratifies the causal relationship between un-

kindness and an extinguishing of the Holy Spirit. Cf also 11.268–9, where, in the narrator's view, Reason knows the connection between poverty and fearlessness of robbers. In Anima's account, Reason links disease in the root of a tree and corruption in fruit and flower (15.101–2). Cf 12.263 and 17.342–4. Although, in each of the following occurrences, 'knowledge of cause and effect' may not become clear as a secondary meaning for 'reson' until its primary sense has been considered, it is expeditious to list them together at this point: C 5.5, 11, 26, 53, 69, 125; B 5.59; C 11.29; B 10.116; C 12.17; B 11.126, 131, 335; C 13.153; B 11.370, 372, 373; C 13.190; B 11.376, 387, 414, 415, 420; C 13.228; B 11.429; C 13.230; B 11.438; B 12.209, 218; B 15.52; B 17.41, 307; C 20.308; B 18.330, 339, 349. Some of the usual ME senses of 'reson' are represented in *Piers*: (a) for deducing conclusions, arranging things in order, reason-finding (cf OED *sv* 'Reason' v 2, 3, 4, 5, 7), see A 8.152, C 13.128, 182 193, 243, and C 15.40; (b) for premises employed in an argument (cf OED *sv* 'Reason' sb 1), see B 12.49, and A 11.40–2 and cf the related occurrences in which 'reson' means a rebuke (C 13.128, 182, 193, 243, and B 12.218). For (a), cf also Ludwig Schütz *Thomas-Lexikon* (Paderborn 1895) *sv* 'ratio' e, f, g; and for (b), cf Schütz ibid *sv* 'ratio' l and m; and G.-Ed. Demers 'Les divers sens du mot "ratio" au moyen âge' *Etudes d'histoires littéraire et doctrinale de XIIIe siècle* 2 (1932) 111–12. But these usual meanings account for fewer than a dozen of the 150 or so occurrences of 'reson' in the poem. At 15.11, Reason is the narrator's means for seeing Anima, and at 15.65, Anima uses 'reson' to mean the process of discovery, or the speculative reason. My argument in this chapter cannot account for these senses. C omits both occurrences, however. In the first case, the omission is part of a larger revision, eliminating the waking interlude between the vision of Haukyn and the vision of Anima. In the second, 'reson' is deleted in favour of 'sciences.'

8 J.L. Austin *How to Do Things with Words* (Cambridge, Mass: Harvard University Press 1962) 112

9 See William J. Courtenay *Schools and Scholars in Fourteenth-Century England* (Princeton: Princeton University Press 1987) 343–4. His logical writings had been of steady interest earlier in the century: see Courtenay *Schools and Scholars* 277, and P.V. Spade, 'Anselm and the Background to Adam Wodeham's Theory of Abstract and Concrete Terms' *Rivista di storia della filosofia* (Milan) 43 (1988) 261–71. George Sanderlin and Edward Vasta have previously related Anselm's 'rectitudo' to the poem. In 'The Character "Liberum Arbitrium" in the C-

Text of *Piers Plowman*,' *Modern Language Notes* 56 (1941) 451–3,
Sanderlin refers to Anselm's having conceived 'liberum-arbitrium' as
seeking rectitude. In *The Spiritual Basis of 'Piers Plowman'* (The Hague,
London, Paris: Mouton 1965), Vasta adduces a tradition including
Anselm to argue that truth in *Piers* 'means to be like God through a
conformity of wills' (63); but he appears to neglect the pre-eminence
Anselm gave to cognition in relation to truth: see Anselm *De veritate*
cap 12 and Imelda Choquette 'Voluntas, Affectio, and Potestas in the
Liber de Voluntate of St. Anselm' *Medieval Studies* 4 (1942) 62.

10   Cf c 13.186–90; Anselm *De veritate* cap 5; and Robert Pouchet *La rectitudo chez Saint Anselme: un itinéraire augustinien de l'âme à Dieu* (Paris:
Etudes Augustiniennes 1964) 86–7.

11   Anselm *De veritate* cap 5 in *Opera omnia* ed F.S. Schmitt, 5 vols (1938;
Edinburgh: Nelson and Sons 1946–51) 1: 182

12   M.J. Lapierre 'Aquinas' Interpretation of Anselm's Definition of
Truth' *Sciences Ecclésiastiques* 18 (1966) 418; cf Anselm *De veritate* cap
7.

13   See Etienne Gilson 'Sens et nature dans l'argument de Saint
Anselme' *Archives d'histoire doctrinale et littéraire du Moyen Age* 9
(1934) 11. See also Hans-Joachim Werner 'Anselm von Canterburys
Dialog *De veritate* und das Problem der Begründung die praktischer
Sätze' *Salzburger Jarhbuch für Philosophie* 20 (1975) 119–30; Gottlieb
Söhngen 'Rectitudo bei Anselm von Canterbury als Oberbegriff von
Wahrheit und Gerechtigkeit' in H.K. Kohlenberger ed *Sola Ratione:
Anselm-Studien für Pater Dr. h. c. Franciscus Salesius Schmitt OSB zum
75. Geburtstag* ... (Stuttgart: Frommann 1970) 71–7; T.F. Torrance 'The
Ethical Implications of Anselm's *De veritate*' *Theologische Zeitschrift* 24
(1968) 309–19; Kurt Flasch 'Zum Begriff der Wahrheit bei Anselm
von Canterbury' *Philosophische Jahrbuch der Görres-Gesellschaft* 72
(1965) 322–52; and Franz Wiedmann 'Wahrheit als Rechtheit' in
F. Wiedmann ed *Epimeleia: Die Sorge der Philosophie um den Menschen*
(Munich: Pustet 1964) 174–82.

14   Thomas Aquinas *Summa theologica* 1.16.1 ed Dominican Fathers, 60
vols (London: Blackfriars 1964–6) 4: 76

15   Lapierre 'Aquinas' Interpretation' 432–3. The dependency of right
knowledge upon a share of the single rectitude of the divine mind
presents an epistemological problem, like Augustinian illuminism
generally, not in question here. (On this, see, eg, Etienne Gilson, *History of Christian Philosophy in the Middle Ages* [New York: Random
House 1955] 76.) We are concerned, not with how rightness is known

to be such, but with the effect of rightness, those moral prescripts
that the narrator, to his sorrow, knows to be binding.

16   Choquette 'Voluntas, Affectio and Potestas' 64. Thus A.V.C. Schmidt
      somewhat oversimplifies the matter when he defines 'reson' in
      11.369–75 as 'natural necessity ... the *naturalis instinctus* of Aquinas':
      'Langland and Scholastic Philosophy' *Medium Aevum* 38 (1969) 148.

17   Lapierre 'Aquinas' Interpretation' 436

18   Cf Aquinas: 'Since ... the idea ['rationem'] of each and every effect
      must pre-exist in him, the divine mind must preconceive the whole
      pattern ['ratio'] of things moving to their end. This exemplar ['ratio']
      of things ordained to their purpose is exactly what Providence is'
      (*Summa theologica* 1.22.1 ed Dominican Fathers 5: 89). Cf also the quo-
      tation from Boethius above, p 34. Cf also Alford: 'In identifying the
      eternal law as *ratio summa*, the Stoics ... were thinking of an objective
      order that would exist even if there were no creatures to perceive it'
      ('Idea of Reason' 204).

19   Gerard Manley Hopkins *Poetical Works* ed N.H. MacKenzie (Oxford:
      Clarendon 1990) 141

20   Anselm *De veritate* tr and ed Richard McKeon in *Selections from Me-
      dieval Philosophers*, 2 vols (New York: Scribner 1929–30) 1: 156–7

21   Anselm *De veritate* cap 12 ed Schmitt 195. Cf Aquinas *Summa theolo-
      gica* 2–2.51.1.

22   Myra Stokes and Gerald Morgan equate 'truþe' in the poem with
      'iustitia.' However, Langland generally uses 'lewte' to signify the rec-
      titude of the human will. When 'Truþe' signifies God, both his intel-
      lect and will are understood to be conditions for this rightness. See
      Stokes *Justice and Mercy* 158, and Gerald Morgan 'The Status and
      Meaning of Meed in the First Vision of *Piers Plowman*' *Neophilologus*
      72 (1988) 457.

23   Cf Söhngen 'Rectitudo bei Anselm' 72.

24   Aquinas *Summa theologica* 1.87.4 *ad* 2 ed Dominican Fathers 12: 119.
      Cf esp F.J. Yartz 'Order and Right Reason in Aquinas' Ethics' *Me-
      dieval Studies* 37 (1975) 407–18.

25   See also the conjunction of 'reson' with 'riȝtwisnesse,' 'riȝtful,' etc:
      eg, c 6.33, b 14.103, c 20.204. Of the eighty-three occurrences of some
      form of 'riȝt' (but excluding 'rights') recorded by Barnet Kottler and
      A.M. Markman *A Concordance to Five Middle English Poems: 'Clean-
      ness,' 'St Erkenwald,' 'Sir Gawain and the Green Knight,' 'Patience,'
      'Pearl'* (Pittsburgh: University of Pittsburgh Press 1966), only eight are
      alliterated with 'reson.' Five of the eight appear in *Cleanness*, where
      on two occasions the hendiadys 'riȝt' and 'reson' seems to signify the

rectitude of the will: see *Purity* ed R.J. Menner (New Haven: Yale University Press 1920) ll 328, 724.

26 C 3.293. Cf C 3.324–6, C 14.148, C 20.308, B 18.349, B 19.460, 478.

27 'Right' is 'related to L "rectus," the base being the root "reg-" to make or lead straight' (OED *sv* 'right' adj). An indication of the tie is given by Conscience, who maintains that 'relacoun rect is a ryhtful custume' (C 3.373).

28 On this sense of 'cause,' see Aquinas: the object 'is a principle of motion in that it determines activity in the manner of a formal cause. Every action throughout the world of nature is specified by its form ... The primordial form for all things is transcendental being and being true, which is the object of mind. And so, in a manner of motion from the formal cause, that is by presenting the object, the mind moves the will to its activity' (*Summa theologica* 1–2.9.1 ed Dominican Fathers 17: 65). Cf esp Torrance 'Ethical Implications' 310–11, 313.

29 Anselm *De veritate* cap 11

30 See eg *Sir Gawain and the Green Knight* 2nd ed, ed J.R.R. Tolkien and E.V. Gordon (Oxford: Clarendon 1967) ll 226, 392, 443. For 'reson' as speech in *Piers*, see 14.311.

31 Accordingly, Anna P. Baldwin has been able to point to the association between Reason and natural-law theory in *Piers*. The *Visio* king, so far as he is restrained only by the natural law, would be an 'absolute' monarch. See her *The Theme of Government in 'Piers Plowman'* (Cambridge: D.S. Brewer 1981) 10, 21–2.

32 For an instance of such disparagement, see Samuel Moore 'Studies in *Piers the Plowman*' *Modern Philology* 11 (1913) 191–2. In an analysis that, at a few points, parallels my own, Willi Erzgräber explains the passage as treating 'das rechte Verhältnis des Menschen zu Gott,' which is of course a person's subordinating himself or herself: *William Langlands 'Piers Plowman': Eine Interpretation des C-Textes* (Heidelberg: Carl Winter 1957) 68–70; but Erzgräber relates neither 'reson' nor rectitude to the passage.

33 See below, p 92. On Conscience's being guided by Reason, see Robertson and Huppé *'Piers Plowman'* 159n. At C 5.6, Conscience leads to Reason.

34 See C 3.293, 309; and cf B 3.239.

35 'Rect,' which the poet joins to both 'relacoun' and 'resonable' (C 3.366), in late-medieval Latin increasingly connoted justice and law: see the *Revised Medieval Latin Word-List from British and Irish Sources*, prepared by R.E. Latham (Oxford: Oxford University Press 1965) *sv*

'rectum.' See also C 11.20 and, for an association of 'reson' with law, see C 3.293. On the relationship between 'reson' and justice, see below pp 42–5.

36 Cf Alford, 'Idea of Reason': 'Concord with Christ means the unification of wills through love ...' (758).

37 S.B. Meech ed 'An Early Treatise in English Concerning Latin Grammar' in *Essays and Studies in English and Comparative Literature* University of Michigan Publications in Language and Literature 12 (Ann Arbor: University of Michigan Press 1935) 108. Where the English treatise has 'certeyn' and 'vncerteyn,' Donatus has 'finita' and 'infinita': see W.J. Chase ed *The Ars Minor* University of Wisconsin Studies in the Social Sciences and History 11 (Madison: University of Wisconsin Press 1926) 32. S.A. Overstreet defines 'relacion ... indirect' as 'ratio indirecta,' instances 'in which the relative pronoun differs from its antecedent in case, but still agrees in gender, number, and person ...': '"Grammaticus Ludens": Theological Aspects of Langland's Grammatical Allegory,' *Traditio* 40 (1984) 254. But this is inconsistent with Langland's writing that 'indirect thyng is ho-so coueytede ... to cache and come to bothe nombres' (C 3.362–4). Cf C 3.370–1.

38 See B 4.1–5.

39 See, for example, B 3.239, where 'ywroght werkes wiþ right and wiþ reson' translates 'operatur iusticiam.' See also B 17.304–10, where 'rightwisnesse,' 'iustice,' 'reson,' and 'equyte' are all closely related.

40 As Overstreet observes, 'rewards are justified by the right relationship of the parties involved' ('"Grammaticus Ludens"' 292). For other occurrences of 'reson' as rectitude, see B 3.239, C 19.3, B 17.263, and B 18.199. For rectitude as a secondary meaning, see B 1.94, C 4.7(?), C 4.29(?), B 4.33(?), 40(?), 42(?), 157, 172, 177, 185; C 4.190, C 4.196, C 5.182, C 6.12, B 5.272, C 6.435, B 6.316, C 12.17, C 13.34 (two occurrences), C 13.193, C 15.52, C 15.151, B 13.166, B 15.52, B 15.513, B 17.349, B 18.278, C 20.308, B 18.330, 334, 350. For earlier comment on the passage, see esp A.V.C. Schmidt 'Two Notes on *Piers Plowman*' *Notes and Queries* ns 16 (1969) 285–6; P.M. Kean 'Justice, Kingship, and the Good Life in the Second Part of *Piers Plowman*,' in S.S. Hussey ed *'Piers Plowman': Critical Approaches* (London: Methuen 1969) 97–9; and Margaret Amassian and James Sadowsky 'Mede and Mercede: A Study of the Grammatical Metaphor in *Piers Plowman* C: IV: 335–409' *Neuphilologische Mitteilungen* 72 (1971) 457–76.

41 But contrast Morgan 'Status and Meaning of Meed' 460; and Robert Adams 'Mede and Mercede: The Evolution of the Economics of

Grace in the *Piers Plowman* B and C Versions' in Kennedy et al eds *Medieval English Studies Presented to George Kane* 222, 229.

42 See Aquinas *Summa theologica* 2–2.58.1.

43 See Aquinas *De veritate* 28.6 *ad* 3.

44 See, eg, 1.25.

45 Because the Harrowing of Hell passus takes up theodicy, 'reson' may confuse the issue here so far as it suggests another sense of justice, viz, equity. Perhaps for this reason, C eliminates 'reson' at this point, even though that word in the primary sense of rectitude occurs frequently in both the B and C versions of the passage.

46 Aquinas *Summa theologica* 2–2.58.11 ed Dominican Fathers 37: 39. See also his comment on 1131a of the *Nicomachean Ethics* (*Commentary on the Nicomachean Ethics* tr C.I. Litzinger, 2 vols [Chicago: Henry Regnery 1964] 1: 402–3).

47 Contrast John Lawlor *'Piers Plowman': An Essay in Criticism* (London: Edward Arnold 1962) 296; see also 62–3, 79, 81. Alford understands 'mesure' as 'moderation' ('Idea of Reason' 213). Gervase Mathew was perhaps the first to stress the importance of equity to the poet's notion of justice: 'Justice and Charity in *The Vision of Piers Plowman*' *Dominican Studies* 1 (1948) 363. And W.J. Birnes was evidently first to connect *Piers* with the growth of 'equity law,' 'the law of the Court of Chancery': 'Christ as Advocate: The Legal Metaphor of *Piers Plowman*' *Annuale Mediaevale* 16 (1975) 72. The Court of Chancery was, Anna Baldwin points out, 'flatteringly referred to as the "Court of Conscience."' When Peace comes into the 'parlement' in passus 4 to complain against Wrong, Baldwin links the power of Reason and Conscience there to a court like Chancery, where the king has the 'prerogative to replace the law by his own equitable notion of justice' (*Theme of Government* 42). Myra Stokes has lately written at length on Langland's 'refusal ever to lose sight of the principles of justice and equity' (*Justice and Mercy* 46). See esp her ch 1.

48 Aristotle *Ethica Nicomachea* 5.3 in *The Works of Aristotle* ed W.D. Ross 12 vols (Oxford: Oxford University Press 1908–52) 9: 1131 a-b. The whole *Nichomachean Ethics* was available after ca 1245, when it was translated by Grosseteste.

49 Raymond Wilson Chambers *Man's Unconquerable Mind: Studies of English Writers from Bede to A.E. Housman and W.P. Ker* (London and Toronto: Jonathan Cape 1939) 112

50 Cf C 11.29 and B 18.339. See also B 6.148–51.

51 See 17.41–3. (Possibly, however, Reason is making an analogy here,

analogies being analogous themselves to proportions.) As the just apportionment of knowledge, see 'reson' at 15.53.

52 See 14.109–10, 126–44. Reason is mensurative also, in a secondary sense, at 14.124. As equity, Reason matches the best rewards with the best servants: see c 18.97–100. See also c 5.69. At c 13.34, 'resoun' matches the length of a delay to the magnitude of a burden. Reason also means justice to oneself – spending on oneself what one deserves: see c 6.33, B 14.103.

53 As chancellor: c 4.185; as otherwise a judge: B 4.108, 177–8. Cf Anima's laying claim to the name 'Racio' 'whan I deme domes' (B 15.27).

54 See May McKisack *The Fourteenth Century, 1307–1399* (Oxford: Oxford University Press 1959) 198. Reason's agreeing to become chancellor provided that 'vnsittynge Suffraunce' does not seal the king's 'pryueie letteres' may allude to the misuse of the privy seal to interfere in the common-law processes represented here by Reason, who as chancellor holds (at the king's discretion) the great seal. Cf H.C. Maxwell-Lyte *Historical Notes on the Use of the Great Seal of England* (London: HM Stationer's Office 1926) esp 116 and his reference to *Rot. Parl.* 3: 247. Cf c 9.138.

55 For other occurrences of 'reson' as signifying primarily the application of law, see c 4.29, B 4.108, 110, 112, 177, 185, c 4.187, 190, 196, B 18.278, 330, 349, 350, and c 20.308. For instances where this is a secondary sense of the word, see B 4.134, 15.513, 19.478. As denoting evidence, 'reson' relates to the application of law at 2.49, 10.55, and 17.307. As personifying a kind of judge, but in any case applying the law, see 'reson' also at 11.126 and c 13.34.

56 Cf Malcolm Godden's interesting suggestion that the *Visio* world is based on Creation, not Redemption. He remarks 'the almost Old Testament emphasis of the *Visio* on justice': *The Making of 'Piers Plowman'* (London and New York: Longman 1990) 158, 85.

57 Walter W. Skeat ed *The Vision of William Concerning Piers the Plowman, in Three Parallel Texts* 2 vols (Oxford: Oxford University Press 1886) 2: 65. Margaret E. Goldsmith believes that the poet intends to make us 'very uneasy about the naked justice being advocated by Reason and the harsh attitude taken by Conscience': *The Figure of Piers Plowman* (Cambridge: D.S. Brewer 1981) 29.

58 'For y made of tho men ['lollares of Londone and lewede ermytes'] as resoun me tauhte' (c 5.5). Moreover, parallels between the speech of Reason here and the conditions of Piers's 'pardon' suggest that, at

a third stage (the pardon scene), the requirements of Reason are applied to Piers.

59 Cf Will:

'Preyeres of a parfit man and penaunce discret
Is the leuest labour þat oure lord pleseth.
Non de solo,' y sayde, 'for sothe *viuit homo,*
Nec in pane et in pabulo, the *pater-noster* wittenesseth;
Fiat voluntas dei – þat fynt vs alle thynges.'   (c 5.84–8)

60 See also B 20.253–72. That this irregularity – waxing beyond limit or establishing oneself apart from an ordained number – means inequity and therefore the loss of rectitude may be clarified through John of Salisbury *The Metalogicon* 2.20, tr D.D. McGarry (Berkeley and Los Angeles: University of California Press 1962) 132–3. Cf Aquinas *Summa theologica* 1.5.5 *ad* 1. Cf also Alford's remark that 'Included in the idea of reason as transcendent order is a strong numerical component' ('Idea of Reason' 205).

61 See T.P. Dunning 'The Structure of the B-Text of *Piers Plowman*' *Review of English Studies* ns 7 (1956) 236.

62 See also the use of 'reson' at 17.258.

63 See also the occurrence at 14.124.

CHAPTER THREE

1 Dream III goes from B 8.68 to B 12.297. The first dream-within-a-dream, called 'Dream IV' by R.W. Frank, takes up B 11.6–406: see 'The Number of Visions in *Piers Plowman*' *Modern Language Notes* 66 (1951) 309–12. Because, in the opinion of the editor of the present standard edition of the A-text, 'the most serious doubts' about the authenticity of passus A 12 'are raised by its poor manuscript support,' I exclude A 12 from consideration here and elsewhere: see George Kane ed *Will's Visions of Piers Plowman and Do-Well* 51.

2 Seriatim: J.J. Jusserand *A Literary History of the English People from the Origins to the Renaissance,* 3 vols (1st Fr ed 1895; London and New York: Putnam's 1909–10) 1: 387; John Norton-Smith *William Langland* (Leiden: E.J. Brill 1983) 23; and Malcolm Godden *The Making of 'Piers Plowman'* (London and New York: Longman 1990) 61

3 See Nevill Coghill 'The Character of Piers Plowman Considered from the B Text' *Medium Aevum* 2 (1933) 112–14. His suggestion is criticized by S.S. Hussey 'Langland, Hilton, and the Three Lives' *Review of English Studies* ns 7 (1956) 132.

4   Godden *Making of 'Piers Plowman'* 193
5   J.A. Alford 'The Design of the Poem' in J.A. Alford ed *A Companion to 'Piers Plowman'* (Berkeley: University of California Press 1988) 50, 47
6   Ibid 50
7   But contrast D.W. Robertson and B.F. Huppé, who believe that 'the poet has cleverly succeeded in satirizing … the superficiality of Will's thought': *'Piers Plowman' and Scriptural Tradition* (Princeton: Princeton University Press 1951) 105. Their key argument, that Thought attempts to define the good life without referring to charity, seems to be groundless, for the 'vertues' taught by Thought presuppose grace and imply charity, which is their form.
8   See Henri de Lubac *Exégèse médiévale: les quatre sens de l'Ecriture*, 2 vols (Paris: Aubier 1959–64) 2: 571–2.
9   Exercising 'Wit and free wil' (rising to steer the boat) is, in their account, a *cause* of sinning venially (ie, falling down). Cf G.W. Stone 'An Interpretation of the A-Text of *Piers Plowman' PMLA* 53 (1938) 667. But contrast T.P. Dunning *'Piers Plowman': An Interpretation of the A Text* 2nd ed, ed T.P. Dolan (Oxford: Clarendon 1980) 134; R.W. Frank *'Piers Plowman' and the Scheme of Salvation: An Interpretation of 'Dowel, Dobet, and Dobest'* (New Haven: Yale University Press 1957) 49; and L.M. Clopper 'Langland's Franciscanism' *Chaucer Review* 25 (1990) 57.
10 Once (2.91) it has to do with lewd imaginings: cf Chaucer's Merchant's Tale (4.2359) and Second Nun's Tale (8.225): Larry D. Benson et al eds *The Riverside Chaucer* 3rd ed (Boston: Houghton Mifflin 1987) 167, 265. However, 'thoughtes' can denote the images of things present as well as images coined by the 'fantasia': see Chaucer's use in *Boece* bk 2, met 10.21 (*Riverside Chaucer* 434) to translate 'mentes': Boethius *Philosophiae Consolatio* Corpus Christianorum, Series Latina 44 (Turnhout, Belg: Brepols 1957). A second occurrence in *Piers* (c 6.100) has to do with imagination also, but as that operates in recollection: cf Chaucer *The Book of the Duchess* 1108–11 and *The House of Fame* 2.523–5 (*Riverside Chaucer* 342, 354). In this second occurrence, however, 'thouhte' may mean judgment brought to bear upon what is imagined (cf *The House of Fame* 3.1174, *Troilus and Criseyde* 2.806, and *Boece* bk 3, met 10.18, translating 'aciem'). Or it may simply mean reflection, the meditative focusing of the mind: cf *Promptorium Parvulorum* … ed Albertus Way, Camden Society 89 (London 1865) 492. Still more broadly, when 'thouȝt' occurs at 5.505 and c 19.109 it appears to mean the total activity of the mind itself: cf *Cursor Mundi*

807, ed Richard Morris, Early English Text Society os 57 (Oxford 1874, 1961), *Boece* bk 1, pr 6.95, where Boethius has 'mentium'; and *Troilus and Criseyde* 3.465.

11 Maisack suggested that Thought is the poet's reminiscence of three stages of life in a Cistercian monastery, with 'dowel' as the lay brother working beside the monks in the fields, 'dobet' the monk himself, and 'dobest' the abbot: see Helmut Maisack 'William Langlands Verhältnis zum zisterziensischen Monchtum: Eine Untersuchung der Vita im *Piers Plowman*' (PHD diss, University of Tübingen, Balingen 1953) 17.

12 Cf Greta Hort, who identifies Thought with Thomas Aquinas' conception of the *intellectus agens*: '*Piers Plowman*' and Contemporary Religious Thought (London: Society for the Propagation of Christian Knowledge [1938]) 89. She defines the latter as 'the link between the knowledge of universal ideas which a man possesses and the concrete instances he observes.' But for the Scholastics, the soul knows no universals until the agent intellect apprehends them in concrete objects. Cf also Raymond St Jacques's comment that Thought 'speaks in abstractions and completely ignores individualizing circumstances': 'The Liturgical Associations of Langland's Samaritan' *Traditio* 25 (1969) 229.

13 James Simpson has related Conscience in passus 2–4 to the 'divisivus' mode of reason: see his 'From Reason to Affective Thought: Modes of Thought and Poetic Form in *Piers Plowman*' *Medium Aevum* 55 (1986) 13.

14 While acknowledging that the content of Thought's speech 'is not fundamentally different from that of the second vision,' Godden suggests 'a shift of emphasis' that results in raising 'the more specifically religious work of the clergy ... to a higher status' (*Making of 'Piers Plowman*' 64).

15 Cf 7.14.

16 These two passages in B are somewhat less similar.

17 It cannot teach its essence: see Aristotle *Posterior Analytics* 2.5.

18 Aristotle *Prior Analytics* 1.31 in his *The Organon* tr O.F. Owen, 2 vols (London: George Bell and Sons 1908) 1: 153–5. The *Analytics* were a staple of university education. For 'determination' in addition to the BA an Oxford student was expected to have heard the *Prior Analytics* twice and the *Posterior Analytics* once: see Hastings Rashdall *The Universities of Europe in the Middle Ages* 2nd ed, ed F.M. Powicke and A.B. Emden, 3 vols (Oxford: Oxford University Press 1936) 3: 153. Of

the four Platonic 'methods' discerned by medieval and Renaissance scholars, division almost exclusively occupied the attention of at least the early Middle Ages: see Neal W. Gilbert *Renaissance Concepts of Method* (New York: Columbia University Press 1960) 5, 140.

19   'Wit and wisdom' occurs in one form or another about seventeen times in the poem, but Langland does not usually, it seems, use 'wit' and 'wisdom' pleonastically: see esp 2.134, 10.393–4, and 19.450. Except when 'wisdomes' are gnomic expressions (eg at 12.137), 'wise' or a form of it merely signifies possession of whatever knowledge from a given viewpoint is decisive and useful. When this is a knowledge of means, 'wisdom' connotes 'wit,' and 'wit and wisdom' is therefore pleonastic.

20   For example, Frank *'Piers Plowman' and the Scheme of Salvation* 50–1. Cf his 'Art of Reading Medieval Personification Allegory' ELH 20 (1953) 245: and P.M. Kean 'Justice, Kingship, and the Good Life in the Second Part of *Piers Plowman*' in S.S. Hussey ed *'Piers Plowman': Critical Approaches* (London: Methuen 1969) 85. Robertson and Huppé, in identifying 'wit' as the Scholastic 'speculative intellect' (*'Piers Plowman' and Scriptural Tradition* 107), confuse the latter with the possible intellect. In 'Langland's Use of *Kind Wit* and *Inwit*' *Journal of English and Germanic Philology* 52 (1953) 182–5, Randolph Quirk attributes to 'wit' the vast range of meaning the word has in ME generally, but associates it especially with the 'ratio particularis,' a Scholastic term for the sensitive soul's power to compare under the guidance of intellect. However, this seems plausible for only a few occurrences of 'wit' in *Piers*: 3.302; 'forwit' 5.166, 11.323, 15.357, 370. Daniel Maher Murtaugh defines 'wit' as simply 'the intelligence considered as a whole': *'Piers Plowman' and the Image of God* (Gainesville: University Presses of Florida 1978) 24.

21   'Quo autem ad diversa instrumenta corporea, ut ad oculum et auditum, et quoad inmutationes in ipsis receptas, diversarum sunt specierum': Iohannes Blund *Tractatus de anima* cap 6 ed D.A. Callus and R.W. Hunt (Oxford: Oxford University Press 1970) 18. Cf Aquinas *Summa theologica* 1.78.3 *ad* 1; and *Piers* 1.15, 10.448. These five 'outer wits,' so far as they are put to a virtuous purpose, are personified in Wit's speech as the 'fyue faire sones' of the constable of the Castle of *Caro*, 'sire Inwit' (9.17–24). Wit calls the six of them together 'inwit and alle wittes' (9.54). I discuss 'inwit' below, pp 60–1.

22   Cf 13.362, 365, 14.166–7. Described from the perspective of those whom he eluded, Christ is 'ful of wit'; from the viewpoint of God's

providential use of Satan's own guile, however, the Incarnation is
done 'by no wit but þoruȝ word one' (19.122). To the contrary, characters representing this viewpoint of grace often seem to use 'wit'
broadly to mean the knowledge of God: see esp 2.129, 134, 138, c
3.211, c 6.311, b 8.9, a 10.75, c 18.28, 190, and b 16.187. Both senses of
'wit' – the less frequent one meaning the knowledge of God and the
predominant one – apply ambiguously to the Franciscans in passus 8.
'Men of grete witte,' they might be thought to know God. They also
assure Will that 'wit' enables man to 'werche wel,' however (8.57).
Many shifts in the action of the poem are marked by the narrator's
mental distress, signified by a phrase like his awakening 'witlees'
(13.1). In addition to the sense of distraction, shared by the word in
ME and modern English, it may also point in the narrator to the absence of this knowledge of God. See also 1.71, 10.6, c 13.183, b 15.3,
and c 18.180.
23   See also b Prol 37, c 9.106, 111, 116, b 11.44, a 10.92, b 12.224, and b
13.291. (The evidence for construing this last occurrence of 'wit' thus
is only the recast line in c.) For more ambiguous examples, see
1.14–16, 8.53, a 10.75, c 13.191, b 15.76, and b 19.216. For 'wit' in the
sense of knowledge of defences against attack, see b Prol 156 and the
secondary meaning of 'wit' at 4.67, 76, 81, and 12.224. Cf MED sv
'engin' n 2 (b) and 3 (c). For uses of 'wit' in a sense similar to its chief
meaning in Piers Plowman, see The Owl and the Nightingale ed E.G.
Stanley (London: Nelson 1960) 681–94; the speech of the second tercel
in Chaucer's Parliament of Fowls 459–62 (Riverside Chaucer 391); and
esp the Parson's Prologue 10.48–51 (Riverside Chaucer 287).
24   See esp 19.229–33. See also 2.134, c 3.211, b 4.27–9, b 7.53. For more
ambiguous uses, see 10.17, c 11.79, c 15.144. Cf William of Auvergne
(d 1249): 'Debes etiam hic reminisci de virtute quae vocatur ingenium
sive ingeniositas, ex que est faciliter inventionis mediorum ad proba-
tiones et probationum sive argumentorum' (De anima 7.8 in Opera
Omnia, 2 vols [Orleans and Paris 1674] 2: 215). For 'wit' as knowledge
of verbal means to an illicit or immoral end, see 4.67, 76, 81, 91, c
6.167; and for a more ambiguous use, see c 20.354. For 'wit' as signifying a knowledge of contrivances in general to an illicit or immoral
end, see 2.153, c 6.261, 264 (cf b 12.362, 365), b 11.45, b 15.400, 409, c
19.243, b 19.354, 450. Cf MED sv 'engin' n 1 (b); and A Glossary of Later
Latin, to 600 A.D. comp A. Souter (Oxford: Oxford University Press
1949, 1964) sv 'ingenium.'
25   See also 5.166, 11.323, 12.169(?), 15.83, 357, 370, 18.234.

26 See B.J. Harwood 'Langland's *Kynde Wit*' *Journal of English and Germanic Philology* 75 (1976) 331. See also below pp 143–9.

27 See also C 14.32, B 12.272, B 18.234.

28 Isidore of Seville *De spiritu et anima* cap 11; *Patrologia Latina* 40: 787. In *Studies in Words* 2nd ed (Cambridge: Cambridge University Press 1967), C.S. Lewis identifies 'wit' as 'the almost invariable translation' of 'ingenium' (89–90). However, he cites only Renaissance examples and takes 'ingenium' in its broad sense of 'quickness to learn and memory,' 'something like cleverness, ability, high intellectual capacity.' Three more recent studies have taken up 'ingenium' also. The most relevant is that by Robert W. Hanning, who shows 'the double perspective' on 'engin,' the French derivative of 'ingenium,' inscribed in chivalric romance: *The Individual in Twelfth-Century Romance* (New Haven: Yale University Press 1977) 135. On the one hand, by 'engin,' characters gild over intractable realities; on the other, 'the artist is a deceiver ... what we witness ... is a society attempting to come to grips with artfulness ...' (136). 'Engin' signifies, among other things, 'problem-solving behavior,' 'manipulation,' and the discovery of expedients (107–10) – a capacity triumphantly shown in Lunette in Chrétien's *Yvain* (118). Less relevantly for a discussion of 'wit' in *Piers*, a poem that also includes the character Imaginative, Winthrop Wetherbee and Kathryn Lynch have drawn attention to the link in Chartrian thought between 'ingenium' and the imagination, and thus the link between 'ingenium' and dreams: see W. Wetherbee *Platonism and Poetry in the Twelfth Century* (Princeton: Princeton University Press 1972) 94–104; and K. Lynch *The High Medieval Dream Vision* (Stanford: Stanford University Press 1988) 35–40, 99–106, 143–4.

29 Hugh of St Cher *Commentary on the Sentences*, as quoted by Odon Lottin *Psychologie et morale au XIIe et XIIIe siècles* 2nd ed, 6 vols in 8 pts (Gembloux, Belg: Ducolot 1957–60) 1: 101. Although Hugh makes 'ingenium' only a function of a faculty, for Roland de Cremona the 'ingenium' is itelf a power of the soul: see Lottin: *Psychologie et morale* 1: 103. Cf Albert Blaise *Dictionnaire Latin-français des auteurs chrétiens* rev Henri Chirat (Turnhout, Belg: Brepols 1954) *sv* 'ingenium' 2–4.

30 Gilbert de Tournai ('Isaac') *Epistola ...: De anima* (*Patrologia Latina* 194: 1879). Cf Jean de la Rochelle *Tractatus de divisione multiplici potentiarum animae* 2.23, 49 ed Pierre Michaud-Quantin (Paris: Vrin 1964) 96, 126; Albertus Magnus *Summa de creaturis*, where 'ingenium' discovers the middle term in a syllogism (*Opera Omnia* ed A. Borgnet, 38 vols [Paris 1890–9] 34: 517); Prevostin de Cremona's 'Per ingenium invenimus et

in ignoti noticiam venimus' (as quoted by Artur M. Landgraf *Dog-mengeschichte der Frühscolastik* 4 vols [Regensburg: Pustet 1952–6] pt 2, 2: 118); and the *Chirurgia Guilielmi de Saliceto* (1476; as quoted by Guy of Chauliac *Ars chirurgica* [Venetiis apud Juntas 1546]), where 'ingenio' denotes means for suturing a wound (329).

31 See Gordon Leff *William of Ockham: The Metamorphosis of Scholastic Discourse* (Manchester: Manchester University Press 1975) 351.

32 See Lottin's excerpts from Albertus' lectures on the *Nicomachean Ethics* (in *Psychologie et morale* 3: 275–6).

33 Aquinas *Summa theologica* 2–2.47.13. A relation between wit and 'prudentia/sapientia/scientia' is documented by R.E. Kaske '"Ex vi transicionis' and Its Passage in *Piers Plowman*' *Journal of English and Germanic Philology* 62 (1963) 46. In *The Abbey of the Holy Ghost*, 'witty' connotes 'be-fore-ware,' that is, forward-looking or prudent: see C. Horstmann ed *Yorkshire Writers: Richard Rolle of Hampole ... and His Followers* 2 vols (London 1895–6) 1: 327.

34 Aristotle *Ethica Nicomachea* 1144a

35 On 'inwit' as synderesis, see B.J. Harwood and R.F. Smith 'Inwit and the Castle of *Caro* in *Piers Plowman*' *Neuphilologische Mitteilungen* 71 (1970) 648–54.

36 For example, the Spirit of God from Gen. 1: 2 as perhaps the third person. On the 'demiurgos' see Tertullian *Adversus Valentinianos* cap 24 (*Patrologia Latina* 2: 578).

37 Frank *'Piers Plowman' and the Scheme of Salvation* 54

38 Cf John Lawlor's remark that '"Wit's" emphasis upon the Flesh only makes clearer the unalterable fact *Qui offendit in vno, in omnibus est reus*': *'Piers Plowman': An Essay in Criticism* (London: Edward Arnold 1962) 93. I am sceptical about the rest of Lawlor's interpretation, however, including his view that 'Intelligence, thoroughly applied, brings the argument to the same level as the Plowman's resolve to be less *bisi* about creature-comforts.'

39 On the meaning of 'wit' here for Patience (esp at 13.154) within the economy of grace, see E.C. Schweitzer '"Half a Laumpe Lyne in Latyne" and Patience's Riddle in *Piers Plowman*' *Journal of English and Germanic Philology* 73 (1974) 323–5.

40 See also B 10.70–6, 104–23, 185–6.

41 Aquinas *Summa theologica* 2–2.167.1 ed Dominican Fathers, 60 vols (London: Blackfriars 1964–6) 44: 203–5. Murtaugh understands Study as the 'intellectual activity' that the virtue 'studiositas' should govern, and refers to 'curiositas' as the opposed vice: see *'Piers Plowman' and*

the Image of God 65. This activity, mental application to a subject, is the usual explanation of Study: eg Frank, *'Piers Plowman' and the Scheme of Salvation* 54. However, when Study writes the Bible for Scripture (10.174) or ordains alchemy and the other dangerous sciences, the mental application that goes into study of the Bible or study of the science has not yet occurred.

42 Lawlor *'Piers Plowman': An Essay in Criticism* 96

43 For evidence of medieval recognition of the wisdom books as a type, see Beryl Smalley 'Some Thirteenth-Century Commentaries on the Sapiential Books' *Dominican Studies* 2 (1949) 318–55; 3 (1950) 41–77, 236–74; and 'Some Commentaries on the Sapiential Books of the late Twelfth and Early Fourteenth Centuries' *Archives d'histoire doctrinale et littéraire du moyen âge* 18 (1950) 105–28. On knowledge and exploitation of the wisdom literature in the fourteenth century – for example by the preacher Thomas Brinton – see also Janet Coleman *'Piers Plowman' and the 'Moderni'* (Rome: Edizioni di Storia e Letteratura 1981) 155–8. As distinct from parts of the Bible mentioned by name, Study's scriptural quotations also come from the wisdom books with relative frequency. Of Wit's seventeen scriptural quotations, for example, only one – Ps 110 – is from wisdom literature; of Study's thirteen, four are: Job 21:13, Ps 48:20, Ps 72:12, and Tob 4:9. (For authority in classifying certain psalms as wisdom psalms, I rely upon H.G. May and B.M. Metzger eds *The Oxford Annotated Bible, with the Apocrypha* [Oxford: Oxford University Press 1965].)

44 In M.C. Davlin's fine account of the relations of the poem to wisdom literature, she points out that in 'medieval times ... a liturgical reading from Proverbs, Wisdom, or Ecclesiasticus was introduced simply as "lectio libri Sapientiae," rather than by the title of the particular book': ('*Piers Plowman* and the Books of Wisdom' *Yearbook of Langland Studies* 2 (1988) 25. She cites Smalley's observation that Dame Study at 10.175 'sums up the learning proper to a clerk as knowledge of the Sapiential books and of the Psalter with its glosses' (24).

45 See W. Baumgartner 'The Wisdom Literature' in H.H. Rowley ed *The Old Testament and Modern Study* (Oxford: Oxford University Press 1951) 210–35.

46 In Jill Mann's excellent discussion of this passage, she points out that 'The image of eating is actually *contained in* the desire to know, since it is an *appetite* ...' Eating has a 'twofold' importance: it is metaphorically 'applied to the texts in the practice of *ruminatio*.' Secondly, 'the texts which are thus "digested" are themselves passages which use

the images of eating and drinking': 'Eating and Drinking in *Piers Plowman' Essays and Studies* ns 32 (1979) 40, 37; her emphasis.

47 Rashdall *Universities of Europe* 1: 174

48 On 'legere ad pennam,' see Istvan Hajnal *L'enseignement de l'écriture aux universités médiévales* 2nd ed, ed Lazlo Mezey (Budapest: Académie des sciences de Hongrie 1959) esp 119–27.

49 When Study says she taught 'Aristotle and opere mo to argue' (10.179), she does not necessarily refer to disputation or debate; she may mean simply lectures on the *Rhetoric*. See Rashdall *Universities of Europe* 3: 155.

50 On 'sacra pagina,' or 'lectio divina,' see Ceslaus Spicq *Esquisse d'une histoire de l'exégèse latine au moyen âge* (Paris: Vrin 1944) 44–5. In B, Theology 'is no Science forsoþe for to sotile Inne,' that is, systematic theology. On the fortunes of 'sacra pagina' as it competed with Scholastic methods in the thirteenth and fourteenth centuries, see Beryl Smalley *The Study of the Bible in the Middle Ages* 2nd ed (Oxford: Blackwell 1952) 73, 79, 281–9, and ch 3–5 passim. Robert Adams has recently suggested that the 'final inspiration' for Langland's 'biblicism' is 'traditional Benedictine spirituality with its emphasis on *lectio divina*': 'Langland's Theology' in J.A. Alford ed *A Companion to 'Piers Plowman'* (Berkeley, Los Angeles, London: University of California Press 1988) 106.

51 H.J. Chaytor translates from *L'hystore Job*: 'When you read the prophet (Jeremiah xxii.29), you will hear him, as you read, admonish the earth three times and say, etc.': *From Script to Print* (Cambridge: Heffer 1945) 16.

52 Hajnal *L'enseignement de l'écriture* 122

53 The 'locus classicus' is Augustine *De doctrina christiana* 2.31–9 ed Joseph Martin (Turnhout, Belg: Brepols 1962) 65–73. James Simpson has recently suggested that Study not only personifies the trivium but points to its limitations as simply a propaedeutic to the study of Scripture: 'The Role of *Scientia* in *Piers Plowman*' in G.C. Kratzmann and J. Simpson eds *Medieval English Religious and Ethical Literature* (Woodbridge, Eng: D.S. Brewer 1986) 54–65.

54 For a study of the manual arts in *Piers* in the light of Benedictine tradition, see Sally Joyce (Cross) 'The Image of God and the Manual Arts in *Piers Plowman*' (PHD diss, Miami University, Oxford, Ohio 1986). The manual arts do not necessarily fall outside the university. In *Mum and the Sothsegger* ed Mabel Day and Robert Steele, Early English Text Society os 199 (Oxford: Oxford University Press 1936),

almost identical pursuits come under geometry and 'þe vij sciences' at Oxford and Cambridge (346–8).

55 See David Knowles *The Religious Orders in England*, 3 vols (Cambridge: Cambridge University Press 1948–56) 1: 25, 2: 61–73.

56 See, for example, 10.415–19.

57 For 'studiare' as 'curare,' see DuCange *Glossarium mediae et infimae Latinitatis* ed Leopold Favre (Niort 1883–7) *sv* 'studere.'

58 Dorothy Owen *'Piers Plowman': A Comparison with Some Earlier and Contemporary French Allegories* (London: Hodder and Stoughton 1912) 105. On Langland's probable knowledge of Guillaume's poem, see Rosemary Woolf 'The Tearing of the Pardon' in Hussey ed *'Piers Plowman': Critical Approaches* 58–9. Roberta D. Cornelius reported that the right name of Leçon is 'Estude': see *The Figurative Castle* (Bryn Mawr, Pa: np 1930). As the pittancer of a Cistercian monastery, Leçon would appeal to Study's good heart. Further, Leçon can be 'Claryffyed by entendement' (Lydgate's translation) in the same way that Study fills the necessary condition for the comprehension personified by Clergy: see Guillaume de Deguileville *The Pilgrimage of the Life of Man* ed F.J. Furnivall, Early English Text Society es 77, 83, 92 (London 1899–1904) 22319–26.

59 Jean Leclercq *The Love of Learning and the Desire for God* tr Catharine Misrahi (1961; New York: Mentor Omega-NAL 1962) 78. Cf Mann 'Eating and Drinking' n 46 above.

60 Lubac *Exégèse médiévale* 1: 524–5, 549–58, 593

61 This seems to modify the line in B (10.226) at the risk of banality in order to distinguish Clergy from clerics. If they were identical, Will need never have left 'clerkes' to find Clergy.

62 The C text replaces 'lewed preestes' with an ironic 'Clergie' (13.128) after Recklessness has raged against bishops who ordain those who 'conne *sapienter* / Nother syng ne rede ne seye a masse of þe day' (C 13.124–5). Latin is suggested also when Sloth, having been 'prest and persoun' for more than thirty years, 'can nat construe Catoun ne clergialiche reden' (C 7.30, 34).

63 For 'clergie' as knowledge generally, see 20.228–31. Cf 15.381 (OFC) and one sense of 'clergie' at 15.209. Having cited a number of thirteenth-century texts, M.T. Clanchy observes that 'A *clericus* in common parlance was ... a person of some scholarly attainments, regardless of whether he was a churchman': *From Memory to Written Record: England 1066–1307* (London: Edward Arnold 1979) 179.

64 Thus, some 'clerkes' by vocation may nevertheless lack 'clergie' be-

cause they are unable to construe. See c 11.280–2, where 'clerkes of þe lawe,' who apparently have mastery of the letter, can be silenced by those who have been given the grace to explain the sentence – 'connyng and clergie to conclude suche alle.'

65 A source for this is Luke 12: 54–7.

66 Eg, Bede: 'Quantum etiam ad historiam pertinet, per hoc quod digito scripsit in terra, illum se fore monstravit qui quondam legem in lapide scripsit': cited by Thomas Aquinas *Catena aurea in quatuor Evangelia* 6 vols (Savona 1889) 6: 285.

67 Robertson and Huppé define 'clergie' at one point as 'spiritual learning' ('*Piers Plowman*' *and Scriptural Tradition* 124). In commenting on 12.139–41, they interpret 'clerkes' as allegorists (152). Yet they also write that 'clergy which is based on Christ's love is good' (152) – as if either 'allegoria' could arise from something else or 'clergie' be more general than 'allegoria.' Finally they seem to understand Clergy simply as 'clerical learning' (153, 157). 'Clergie' is one of the objects of the faculty Imaginative. On 'clergie' as an object of knowledge, 'the *result* of a mental activity,' see A.V.C. Schmidt 'Langland and Scholastic Philosophy' *Medium Aevum* 38 (1969) 153. For earlier views of 'clergie,' see B.J. Harwood '"Clergye" and the Action of the Third Vision in *Piers Plowman*' *Modern Philology* 70 (1973) 280n10, 283n24.

68 Lubac *Exégèse médiévale* 1: 489. Langland himself refers to the *Moralia* (10.298–9).

69 That the earlier event typifies the church may clarify some otherwise puzzling words in c: 'Crist cam and confermede [the New Law, that is] and holy kyrke made / And in soend a signe wroet ...' (14.39–40).

70 See Augustine *De doctrina christiana* 2 and 3. Beryl Smalley reviews Hugh of St Victor's attempt to press the new sciences, particularly history and geography, into the service of exegesis; likewise the twelfth-century masters of the sacred page (eg, Peter Comestor) tried to adapt the 'artes' to spiritual exposition: *Study of the Bible in the Middle Ages* 86–7, 216–17. Dame Study may be indicating the breadth of knowledge required by exegesis when she says that both Clergy and Scripture know 'lore and ... lettrure ... lawe and ... resoun' (c 11.100).

71 Augustine *On Christian Doctrine* 2.62 tr D.W. Robertson Jr (Indianapolis: Bobbs-Merrill 1958) 77

72 Lubac *Exégèse médiévale* 1: 515

73 This single line on 'dobest' is expanded, of course, with a long passage on covetous priests and lordly monks. The latter, says Clergy, will be disendowed and have 'a knok of a kyng' (10.332). 'Ac er þat

kyng come Caym shal awake, / Ac dowel shal dyngen hym adoun and destruye his myƷte' (10.334–5). This violent punishment executed by 'dowel' is so far from the understanding of 'dowel' with which Clergy began that Will (acting out, perhaps, the narrator's chagrin at his own satiric detour) makes fun of it: 'Thanne is dowel and dobet … dominus and knyƷthode?' (10.336). Scripture steps in at this point to take Will's question seriously. Clergy may have defined 'dowel,' 'dobet,' and 'dobest' 'just as Thought had done, that is, in terms of the Active, Contemplative, and "Mixed" Lives' (Dunning 'Piers Plowman': An Interpretation of the A Text 140). But before he gave himself over to 'some comments on the conduct of the religious of his times' (Dunning ibid 140), Clergy's greatest interest was clearly in a perception of the Trinity. The treatment of 'dobet' and 'dobest' is collapsed in c into two lines (c 11.161–2), and the comments on priests and monks are dropped or transferred.

74 Cf c 11.149–56a, esp 152–4.
75 See Augustine De doctrina christiana 2.10. So far as exegesis was once the means of contrition, it thus led to rectitude as well. Accordingly, 'clergie' is related to 'resoun' (11.415) or a means for coming to 're-soun' (c 15.26), since the most important moral sense of 'resoun' in Piers, as we have seen, is 'rectitude.'
76 Similarly, two occurrences that signify an approach to 'clergie' through Conscience are omitted from c: see 13.23, 24.
77 See Smalley Study of the Bible 281, 292–4, 308–28. While Aquinas allows that assigning multiple meanings to a text may be useful, eg, in homiletics, he denies that any single word in Scripture properly has a number of senses: cf Spicq Esquisse d'une histoire de l'exégèse latine au moyen âge 280. Paul de Vooght remarks the general disaffection with Scripture among fourteenth-century theologians, as if the full study of Scripture and tradition had already been accomplished: Les sources de la doctrine chrétienne d'après les théologiens du XIVe siècle et du début de XVe … (Bruges: Desclée, De Brouwer 1954) 256–8.
78 See also Johan Huizinga The Waning of the Middle Ages (1924) tr F. Hopman (Garden City NY: Doubleday nd) 213–14, 221, 284. Cf Godden: 'clergie is a kind of knowledge that has broken free from holiness of life and fails for that reason' (Making of 'Piers Plowman' 105).
79 See c 13.130–2.
80 Elizabeth Doxsee '"Trew Treuthe" and Canon Law: The Orthodoxy of Trajan's Salvation in Piers Plowman c-Text' Neuphilologische Mitteilungen 89 (1988) 297. Cf also Pearsall's note in his edition of the c text to

11.196. According to Joseph Wittig, Recklessness is 'arguing that [Solomon's and Aristotle's] knowledge availed them nothing – a point his informants have been desperately trying to get across to him': *'Piers Plowman* B, Passus IX–XII: Elements in the Design of the Inward Journey' *Traditio* 28 (1972) 230. Wittig misses Recklessness's claim that their good works availed them nothing either: see C 11.219–20, 223.

81 See Dietrich Bonhoeffer *The Cost of Discipleship* (1937) 2nd ed, tr R.H. Fuller (New York: Macmillan 1959) 35.

82 Cf Godden: 'On the surface ... the narrator's objections to Scripture's emphasis on salvation through living a good life seem to be gross examples of misapplied knowledge. Yet possibly beneath them lurks something serious and important, a genuine yearning for theology which places less reliance on doing well and knowing much, and more on God, grace and simplicity' (*Making of 'Piers Plowman'* 69).

83 However, for contrasting views of Will's reference to the penitents, see Marie Collins 'Will and the Penitents: *Piers Plowman* B X 420–35' *Leeds Studies in English* ns 16 (1985) 303–4, and D.G. Allen 'The Dismas *Distinctio* and the Form of *Piers Plowman* B.10–13' *Yearbook of Langland Studies* 3 (1989) 32, 45.

84 Pamela Gradon 'Langland and the Ideology of Dissent' *Proceedings of the British Academy* 66 (1980) 201. Rose Bernard Donna believes that Will's indulgence with Fortune and the Three Temptations leads 'naturally to discouragement and despair': *Despair and Hope: A Study in Langland and Augustine* (Washington DC: Catholic University of America Press 1948) 21. To the contrary, I believe he represents himself as indulgent because he is desperate.

85 The prevailing critical view, however, is that the inner dream is meant to be 'retrospective': see eg, Wittig *'Piers Plowman* B, Passus IX–XII' 245; and esp now L.M. Clopper 'The Life of the Dreamer, the Dreams of the Wanderer in *Piers Plowman' Studies in Philology* 86 (1989) 261–6.

86 Cf Godden, who believes that Recklessness is introduced in c 'primarily as a figure of irresponsible carelessness.' 'But as his speech develops Recklessness begins to be associated with the virtue of poverty and with taking no thought for the world ...' (*Making of 'Piers Plowman'* 192).

87 Cf esp Clopper 'Life of the Dreamer' 277–8.

88 H.A. Oberman *The Harvest of Medieval Theology: Gabriel Biel and Late Medieval Nominalism* (Cambridge, Mass: Harvard University Press 1963) 73. In Oberman's account, the fifteenth-century theologian Biel distinguishes 'acquired faith' in 'the objective factuality of God's re-

vealing acts in history' from 'infused faith,' sacramentally transform-
ing 'intellectual faith into living faith' (73–4).
89   Contrast Augustine *Epistolae* Classics 3.13 (*Patrologia Latina* 33: 714).
90   The speech at issue is 11.154–319 (Line 171 is direct speech of Trajan's
being quoted by Will: but see Michael Peverett '"Quod" and "Seide"
in *Piers Plowman*' *Neuphilologische Mitteilungen* 98 [1986] 126.) Because
the lines include statements such as 'Loue and lewtee is a leel science'
(11.167), Will could not be speaking them, certain readers have maintained, because this is exactly what he must learn. Thus, Wittig follows Skeat in calling the speaker 'Lewte' ('*Piers Plowman* B, Passus
IX–XII' 255n143). Cf Robert Adams, who calls the speaker 'anonymous': 'Piers's Pardon and Langland's Semi-Pelagianism' *Traditio* 39
(1983) 390. Frank ('*Piers Plowman*' *and the Scheme of Salvation* 60), followed by David C. Fowler ('*Piers the Plowman': Literary Relations of the*
A and B Texts [Seattle: University of Washington Press 1961] 219),
thinks Will is more likely the speaker than 'Leute,' but assigns the
speech to Trajan. This would involve Trajan's repeatedly speaking of
himself in the third person (eg, 11.157, 165), unlike, I believe, any
other speaker in the poem. I follow R.W. Chambers (*Man's Unconquer-*
able Mind: Studies of English Writers from Bede to A.E. Housman and W.P.
Ker [London and Toronto: Jonathan Cape 1939] 136), E. Talbot Donaldson ('*Piers Plowman: the C-Text and Its Poet* [New Haven: Yale University Press 1949] 173), and now Clopper ('Life of the Dreamer'
277–8) in assuming that Will is speaking. To begin with, the speech is
more about patient poverty than about 'leute.' Further, as Clopper
rightly observes, 'Langland makes it more obvious in the c-Text that
the speech is uttered by Rechelesnesse and that Rechelesnesse is the
Dreamer' (277). The best argument, of course, will lie in understanding the context in which the speech occurs and following the turns of
the thought itself.
91   See Robert Adams: 'Langland believed fervently in man's obligation
to do his very best (*facere quod in se est*) and in its guaranteed complement, divine acceptation' ('Piers's Pardon' 377). Cf Frank '*Piers Plow-*
man' and the Scheme of Salvation 65. Adams holds that 'No episode in
the poem marks Langland more clearly as a semi-Pelagian than this
one' – ie, the episode with Trajan (390). Adams' position is generally
shared by Coleman '*Piers Plowman' and the 'Moderni*' 85–7, 118–24, 135,
222; Pamela Gradon '*Trajanus Redivivus*: Another Look at Trajan in
Piers Plowman' in Douglas Gray and E.G. Stanley eds *Middle English*
Studies Presented to Norman Davis in Honour of His Seventieth Birthday

(Oxford: Clarendon 1983) 93–114; and Doxsee "'Trew Treuthe" and Canon Law' 299. See esp the carefully detailed article by Gordon Whatley 'The Uses of Hagiography: The Legend of Pope Gregory and the Emperor Trajan in the Middle Ages' *Viator* 15 (1984) 25–63.

92   Trajan's line in B – 'al þe clergie vnder crist ne myȝte me cracche fro helle' (11.143) – is replaced in C with 'al þe cristendoem vnder Crist ne myhte me crache fro thenne' (12.77), perhaps for the reason that Pope Gregory's belief in the possibility of mercy for Trajan was arguably predicated on the knowledge called 'clergie.' 'Clergie' is not altogether abandoned with 'cristendoem,' since one sense of that word is 'Christian wisdom' (eg, 19.330). Whatley believes that Langland lumps Trajan with righteous heathen who are invincibly ignorant of Christ, but saved by an implicit faith: 'The possessor of such a faith when he died would not have to go to hell, as Trajan did.' Hence, for Whatley it is 'inconsistent' for Langland to have put Trajan in hell ('Uses of Hagiography' 55, 59).

93   Cf Denise Baker 'Dialectic Form in *Pearl* and *Piers Plowman*' *Viator* 15 (1984) 270.

94   Whatley 'Uses of Hagiography' 42

95   But see Gordon Whatley '*Piers Plowman* B 12.277–94: Notes on Language, Text, and Theology' *Modern Philology* 82 (1984) 6.

96   On the second of these, however, see ibid 7–8.

97   However, contrast Whatley, who believes that Dunning erred in attributing baptism of the spirit to Trajan, since Trajan is said (12.282) to have died unbaptized (ibid 7). Yet Trajan's own references to Gregory's necessary help are consistent with the 'resuscitation motif' (as Whatley calls it elsewhere) of the legend.

98   On 'fides implicta' see Aquinas *Summa theologica* 2–2.2.7 ad 3.

99   T.P. Dunning 'Langland and the Salvation of the Heathen' *Medium Aevum* 12 (1943) 48. Cf Coleman: 'the Wisdom Commentaries of the Dominican Robert Holcot frequently point out that God would give *sufficient* knowledge of Himself by revelation or inspiration to *anyone* who sincerely sought Him through the use of natural reason' ('*Piers Plowman*' and the '*Moderni*' 118).

100   Whatley 'Uses of Hagiography' 41

101   Whatley '*Piers Plowman* B' 7

102   This tactical emphasis on Will's part would explain C's omitting from his long speech in passus 11 a passage (11.216–23) taking the contrary position, reserved for Imaginative.

103   See 11.276, C 13.98.

104 See esp C 12.153–69a.

105 For example, Chambers *Man's Unconquerable Mind* 138–42; Frank *'Piers Plowman' and the Scheme of Salvation* 63–7; Lawlor *'Piers Plowman': An Essay in Criticism* 116–18; Barbara Raw 'Piers and the Image of God in Man' in Hussey ed *'Piers Plowman': Critical Approaches* 172; and Anne Middleton 'Narration and the Invention of Experience: Episodic Form in *Piers Plowman*' in Larry D. Benson and Siegfried Wenzel eds *The Wisdom of Poetry: Essays in Early English Literature in Honor of Morton W. Bloomfield* (Kalamazoo: Medieval Institute Publications 1982) 111

106 Frank *'Piers Plowman' and the Scheme of Salvation* 62

107 Morton W. Bloomfield *'Piers Plowman' as a Fourteenth-Century Apocalypse* (New Brunswick: Rutgers University Press [1961]) 173–4. I discuss Bloomfield's suggestion, as well as explanations of Imaginative as memory, the 'sensus communis,' etc, in my 'Imaginative in *Piers Plowman' Medium Aevum* 44 (1975) 249–63. More recently, in a pair of related articles, E.N. Kaulbach has defined imaginative as 'sense reasoning in animals': 'The "Vis Imaginativa" and the Reasoning Powers of Ymaginatif in the B-Text of *Piers Plowman' Journal of English and Germanic Philology* 84 (1985) 23. See also his 'The "Vis Imaginativa Secundum Avicennam" and the Naturally Prophetic Powers of Ymaginatif in the B-Text of *Piers Plowman' Journal of English and Germanic Philology* 86 (1987) 496–514. In my opinion, much in Kaulbach's position rests on a misunderstanding of what 'reason in the imagination' could mean. The imaginative power is not in itself rational; rather, the reason can make use of the powers of the imagination. In fact, Kaulbach's view of the 'imaginativa' puts it very close to the 'vis cogitativa' as that latter power was traditionally conceived. See George P. Klubertanz *The Discursive Power: Sources and Doctrine of the 'Vis Cogitativa' According to St. Thomas Aquinas* (St Louis, Mo: Modern Schoolman [1952]) 212–14, 231–7, 242, 265–94. By insisting upon the 'imaginativa' as animal rather than human (and therefore as uninformed by reason), Kaulbach appears to be describing the 'vis aestimativa,' as the 'cogitativa' was called in animals. See also A.J. Minnis 'Langland's Ymaginatif and Late-Medieval Theories of Imagination' *Comparative Criticism: A Yearbook* 3 (1981) esp 81–6. Minnis appears to confuse the imagination's responsibility for reproducing sensory images (see the opening of passus 13 as it harks back to the vision of Middle Earth) with reason's use of imagination, or 'phantasia,' to manipulate images (eg, to move from the known to the unknown).

108 See Aristotle *De anima* 428a.6. Cf M.W. Bundy *The Theory of Imagination in Classical and Medieval Thought* University of Illinois Studies in Language and Literature 12.2–3 (Urbana 1927) 182–3; and Bloomfield *'Piers Plowman' as a Fourteenth-Century Apocalypse* 172. This connection with dreams may explain why Imaginative is not 'Imagination' instead, for the adjective was used in ME in relation to the second of the three Augustinian classes of visions, the one in which images of things are beheld with the spiritual eye (as distinct from the bodily vision, in which the bodily eye beholds corporeal things themselves, and the intellectual vision, which dispenses with imagery altogether). See Edward Wilson 'The "Gostly Drem" in *Pearl*' *Neuphilologische Mitteilungen* 69 (1968) 90–101. However, Robert Holcot, in *Super sapientiam Salomonis*, used 'imaginatio' as well as such cognates as 'imaginativi' in connection with dreams: see R.A. Pratt 'Three Old French Sources of "The Nonnes Preestes Tale" (Part II)' *Speculum* 47 (1972) 666. The two terms were put to other uses: eg Jean de la Rochelle related 'imaginativa' to the compounding and dividing function of the imagination, 'imaginatio' to the retentive function: *Tractatus de divisione multiplici potentiarum animae* 2.7–8 ed Michaud-Quantin 75–6.

109 Cf Frank 'The Number of Visions in *Piers Plowman*' 311.

110 For other views, however, of the chronological relation of the dream-within-a-dream to Will's life, see Wittig '*Piers Plowman* B, Passus IX–XII' 245; and Clopper 'Life of the Dreamer' 261.

111 Defined by Iohannes Blund (d 1248) in a typical and technical way: 'similitudines rerum singularium, per ymaginationem rerum absentium potest fiere apprehensio' (*Tractatus de anima* 18 ed Callus and Hunt 67). Cf Isidore of Seville *De spiritu et anima* 11 *Patrologia Latina* 40: 787. Cf also H.S.V. Jones's valuable hint that Imaginative teaches the use of natural 'phenomena as similitudes of spiritual truth …': 'Imaginatif in *Piers Plowman*' *Journal of English and Germanic Philology* 13 (1914) 583, 584.

112 See Plato *De memoria et reminiscentia* 450b.12–451a.12; (on Plato) Bundy *Theory of Imagination* 28–59.

113 In the Boethian tradition, however, imagination would help in the formation of the intelligible only, not of the intellectible: see M.-D. Chenu 'Imaginatio: Note de lexicographie philosophique médiévale' in *Miscellanea Giovanni Mercati* Studi e Testi 122 (Vatican City: Biblioteca Apostolica Vaticana 1946) 597–8.

114 Thomas Aquinas *Summa theologica* 1.1.10; ibid art 9 (ed Dominican Fa-

thers, 60 vols [London: Blackfriars 1964–6] 1: 37, 33, 35). Cf Richard of
St Victor *Benjamin Minor* 15 *Patrologia Latina* 194: 10–11.

115 R.E. Kaske makes this point, in counting 15 in slightly over 300 lines:
'The Use of Simple Figures of Speech in *Piers Plowman* B: A Study in
the Figurative Expression of Ideas and Opinions' *Studies in Philology*
48 (1951) 588.

116 By 'kynde wit,' a power of the sensitive soul, Langland means the apprehension of the beneficial. (Imaginative evidently sees this power
co-operating with another sensitive power, the 'imaginativa.') Known
in animals as the 'aestimativa' and in humans as the 'cogitativa,' this
power can supply material for use by the rational soul, and in turn it
can be guided by it. Thus, it can be guided by revealed knowledge.
For a fuller discussion of its twenty-five or so appearances in B, see
B.J. Harwood 'Langland's *Kynde Wit' Journal of English and Germanic
Philology* 75 (1976) 330–6. See also Gerald Morgan 'The Meaning of
Kind Wit, Conscience, and Reason in the First Vision of *Piers Plowman'
Modern Philology* 85 (1987) 351–8. Having pointed out that 'kynde wit'
is the teacher of Conscience, Morgan appears to infer that 'kynde wit'
is a habit of the intellect (352–3). But in scholastic psychology, the
'cogitativa,' by discovering 'sensible good or evil under the guidance
of reason,' 'presents to reason the material for the particular premise
of the practical syllogism' (Klubertanz *Discursive Power* 288). The act
of conscience would be an instance of such a practical syllogism.
Hugh White believes that the meaning of 'kynde wit' changes as the
poem progresses: *Nature and Salvation in 'Piers Plowman'* (Cambridge:
D.S. Brewer 1988) 6. On appearances of 'kynde wit' early in Piers,
White makes the same inference as Morgan (11–12). White acknowledges, however, that 'kynde wit' is 'deeply implicated in the unsatis-
factoriness that Piers perceives [in the pardon scene] in the life he has
been leading' (24); and in passus 12 the poet comes to see 'kynde wit'
'as natural wisdom ... unillumined by divine revelation' (29).

117 I cannot account for Aristotle's and Solomon's inclusion among 'thise
clerkes' *and also* among those encumbered by 'kynde wit' (12.41, 43).
The difficulty is removed in c by the omission of B 12.40–50a.

118 Because they are Christian clerics for having recognized Christ in
prophecies of him, they see him in nature as well: 'Clerkes knewe þe
comet and comen with here presentes' (c 14.97).

119 I have no idea what Imaginative means by 'dobest.' Perhaps, like 'an-
agogia,' it is beyond his competence.

120 See 10.119. Dame Study has been scorning the 'motyues' advanced for

discussion by vain and facetious 'maistres,' one of the questions being 'why wolde oure Saueour suffre swich a worm in his blisse / That biwiled þe womman and þe wye after?' (10.108–9). It is these intellectually proud men whom Study may apostrophize when she says, 'Ymaginatif herafterward shal answere to youre purpos.' (Cf the Nun's Priest's apostrophe to lords who allow 'many a fals flatour / ... in youre courtes, and many a losengeour.') The suggestion that the 'purpos' concerns something broader, such as the nature of 'dowel,' involves an implausible vagueness of reference and the difficulty that other characters before Imaginative deal with it at least as fully as he does.

121 See esp C 14.30–6.

122 See Ernst Curtius *European Literature and the Latin Middle Ages* (1948) tr Willard Trask (New York and Evanston: Harper 1963) 12. Cf Morton W. Bloomfield 'Symbolism in Medieval Literature' *Modern Philology* 56 (1958) 78.

123 Cf Middleton: 'Ymaginatif presents an authorized version of what Will as visionary and maker aspires to do, to integrate what books and experience can show' ('Narration and the Invention of Experience' 112).

124 See Hugh of St Victor *De unione corporis et spiritus* (*Patrologia Latina* 177: 269).

125 Walter Hilton 'Of Angels' Song' in Horstmann ed *Yorkshire Writers* 1: 178. My emphasis.

126 Etienne Gilson *The Philosophy of St. Bonaventure* (1924) tr Illtyd Trethowan and F.J. Sheed (New York: Sheed and Ward 1938) 376.

CHAPTER FOUR

1 On Conscience, see Günter Spitzbart 'Das Gewissen in der mittelenglischen Literatur, mit besonderer Berucksichtigung von *Piers Plowman*' (PHD diss, University of Cologne 1962); Priscilla Jenkins 'Conscience: The Frustration of Allegory' in S.S. Hussey ed *'Piers Plowman': Critical Approaches* (London: Methuen 1969) 125–42; and Mary Carruthers (Schroeder) 'The Character of Conscience in *Piers Plowman*' *Studies in Philology* 67 (1970) 13–30. Spitzbart fails to relate the ME senses of 'conscience' he derives to actual occurrences of the word in the poem. While Carruthers rightly stresses the complexity of Conscience, she is unpersuasive in arguing (1) that Conscience is related to the scholastic notion of the speculative intellect, (2) that

Conscience lacks a full knowledge of Christian law at the outset (see, eg, 3.230–45), and (3) that Conscience picks up a mystical kind of knowledge behind the scenes with Patience only to lose it shortly after the opening of passus 19.

2 Cf Willi Erzgräber *William Langlands 'Piers Plowman': Eine Interpretation des c-Textes* (Heidelberg: Carl Winter 1957) 61; and Odon Lottin's description of the third of the three senses of 'conscience' according to Jean de la Rochelle: 'la conscience est l'opinion, *opinio*, que l'on se forme de ce qu'il faut faire ou ne pas faire, opinion qui peut évidemment être erronée; en ce sens, la conscience est un habitus acquis': *Psychologie et morale au xiie et xiiie siècles* 2nd ed, 6 vols in 8 pts (Gembloux, Belg: Ducolot 1957–60) 2: 171. For Bernard, this is the 'conscientia antecedens,' the conscience of moral obligation: see Philippe Delhaye *Le problème de la conscience morale chez S. Bernard, étudié dans ses oeuvres et dans ses sources* Analecta Mediaevalia Namurcensia 9 (Louvain: Nauwelaerts 1957) 40.

3 Cf Janet Coleman on Ockham's conception of the relation between reason and conscience: *Medieval Readers and Writers, 1350–1400* (New York: Columbia University Press 1981) 246. T.P. Dunning (*'Piers Plowman': An Interpretation of the A Text* 2nd ed, ed T.P. Dolan [Oxford: Clarendon 1980] 86), Greta Hort (*'Piers Plowman' and Contemporary Religious Thought* [London: Society for the Propagation of Christian Knowledge (1938)] 84), and Gerald Morgan ('The Meaning of Kind Wit, Conscience, and Reason in the First Vision of *Piers Plowman' Modern Philology* 85 [1987] 354–5, 358) describe Conscience simply from the Dominican point of view, viz, as an act of the practical reason. This seems untenable, however. Eg, at c 15.151–2, Conscience continues to act even though Reason has gone off.

4 See c 4.30, 195, b 3.283, c 5.113, and a secondary sense of the term at b 4.4, 6, 11, and c 4.13, 186. Thus subordinated, Conscience is properly linked with 'counseil' (20.147), if that is taken in the sense, for instance, of Bernard's 'liberum consilium': see Bernard of Clairvaux *Concerning Grace and Free Will* tr W.W. Williams (London: Society for the Propagation of Christian Knowledge 1920) 16, 52–5; and Etienne Gilson *The Mystical Theology of Saint Bernard* (1934) tr A.H.C. Downes (London: Sheed and Ward 1940) 47–51.

5 See 3.299, 4.24, 193 (ofc), c 5.104, and a secondary meaning at c 5.181.

6 See the primary sense of 'conscience' at c 4.186, c 5.89, c 15.53, and c 17.149. See also a secondary sense at b 4.182, c 4.195, and c 5.83.

7 See C 5.6, B 5.539, C 15.26. At B 20.242, 268, Conscience attempts to impose rectitude.

8 See 2.139.

9 See 2.191, 192, 5.328, and a secondary sense of the word at 4.32, 41 (OFC), 43, 182, C 4.33, 195.

10 See 19.412. Conscience is associated with the cardinal virtue justice at 19.398, 401, 403, 424 and with the cardinal virtues generally at 19.452 and 20.21, 303. See also secondary senses of the word at 19.407 and 20.72, 122.

11 See C 8.13–14.

12 See 11.66 (OFC). A secondary sense of 'conscience' at 3.120 is 'knowledge of the law.' Among the circumstances from which the moral conscience must prescind are considerations of temporal welfare: eg, at 19.360, 364 (and in a secondary sense at 20.268) Conscience can be taught by Kynde Wit.

13 See 3.110, 114, 116.

14 See C Prol 142.

15 See 20.74. 80, 106.

16 See 3.178 and a secondary sense at 19.212.

17 At 19.214, Conscience acts without having yet received grace.

18 Cf Jean Leclercq on the 'Liber Conscientiae,' in his 'Aspects spirituels de la symbolique du livre au XIIe siècle ' in L'homme devant Dieu: Melanges ... Henri de Lubac (Paris: Aubier 1963–4) 64–9; and A.V.C. Schmidt 'Langland's "Book of Conscience" and Alanus de Insulis' Notes and Queries ns 29 (1982) 482–4.

19 See Euryale Fabre 'De l'origine et de l'institution du notariat, précis historique' Annales scientifiques, littéraires et industrielles de l'Auvergne 22 (1849) 23, 54. B.B. Gilbert takes up the place of notaries in Langland's satire, in '"Civil" and the Notaries in Piers Plowman' Medium Aevum 50 (1981) 58–61.

20 Augustine Confessionum libri XIII 10.2 ed Lucas Verheijen, Corpus Christianorum, Series Latina 23 (Turnhoult, Belg: Brepols 1981) 155

21 A. Chollet notes the certainty of the psychological conscience: 'Conscience' J.M.A. Vacant et al eds Dictionnaire de théologie Catholique 15 vols (Paris: Letouzey et Ané 1899–1950) 3: 1168. See also 3: 1157–8. Conscience is evidently alone among the mental powers in knowing persons – that is, present and existing things. See eg, 13.131, 272–3, 19.9, 12.

22 A 'clene conscience' is, of course, what Langland conventionally calls the knowledge of a rationally governed choice: see 7.22. Cf 4.80. This

is probably the sense of 'conscience' also at C 4.195, B 15.242 (OFC), and, secondarily, at B 5.562, A 10.88 (OFB and C), and B 19.348.

23 Cf Delhaye *Le problème de la conscience* 21; Chollet 'Conscience' 3: 1159–60. Cf also Judith H. Anderson *The Growth of a Personal Voice: 'Piers Plowman' and 'The Faerie Queene'* (New Haven: Yale University Press 1976) 91.

24 See C Prol 95, 138, C 2.245, B 3.174.

25 This corresponds to New Testament 'conscientia' (συνείδησις), which 'can be said (a) to be a pain; (b) to inflict pain … and (c) to feel pain': C.A. Pierce *Conscience in the New Testament* Studies in Biblical Theology 15 (London: Student Christian Movement Press 1955) 46, also 45–8, 111. The poet drew upon well-established opinion in making conscience an emotion – 'synderesis' in the Franciscan tradition, as Bonaventure stamped that term with the meaning of 'guilt' (see Lottin *Psychologie et morale* 2: 206–7). In general, from the time of Jerome's commentary on Ezechiel (1.1 *Patrologia Latina* 25: 22, as quoted by Lottin *Psychologie et morale* 2: 103), the 'spark of conscience' was understood in part as a 'habitus' of the will that approves the good by impelling one towards it and reproves the evil. Bernard conceived this meaning of remorse as dominant in the psychological conscience: see Delhaye *Le problème de la conscience* 42–3; cf 23.

26 More exactly, it fulfils a necessary condition for it. At 19.381, 383, and 393, Conscience recognizes contrition as a precondition for sanctifying grace. Conscience's expressing *himself* as contrition may be premature within the development of the poem; this speech is omitted from C.

27 See 13.179 (OFC), 198, 205 (OFC), 215, C 15.182, 183, and a secondary sense of 'conscience' at B 13.188 (OFC) and 218.

28 See 13.211–14. Cf the occurrences of 'conscience' where it signifies a relinquishing of various forms of the goods of earth: C 3.238, 241, 243, 254, 255. Cf also other instances of 'conscience' relating to contrition, rigorism, penance, and reck-less-ness: 7.139 (OFC), C 9.239, B 20.214, 216. 329.

29 Henry Charles Lea *A History of Auricular Confession and Indulgences in the Latin Church* 3 vols (Philadelphia 1896) 2: 11. Cf P. Bernard 'Contrition (aspect dogmatique)' in Vacant et al eds *Dictionnaire de théologie Catholique* 3: 1673–4. With conscience as attrition, cf the 'right drede' which 'sal prikke' the 'conscience' of 'laude men' in Richard Rolle 'The Pricke of Conscience (Stimulus Conscientiae)' ed Richard Morris, in *The Philological Society's Early English Volume, 1862–64* (London and Berlin 1865) ll 3342–4; 'of þat drede may a lofe bygyn'

(l 345) – ie, contrition. For 'attricioun' as fear, see Chaucer *Troilus and Criseyde* 1.557 (Larry D. Benson et al eds *The Riverside Chaucer* 3rd ed [Boston: Houghton Mifflin 1987] 481. While Scotus taught that attrition might lead to confession, in which case justification would come through the sacrament ('ex pacto divino' rather than 'ex merito'), *Piers* seems to express the received view, held from Peter Lombard to Biel, that justification through the sacrament prerequires an interior disposition to love God for his own sake. Cf H.A. Oberman *The Harvest of Medieval Theology: Gabriel Biel and Late Medieval Nominalism* (Cambridge, Mass: Harvard University Press 1963) 147–8, 152–5.

30 J.A. Alford suggest that Haukyn's 'solicitude is ... evidence of disbelief, of a lack of faith': 'The Role of the Quotations in *Piers Plowman*' *Speculum* 52 (1977) 91.

31 See 14.281–4 (OFC).

32 See esp 19.219–20. See also 19.341 and 20.72. As the capacity for bearing guilt, with this reason for resisting sin, Conscience is the central character in passus 20.

33 See 19.355–9.

34 See the parallel text in B 3.42. See also B 20.228–9 and (when Pride threatens 'Confessioun and Contricioun') B 19.344–8.

35 Cf the ancient tradition in which conscience is taken to be a kind of god dwelling in the soul: eg, 'nihil homini dedit Deus ipse divinius' (Lactantius *De vero cultu* 6.24 *Patrologia Latina* 6: 725).

36 Morton W. Bloomfield held that in the *Vita* 'Conscience's role has been considerably widened and in terms of monastic philosophy': '*Piers Plowman*' as a Fourteenth-Century Apocalypse (New Brunswick: Rutgers University Press [1961]) 168. But Bloomfield seems to have been mistaken in thinking that the notion of conscience as 'a moral guide and judge of human actions' came only with the scholastics. See, eg, Ambrosius *Sermo* LII (*Patrologia Latina* 17: 710); Cassianus *Collatio undecima* 11 (Alardi Gazaei Commentarius *Patrologia Latina* 49: 857); and Gregory *Moralia* 24.16 (*Patrologia Latina* 76: 295). Even for Bernard, the mystic's awareness of the sweetness of God's presence in the soul may arise only as an extrapolation from the moral conscience: see Delhaye *Le problème de la conscience* 17; cf René Carpentier 'Conscience' in Marcel Viller, F. Cavallera, J. de Guibert eds *Dictionnaire de spiritualité ascétique et mystique, doctrine et histoire* 6 vols (Paris: Beauchesne 1937–67) 2: 1549. (See Carpentier's whole section 'Existe-t-il une antinomie entre la conscience morale et la conscience spirituelle?' [2: 1552–5].) Bloomfield's claim that monasticism gives 'the

final and richest part' (169) to the concept of Conscience rests on a suggested similarity between the role of Conscience in *Dobest* and in the Bernardine *Tractatus de interiori domo seu de conscientia aedificanda* and *The Abbey of the Holy Ghost*. This similarity is hard to see. To the authors of the treatises we can apply what Delhaye said of Bernard: 'la conscience n'est autre chose que l'âme elle-meme' (11). In *Piers*, to the contrary, Conscience is never more or less the entire soul than Reason, Imaginative, or Wit is – one possible exception occurring at 20.151.

37 See Delhaye *Le problème de la conscience* 24.

38 The change is perhaps briefly anticipated at the very moment of Piers's conversion. As against the moral conscience, whom Piers believed to be leading him to Truth (see ch 6), Piers invokes, after tearing his pardon, a conscience associated with 'Abstinence' (7.138–9).

39 'Resoun stoed and styhlede, as for styward of halle' (c 15.40). Shortly thereafter, in a change that spoils the rhythm in c, Reason is introduced to give orders to Conscience (15.52–3; cf B 13.46).

40 The turn of the action here has been variously interpreted, perhaps most fully and cogently by E. Talbot Donaldson, who believed that near the end of *Dowel* the c reviser changed his conception of 'dowel' from the active life (as represented by Haukyn) to patient poverty ('Piers Plowman': The c-Text and Its Poet [New Haven: Yale University Press 1949] 177). However, several difficulties remain. Donaldson believed that, in the poem, patience is made the ground of charity. But in *Piers* as in orthodoxy, the reverse seems true. E. Vansteenberghe, referring to Aquinas (*Summa theologica* 2–2.136.3), writes that a person must love God above all things before patience is possible ('Patience' Vacant et al eds *Dictionnaire de théologie Catholique* 11: 2249). Further, it is doubtful that a distinction between mere salvation and perfection, of which Patience would be the first stage (Donaldson 'Piers Plowman' 163–8), is essential to the *Vita*. For other views of the nature of the turn in the action, see R.W. Frank 'Piers Plowman' and the Scheme of Salvation: An Interpretation of 'Dowel, Dobet, and Dobest' (New Haven: Yale University Press 1957) 68, 70–1, 77; Stella Maguire 'The Significance of Haukyn, Activa Vita, in Piers Plowman' Review of English Studies os 25 (1949) 99–100; John Lawlor 'Piers Plowman': An Essay in Criticism (London: Edward Arnold 1962) 120–2; D.W. Robertson and B.F. Huppé 'Piers Plowman' and Scriptural Tradition (Princeton: Princeton University Press 1951) 158; Fowler 'Piers the Plowman':

Literary Relations of the A and B Texts (Seattle: University of Washington Press 1961) 82–3; Donald R. Howard *The Three Temptations: Medieval Man in Search of the World* (Princeton: Princeton University Press 1966) 186–9; and Hugh White *Nature and Salvation in 'Piers Plowman'* (Cambridge: D.S. Brewer 1988) 112.

41   Cf B.F. Huppé 'The Authorship of the A and B Texts of *Piers Plowman*' *Speculum* 22 (1947) 619; and Malcolm Godden *The Making of 'Piers Plowman'* (New York and London: Longman 1990) 114.

42   Augustine *Patience* tr Luanne Meagher in *Treatises on Various Subjects* The Fathers of the Church, a New Translation 16 (Washington: Catholic University of America Press 1952) 237.

43   See Vansteenberghe 'Patience' 11: 2250. In Guillaume de DeGuileville's *The Pilgrimage of the Life of Man* (ed F.J. Furnivall [London: Early English Text Society 1897–1904] 44), 'patient poverty' has forsaken all temporal possessions 'ffor goodes that ben celestyall' (22704).

44   'Supporter avec patience les peines et les épreuves d'ici-bas, c'est donc faire acte de soumission à la volonté de Dieu et de confiance en sa bonté comme en sa justice': Vansteenberghe 'Patience' 11: 2249. For patience as a virtue elsewhere in the poem, see 13.164–71, c 21.248–9, and B 19.295.

45   Vansteenberghe 'Patience' 11: 2250. Such a critique of 'pouerte' is made explicit by Anima a little later (15.205–8).

46   *Patience* 45 ed J.J. Anderson (Manchester: Manchester University Press 1969). Elizabeth D. Kirk's discussion of patience in the two poems takes a much different direction: see '"Who Suffreth More Than God?"': Narrative Redefinition of Patience in *Patience* and *Piers Plowman*' in G.J. Schiffhorst ed *The Triumph of Patience: Medieval and Renaissance Studies* (Orlando: University Presses of Florida 1978) 88–104.

47   Cf Malcolm Godden 'Plowmen and Hermits in Langland's *Piers Plowman*' *Review of English Studies* ns 35 (1984) 147.

48   See the omission from c of 14.142–57, 168–73. See also c 16.19–21.

49   See the omission from c of 14.83–97.

50   See, eg, 14.157–65.

51   William Lynch *Christ and Apollo: The Dimensions of the Literary Imagination* (New York: Sheed and Ward 1960) 149

52   See A.C. Spearing 'The Development of a Theme in *Piers Plowman*' *Review of English Studies* ns 11 (1960) 241–53.

53   Anderson *Growth of a Personal Voice* 94.

54   Cf 17.100, 19.385. Elsewhere the poet explicitly calls the redemptive

power of the Passion 'pacience': see 18.168, 172, 415. Patience, the
'riche clopyng' of Peace is to be identified with Piers's bleeding flesh
– paradoxically, the armour of Christ.

55 For recent instances see Steven Justice 'The Genres of *Piers Plowman*'
Viator 19 (1988) 294; John Bowers *The Crisis of Will in 'Piers Plowman'*
(Washington: Catholic University of America Press 1986) 204–5; Godden 'Plowmen and Hermits' 161–2; and Marta Powell Harley 'The
Derivation of *Hawkin* and Its Application in *Piers Plowman*' *Names* 29
(1981) 98. Harley's brief article, which suggests that Haukyn stands
to Piers as David does to Christ, is full of interest.

56 *Middle English Dictionary sv* 'minstral' 2. For this sense, the MED cites
'menestrales' at C 5.60 in the Vespasian ms of *Piers*. While the MED
records no other instance later than the thirteenth-century, Frederic
Godefroy gives fourteenth-century uses of 'menestrel' as 'artisan, ou-
vrier, serviteur': *Dictionnaire de l'ancienne langue française et de tous ses
dialectes du IXe au XVe siècle* 10 vols (Paris 1880–1902) *sv*.

57 Maguire 'The Significance of Haukyn' 100–3. Contrast R.W. Chambers' comment: '*Allegorically*, Hawkyn stands for the whole body of
sinning, penitent laity' (*Man's Unconquerable Mind: Studies of English
Writers from Bede to A.E. Housman and W.P. Ker* [London and Toronto:
Jonathan Cape 1939] 152). Cf Frank '*Piers Plowman' and the Scheme of
Salvation* 76; and G.H. Gerould 'The Structural Integrity of *Piers Plowman* B' *Studies in Philology* 45 (1948) 68.

58 Cf Godden: 'In representing the active life by the figure of the
stained and sinful Haukyn, Langland is at last giving full expression
to that repudiation of the ideal of labor so dramatically but crypti-
cally signalled by Piers' rejection of plowing at the end of the Visio'
(*The Making of 'Piers Plowman'* 112). Middleton calls Haukyn 'a sad
afterimage of a possibility from which sustained conviction has been
drained': 'Narration and the Invention of Experience: Episodic Form
in *Piers Plowman*' in Larry D. Benson and Siegfried Wenzel eds *The
Wisdom of Poetry: Essays in Early English Literature in Honor of Morton
W. Bloomfield* (Kalamazoo: Medieval Institute Publications 1982) 109.

59 With this 'memento mori,' cf esp c 8.349.

60 In C, when Patience describes the three parts of the sacrament of
penance (16.25–33), he does not mention Conscience. By contrast, in
B, it is Conscience who offers to teach Haukyn how to be contrite
(14.16–17a).

61 Baptism, as symbolized by his coat, now soiled. For sins other than
the original one, penance is necessary. On Haukyn's coat, see esp

Apoc 22.14; R.E. Kaske "'*Ex vi transicionis*" and Its Passage in *Piers Plowman' Journal of English and Germanic Philology* 62 (1963) 46; Bloomfield review of Robertson and Huppé '*Piers Plowman' Speculum* 27 (1952) 248; and Bloomfield '*Piers Plowman' as a Fourteenth-Century Apolcalypse* 108, 209. Skeat suggested that 'Haukyn's one garment symbolises the carnal nature of man ...': Walter W. Skeat ed *The Vision of William Concerning Piers the Plowman, in Three Parallel Texts* 2 vols (Oxford: Oxford University Press 1886) 2: 204; yet this nature is surely reciprocal with his baptism, his 'beste cote,' 'a coat of cristendom' (13.313, 273). Haukyn's coat also anticipates the 'cote Armure,' Piers's 'haubergeon, *humana natura*,' which is the suffering flesh of Christ: 'Culpat caro, purgat caro, regnat deus dei caro' (18.407b).

62 See Lea *History of Auricular Confession* 2: 6.

63 T.P. Dunning, in fact, speaks of this point as 'the climax of the poem': 'Action and Contemplation in *Piers Plowman'* in Hussey ed '*Piers Plowman': Critical Approaches* 221.

64 See, eg, R.E. Kaske 'Holy Church's Speech and the Structure of *Piers Plowman'* in Beryl Rowland ed *Chaucer and Middle English Studies in Honour of Rossell Hope Robbins* (London: Allen and Unwin 1974) 325.

65 The way that the first vision of *Dobet* may partly represent something fundamental to – in a sense, presupposed by – *Dowel* is expressed concretely enough in C's transition from *Dowel* to *Dobet*: 'Thenne hadde Actyf a ledare þat hihte *Liberum Arbitrium*' (16.157). Cf B 16.2.

66 For the relevant texts and fuller discussion, see B.J. Harwood '*Liberum-Arbitrium* in the C-Text of *Piers Plowman' Philological Quarterly* 52 (1973) 680–95.

67 See Lottin *Psychologie et morale* on Peter of Capua (1: 55–6), Godfrey of Poitiers (1: 62), an anonymous Parisian master of the thirteenth century (1: 83), and Albertus Magnus (1: 121–2).

68 See ibid 1: 207–11, and the reference (1: 211) to *In* II *Sent*, 24.1.2.

69 See ibid 1: 47–50, 60, 92, 98, 154, 203–4. See also Alexander of Hales *Summa theologica* Inq 4, Tract 1, Sect 4, Q 3, Tit 3, Memb 4, Cap 4, A 2, ed Collegium S. Bonaventurae, 3 vols (Quaracchi 1928) 2: 489. Although this *Summa* is traditionally attributed to Alexander, much of it was evidently written by his followers.

70 See Lottin *Psychologie et morale* 1: 160. However, contrast the comments by A.V.C. Schmidt 'Langland and Scholastic Philosophy' *Medium Aevum* 38 (1969) 142–3.

71 See George Sanderlin 'The Character "Liberum Arbitrium" in the C-Text of *Piers Plowman' Modern Language Notes* 56 (1941) 450. This posi-

tion has been challenged by Schmidt 'Langland and Scholastic Philosophy' 135–7.

72 Donaldson *'Piers Plowman': The c-Text and Its Poet* 193. The identification of 'liberum-arbitrium' with the will likewise weakens Erzgräber's treatment of will in the poem: *Eine Interpretation des c-Textes* 190–209.

73 See Bernard of Clairvaux *De gratia et libero arbitrio* 2 in *Opera* ed J. Leclercq, C.H. Talbot, and H.M. Rochais, 8 vols to date (Rome: Editiones Cistercienses 1957–) 3: 67.

74 The relation of 'animus' to volition is clearly suggested earlier in the same pseudo-Augustinian tractate from which (as Erzgräber has shown, *Eine Interpretation des c-Textes* 170) Langland drew this catalogue of faculties for B. 'Animus' is called the 'dominator' and 'rector' of the body: 'moverat se apud se'; 'modo vult, modo non vult': Isidore of Seville *De spiritu et anima* 1.2 *Patrologia Latina* 11: 781. Cf Otto Prinz ed *Mittellateinisches Wörterbuch bis zum Ausgehenden 13. Jahrhundert* (Munich: Beck 1967–) *sv* 'Animus' II, c.

75 See Harwood 'Liberum-Arbitrium in the c-Text' 684n14.

76 See Lottin *Psychologie et morale* 1: 141–5.

77 Frank, for one, seems to interpret Sanderlin in this way: *'Piers Plowman' and the Scheme of Salvation* 84.

78 See John of Damascus *The Orthodox Faith* 2.22 in his *Writings* tr F.H. Chase Jr, The Fathers of the Church, a New Translation 37 (New York: Fathers of the Church Inc 1958) 249.

79 Hugh of St Cher 'Commentary on the *Sentences*' printed by Lottin *Psychologie et morale* 1: 100. In an earlier printing, on which Sanderlin had relied ('La théorie du libre arbitre pendant le premier tiers de xIIIe siècle' *Revue Thomiste* 32 [1927] 378), Lottin quoted Hugh as using the nominative case in translating John Damascene: 'Liberum arbitrium appetit' etc. But 'liberum-arbitrium' then becomes the subject of a series of different acts, while actually the subject in John Damascene is a human being.

80 Bernard of Clairvaux seems to typify medieval theologians in distinguishing the sense in which 'liberum-arbitrium' is free in fallen humanity from the senses in which it is not. 'Liberum-arbitrium' is always free insofar as the soul has the inalienable power both to judge its choice and to consent to its choice. Nevertheless, in fallen humanity 'liberum-arbitrium' is enslaved so far as the human will is corrupt through evil habits, and human reason through blindness that stultifies the deliberation ('consilium') preceding judgment. See

Gilson *Mystical Theology of Saint Bernard* 47–51; and George Bosworth Burch tr *The Steps of Humility* by Bernard of Clairvaux (Cambridge, Mass: Harvard University Press 1940) 13–23.

81 On the sense in which all Three Persons engrafted love in humanity, see the passage in which Augustine inquires whether the entire Trinity might not be implicit in the 'Fiat' of Genesis: *De civitate Dei* Corpus Christianorum Series Latina 48 (Turnhout, Belg: Brepols 1955) 343–4.

82 For brief discussion of earlier interpretations of the passage, see my '*Liberum-Arbitrium* in the c-Text' 689. For a view that contrasts with the one I am proposing, see Robert Adams 'Piers's Pardon and Langland's Semi-Pelagianism' *Traditio* 39 (1983) 377–82.

83 Alexander of Hales *Summa* Inq 4, Tract 1, Sect 2, Q 3, Tit 3, Cap 1, A 3, ed Collegium S. Bonaventurae 2: 470.

84 Liberum Arbitrium's taking up all three planks coincides in c with his assumption of what, rightly understood, is indeed a universal power of the soul ('when y wilne and wolde *Animus* y hatte' etc). As a universal power, 'liberum-arbitrium,' when unfettered, elicits the activity of all other powers of the mind so that a person might do what he or she ought.

85 For another view of Liberum Arbitrium's having 'þe lond to ferme, / Vnder Piers þe Plowman,' see A.J. Bowers 'The Tree of Charity in *Piers Plowman*: Its Allegorical and Structural Significance' in Eric Rothstein and J.A. Wittreich Jr eds *Literary Monographs* 6 (Madison: University of Wisconsin Press 1975) 25.

86 Augustine *Confessionum libri* XIII 10.10 (17) ed Verheijen 163

87 In B the fruit is simply 'Charite' while in c it is 'werkes / Of holynesse,' called '*Caritas*' (18.12–13, 14). The change coincides with an earlier one in which, in B, charity is visible only in the will, while in c it is visible in charitable works: see B 15.198–210, c 16.337–9. The change may come from c's clear understanding that the freedom of 'liberum-arbitrium' presupposes the habit of charity in the will and that the choices of 'liberum-arbitrium' are therefore of means, ie, specific charitable acts. Bowers compares the 'commonplace tradition of equating the states of Marriage, Widowhood, and Virginity with thirty, sixty, and one-hundred-fold harvest of Christian works,' deriving from the parable of Matt 13.23 ('Tree of Charity in *Piers Plowman*' 27).

88 The fruit is not explicitly rotten, but Piers's description of it as, for example, 'swete wiþouten swellyng; sour worþ it neuere' (16.72) con-

trasts ironically with the unexpectedly 'foul noise' (16.77) at the moment of its falling. The weeping at all levels surely signifies regret.

89 Cf Werner Klett *Wörter im Sinnbereich der Gemeinschaft bei William Langland* (PHD diss, University of Bonn 1939) 24.

90 Dante 'Paradiso' 26.91–2. I am not convinced of 'a general desire on Langland's part to see the natural as a force for good' (White *Nature and Salvation* 92).

91 Cf Robert Adams 'Langland and the Liturgy Revisited' *Studies in Philology* 78 (1976) 283–4.

92 Cf Margaret E. Goldsmith: 'It is often supposed that his [ie, Liberum Arbitrium's] seizing of the staff precipitates the Incarnation ... But there can be no temporal sequence here: the facts entirely preclude it' (*The Figure of 'Piers Plowman'* [Cambridge: D.S. Brewer 1981] 68).

93 The B text summarizes the Passion and Resurrection swiftly and distantly; c stops abruptly with 'This Iewes to þe iustices Iesus they ladde' (18.178), after which Will awakens 'nere frentyk.'

94 I mean this term in the sense well known from Anders Nygren. For a convenient summary of its significata, see Nygren's *Agape and Eros* (1930–6) tr P.S. Watson (Philadelphia: Westminster Press 1953) 208–10. Cf the earlier work by Max Scheler *Ressentiment* (1912) 4th ed, ed L.A. Coser tr W.W. Holdheim (New York: Free Press 1961) 84–8. Like other heuristic works, *Agape and Eros* has drawn serious criticism: see, eg, Gustaf Wingren *Theology in Conflict: Nygren – Barth – Bultmann* tr E.H. Wahlstrom (Philadelphia: Muhlenberg Press 1958) 85–101. Such critics, however, recognize the existence of a dichotomy even while quarrelling with Nygren's method or formulation. I cite Nygren because of the clarity and unchallenged adequacy of his definition of *agape*. The poet seems to sense the difficulty of theocentric love much as he does (cf 15.158–60). Cf W.O. Evans 'Charity in *Piers Plowman*' in Hussey ed '*Piers Plowman': Critical Approaches* 261–2; Gordon Leff *Bradwardine and the Pelagians: A Study of His 'De causa Dei' and Its Opponents* (Cambridge: Cambridge University Press 1957) 19; and J.A. Burrow *Ricardian Poetry: Chaucer, Gower, Langland and the 'Gawain' Poet* (London: Routledge and Kegan Paul 1971) 102–11.

95 On the six principal movements of the mind (beginning with 'foi [qui] montre Dieu') constituting conversion in orthodox Catholic theology, see Edouard Hugon 'La notion théologique de la "psychologie de la conversion"' *Revue Thomiste* 24 (1914) 232–4.

96 See 17.115–17 (where the Samaritan, symbolic of Christ, will be known by Faith under the New Dispensation) and 125–6. Faith

under the New Dispensation speaks at 18.92–109 (note the past tense in lines 98–100).

97 Cf Ruth H. Ames *The Fulfillment of the Scriptures: Abraham, Moses, and Piers* (Evanston, Ill: Northwestern University Press 1970) 90.

98 Cf esp Paul's teaching that 'faith was credited as justice' to Abraham (Rom 4.9).

99 Cf Faith's other generative metaphors for the Trinity (16.202–24) and esp his own relationship with Sarah and Isaac in the c revision, 18.246–51.

100 Jean Daniélou *God and the Ways of Knowing* tr W. Roberts (New York: Meridian 1957) 117

101 The equating of contrition, or penitence, with conversion has been standard since Tertullian: see *On Penitence* 2, 4 tr W.P. Le Saint in *Tertullian Treatises on Penance* Ancient Christian Writers 28 (Westminster, Md, and London: Newman Press and Longmans, Green 1959) 15–16, 20–1; cf esp 140.

102 See Deut 6.5, Lev 19.18, Matt 22.34–40. Cf *Piers* B 15.584.

103 In addition to the discussion of 'redde quod debes' in the following chapter, see Will's summary of Hope's teaching as the command to 'loue a sherewe' (16.45). The c revision of this (19.101–5) recalls Augustine's doctrine that 'only those [things] pertain to hope which are contained in the Lord's Prayer,' notably 'forgive us our debts, as *we also forgive our debtors*': 'Faith, Hope, and Charity' (the *Enchiridion*) 114–15 tr B.M. Peebles in *Writings of Saint Augustine* 2nd ed The Fathers of the Church, a New Translation, 22 vols (Washington: Catholic University of America Press 1947–) 4: 465–6. In Hope's saying 'thogh y myhte venge / Y sholde tholye and thonken hem þat me euel wolden' (19.104–5), c anticipates the Samaritan's asking, 'How myʒte he aske mercy, or any mercy hym helpe, / That wikkedliche and wilfulliche wolde mercy aniente?' (B 17.189–90). Cf the context of the second great commandment (Lev 19.18). The usual interpretation of Hope may be represented by Ben H. Smith's remark: 'The law ... must be fulfilled by good works; and good works nourish the virtue of hope' (*Traditional Imagery of Charity in 'Piers Plowman'* [The Hague and Paris: Mouton 1966] 82).

104 Frank *'Piers Plowman' and the Scheme of Salvation* 91.

105 c omits B 16.189–90, which tend to draw grace and nature together in a way that the poet seems to reserve for the Samaritan.

106 Contrast Liberum Arbitrium's use of 'kynde' at c 18.78 with the Samaritan's at B 17.348, 349.

107 See 17.303–20. By 'restitucioun' (17.319), the Samaritan surely means

that one who is contrite shows mercy where the unconverted does not (see 17.289–98).

108 See Frank *'Piers Plowman' and the Scheme of Salvation* 92.

109 Cf Mary-Jo Arn: 'More than any other section of the poem, *Dobest* is the meeting-place of divinity and humanity ...' ('Langland's Triumph of Grace in *Dobest' English Studies* 63 [1982] 506).

CHAPTER FIVE

1 By contrast, for another way 'to fiȝte' with the cross, see 19.63–8. At the beginning of the next dream, Will emphasizes the talismanic quality of the name of Jesus (19.21).

2 Malcolm Godden *The Making of 'Piers Plowman'* (London and New York: Longman 1990) 136. R.A. Waldron reports 'an element of puzzlement' on the reader's part when the latter finds in the Harrowing of Hell 'the very relief ... of the familiar. Have we really come through so much questioning to find the answer under our very nose?': 'Langland's Originality: The Christ-Knight and the Harrowing of Hell' in Gregory Kratzmann and James Simpson eds *Medieval English Religious and Ethical Literature* (Cambridge: D.S. Brewer 1986) 66.

3 With the following interpretation, contrast that of D.W. Robertson and B.F. Huppé *'Piers Plowman' and Scriptural Tradition* (Princeton: Princeton University Press 1951) 218; and David Fowler *'Piers the Plowman': Literary Relations of the A and B Texts* (Seattle: University of Washington Press 1961) 153–4.

4 Cf Anna P. Baldwin: in c 18–20, 'we are shown a ruler who obeys the law as if He were His humblest subject' (*The Theme of Government in 'Piers Plowman'* [Cambridge: D.S. Brewer 1981] 56). Cf also Helen Barr: 'The only character in the poem whose actions are fully *shown* to be proportionate to Biblical texts is Piers as Christ. He fulfills the law, pays what he owes according to the injunction in Matthew only by paying more than he owes ...' ('The Use of Latin Quotations in *Piers Plowman* with Special References to Passus XVIII of the "B" Text' *Notes and Queries* ns 33 [1986]: 448).

5 'Dowel' is achieved only 'þoruȝ word,' ie, Christ's knowledge of God. 'Dès l'instant premier de son existence, c'est dans la claire vision directe de Dieu que s'éveiller l'âme du Christ ...': Léon Seiller *L'activité humaine du Christ selon Duns Scot* Etudes de science religieuse 3 (Paris: Editions franciscaines 1944) 68. On Jesus as 'dowel,' cf Hugh of St Victor: '*Lex per Moysen data est; veritas per Jesum Christum facta*

est. Quia quod Moyses docuit, ipse adimplere nequaquam potuit; unde dedit quod ipse facere non potuit; sed Jesus Christus quod docuit, hoc ipsum etiam opere adimplevit ...' *(Allegoria in Novum Testamentum* 5 *Patrologia Latina* 175: 838).

6 The Samaritan's wine and the oil represent, respectively, redemption from original sin, in which humanity participates by the Eucharist, and sacerdotal healing of subsequent sin, signified by the oil of Isaiah 61:1. The Samaritan explicitly ascribes to Christ the origin of baptism and penance (17.94–7).

7 Anders Nygren *Agape and Eros* (1930–6) tr P.S. Watson (Philadelphia: Westminster Press 1953) 206

8 See 1.85–7, 91, 90 (see also 2.29–35), 143, 153–8 (cf Nygren *Agape and Eros* 518–32, esp 527), 181–4, 201, 159–62.

9 See c 17.136.

10 Cf Martin D'Arcy's succinct paraphrase of Nygren: 'in these two commandments ['love God and your neighbour'] ... is Agape comprised, and there is no third commandment, such as "love thyself." The intrusion of this last into Christianity and its theology is due to Eros and not Agape, and its presence is an infallible mark of Eros' *(The Mind and Heart of Love: Lion and Unicorn, A Study in Eros and Agape* 2nd ed [Cleveland and New York: Meridian 1956] 65).

11 Nygren *Agape and Eros* 629–30

12 See ibid 655–8.

13 See ibid esp 115–20.

14 See also 19.14, 41, 63–8, 142, 170–5, and 321–4.

15 Helen Barr observes that, in portions of *Piers* lying outside passus 18, 'exhortations to do well, emphasized through the use of learned quotations, are shown finally to be inadequate.' The use of such quotations in the Harrowing of Hell 'represents almost a withdrawal from the intricacies of a real human struggle' ('The Use of Latin Quotations' 448).

16 Cf Conrad Pepler: 'As Dobet [Christ's] life was one of the ministry ... and this included the Crucifixion and Resurrection ...' *(The English Religious Heritage* [St Louis, Mo: Herder 1958] 64). Lines 19.50–2 make the Resurrection the act of Christ the conqueror; yet it is probable that Conscience distinguishes between the Passion itself (see esp 19.41) and the conquest achieved when sinful people identify themselves with it (see esp 19.36–40). Thus, it is only after the Resurrection and the appearance to the apostles that Christ decides to 'do best' – begins to conquer, as it were (19.182).

17 That is, Bernard of Clairvaux's sermon on Psalms 84.10–11. See Hope Traver *The Four Daughters of God, A Study of the Versions of This Allegory with Especial Reference to Those in Latin, French, and English* (Philadelphia: Winston 1907) 16.

18 Ibid 31

19 See, for example, John Norton-Smith *William Langland* (Leiden: E.J. Brill 1983) 68. For other recent comment on Langland's treatment of the quarrel among the Four Daughters, see esp Waldron 'Langland's Originality' 76–80; and Godden *The Making of 'Piers Plowman'* 144–5.

20 On the meaning of *Dobest*, see also H.W. Wells 'The Philosophy of *Piers Plowman' PMLA* 53 (1938) 343, 346–7 and 'The Construction of *Piers Plowman' PMLA* 44 (1929) 134; R.W. Frank 'The Conclusion of *Piers Plowman' Journal of English and Germanic Philology* 49 (1950) 309–16 and *'Piers Plowman' and the Scheme of Salvation: An Interpretation of 'Dowel, Dobet, and Dobest'* (New Haven: Yale University Press 1957) 110–18; and Fowler *'Piers the Plowman': Literary Relations* ch 5.

21 For the view that the poem ends in a mood of despair, see, eg, E. Talbot Donaldson, review of R.B. Donna *Despair and Hope* in *Modern Language Notes* 68 (1953) 141–2; and Pepler *English Religious Heritage* 44. To the contrary, A.H. Smith believes that, at the end, Conscience is 'fortified by Hope': *'Piers Plowman' and the Pursuit of Poetry* (London: H.K. Lewis 1952) 12. Konrad Burdach (*Der Dichter des Ackermann aus Böhmen und seine Zeit* [Berlin: Weidmann 1926–32] 313–14), Frank (*'Piers Plowman' and the Scheme of Salvation* 118), and John Lawlor (*'Piers Plowman': An Essay in Criticism* [London: Edward Arnold 1962] 185) see the situation as ambiguous.

22 Kenneth Kirk's paraphrase (*The Vision of God: The Christian Doctrine of the Summum Bonum* [1931; New York: Harper Torchbook 1966] 66) of *Jesus and the Word*. Cf Kirk *Vision of God* 95; and Ruth H. Ames *The Fulfillment of the Scriptures: Abraham, Moses and Piers* (Evanston, Ill: Northwestern University Press 1970) 191. Similarly, R.E. Emmerson remarks that 'there is no indication in *Dobest* that evil can be overcome by any human agency, no matter how ideal.' The poem moves 'to the apocalyptic hope of individual salvation ... in another, divine, world': 'The Prophetic, the Apocalyptic, and the Study of Medieval Literature' in Jan Wojcik and Raymond-Jean Frontain eds *Poetic Prophecy in Western Literature* (Rutherford NJ: Fairleigh Dickinson University Press 1984) 53, 54.

23 Donald R. Howard *The Three Temptations: Medieval Man in Search of the World* (Princeton: Princeton University Press 1966) 203

24 Frank argues that love of God and neighbour is the full meaning of '*redde quod debes*,' into which the narrower one of restitution (within the sacrament of penance) moves ('*Piers Plowman' and the Scheme of Salvation* 106–9). Frank is echoed by Margaret E. Goldsmith *The Figure of Piers Plowman* (Cambridge: D.S. Brewer 1981) 90; and by Penn R. Szittya: 'The payment must be love. Love of God and love of our neighbor – only these fulfill the command of *Redde quod debes*' (*The Antifraternal Tradition in Medieval Literature* [Princeton: Princeton University Press 1986] 260.

25 Cf Prol 100–4 and the protective role of the four cardinal virtues as the turrets on the Castle of Love (ie, Mary) in *Cursor Mundi* 10005–12 ed Richard Morris, Pt 2 Early English Text Society os 59 (London, New York, Toronto 1875; 1966) 576–7.

26 See Thomas Aquinas *Summa theologica* 1–2.65.2, 3; 1–2.63.3. Cf Prol 102–4.

27 See Romans 13 and Frank's discussion of it in relation to '*redde quod debes*' ('*Piers Plowman' and the Scheme of Salvation* 109).

28 Cf Kirk *Vision of God* 384–8.

29 See Anima's speech, 15.344–84, and cf 19.344–51. See also Thomas Aquinas *Summa contra gentiles* 4.72 ed English Dominican Fathers, 4 vols (London: Burns, Oates 1924–9) 4: 249. On the presupposition of the theological virtues by the gifts also, see Odon Lottin *Psychologie et morale au xiie et xiiie siècles* 2nd ed, 6 vols in 8 pts (Gembloux, Belg: Ducolot 1957–60) 3: 433.

30 Cynewulf *Christ* ii 659–88: G.P. Krapp and E.K. Dobbie eds *The Exeter Book* The Anglo-Saxon Poetic Records 3 (New York: Columbia University Press 1936) 21–2. Cf the 'woruldcræftas' in *The Gifts of Men* 22 (*Exeter Book* 138).

31 Howard *Three Temptations* 203. Cf S.A. Barney 'The Plowshare of the Tongue: The Progress of a Symbol from the Bible to *Piers Plowman*' *Medieval Studies* 35 (1973) 288–9.

32 'Conscience' is also coupled with 'kynde wit' at c Prol 142, c 4.152, B 15.553, and B 17.138. Cf B 1.54–7.

33 Godden *Making of 'Piers Plowman'* 153; cf 158.

34 See also 6.7–69, 139–47, and 247–9.

35 See 7.13–37, 61–6. For a comparison of Piers's activity in *Dobest* with his activity in the *Visio*, see Barbara Raw 'Piers and the Image of God in Man' in S.S. Hussey ed '*Piers Plowman': Critical Approaches* (London: Methuen 1969) 146.

36 Cf J.A. Burrow's remark that in *Dobest* the Church is represented as

undergoing a process that he calls 'entropic' ('Words, Works, and Will: Theme and Structure in *Piers Plowman*' in Hussey ed *'Piers Plowman': Critical Approaches* 120).

37   Kirk *Vision of God* 147 ·
38   With the second verse of this line, cf Gal 6: 10.
39   See Robert Adams 'The Nature of Need in *Piers Plowman*' *Traditio* 34 (1978) 278.
40   See 5.260–75, 280–95, 455–70, 598; 6.87–90; 7.80–1. Stokes and Coleman, among others, see this as dominant in Langland's view of penance. 'Eternal life must be worked for.' Christ 'did not so much redeem men, as make it possible for them to redeem themselves, by cancelling the unredeemable deficit' of original sin. 'To pardon, or forgive, only such debts as have been paid could be regarded as a contradiction in terms': Myra Stokes *Justice and Mercy in 'Piers Plowman'* (London and Canberra: Croom Helm 1984) 29, 15, 14; but see also 91–4, 266. Coleman believes that *'redde'* owes much to the 'ethical injunction,' formulated by the 'moderni,' *'facere quod in se est'* *'Piers Plowman' and the 'Moderni'* (Rome: Edizioni di Storia e Letteratura 1981) 41. Wendy Scase has recently remarked the prevalence in contemporary texts of an insistence on restitution, which she traces to an anti-clericalism: 'Insisting on the claims of justice ... was potentially antisacerdotal, since it implied a limit to the priest's power, for even if properly administered by him the sacrament was not effective without restitution to the victim of the crime' (*'Piers Plowman' and the New Anticlericalism* [Cambridge: Cambridge University Press 1989] 28).
41   Frank *'Piers Plowman' and the Scheme of Salvation* 109. Cf Peter Lombard *Sententiae* 4.15.7; Raymond St-Jacques 'Conscience's Final Pilgrimage in *Piers Plowman* and the Cyclical Structure of the Liturgy' *Revue de l'Université d'Ottawa* 40 (1970) 218; and esp E.D. Higgs: 'now that [Will] has seen that God uses man's sins as a means of revealing His love, Will can understand that "paying what he owes" (*reddere quod debet*) to Piers's pardon consists first of admitting that he can never pay his own debt of righteousness, then of laying hold of Christ's perfect satisfaction of that debt; and subsequently, it means doing his best and trusting God for the increase' ('The Path to Involvement: The Centrality of the Dreamer in *Piers Plowman*' *Tulane Studies in English* 21 [1974] 30).
42   But see 17.238–42.
43   See esp C 19.101–5.

44 See eg, 15.511–18. Cf Piers on the wasters: 'it are my blody breþeren for god bouȝte vs alle' (6.207).

45 Matt 18: 23–34 Challoner-Rheims Version, rev Confraternity of Christian Doctrine (Paterson NJ: St Anthony Guild Press 1941). St-Jacques argues that, in linking passus 19 and 20, Langland selects the 'redde quod debes' tag from the liturgy for the twenty-second Sunday after the Feast of the Holy Trinity, the liturgy of which looks back to Pentecost and forward to 'the Advent of Antichrist and Christ's Second Coming.' For this Sunday, The Gospel and Epistle (Phil 1: 6–11), claims [the liturgical commentator William] Durand, urge us to practice perfect charity since unity can exist in the Church only if we forgive the wrongs done to us by others': 'Conscience's Final Pilgrimage in *Piers Plowman* and the Cyclical Structure of the Liturgy' *Studies in Medieval Culture* 4 (1974): 381–2.

46 On the role of Conscience in *Dobest*, see Rose Bernard Donna *Despair and Hope: A Study in Langland and Augustine* (Washington DC: Catholic University of America Press 1948) 68–71; Willi Erzgräber *William Langlands 'Piers Plowman': Eine Interpretation des C-Textes* (Heidelberg: Carl Winter 1957) 62, 218, 220; and Morton W. Bloomfield *'Piers Plowman' as a Fourteenth-Century Apocalypse* (New Brunswick: Rutgers University Press [1961]) 142. C.W. Whitworth Jr proposes that Conscience in *Dobest* represents 'the act of mind proceeding from the innate habit, *synderesis*, without the deliberation of reason': 'Changes in the Roles of Reason and Conscience in the Revisions of *Piers Plowman*' *Notes and Queries* ns 19 (1972) 7. Whitworth attempts to distinguish an 'act of judgment' from 'lengthy cogitation'; but so far as conscience signifies a conclusion about something to be done, it is, in scholastic thought, an act of the practical reason. Like Will, Conscience seeks 'dowel' (13.112, 119) and grace (C Prol 151, B 19.199, 204, 207, 20.386). He will ultimately be capable of belief: see A 11.309, where the later texts substitute 'belief.' He has hope (14.189, omitted from C as part of a large cut) and gives comfort (13.58, 20.358).

47 See Peter Lombard *Sententiae* 4.17.3.4.

48 If G.L. Wilkes is right in pointing to a castle in the *Ancrene Riwle* as a source for Unity, it is interesting that a lengthy adjacent passage in the *Riwle* insists on 'herdi bileaue' as the only successful defence against sin. No such protection is apparent at Unity, which, unlike the *Riwle* castle, evidently falls to the devil. Wilkes assumes Unity to symbolize 'unified belief': see 'The Castle of Vnite in *Piers Plowman*' *Medieval Studies* 27 (1965) 334–6.

49 Cf Godden: 'The central position of the friars in the fall of Unitee and the climactic last section of the poem is hard to explain' (*Making of 'Piers Plowman'* 166).

50 On Need, see the excellent passage in Frank's *'Piers Plowman' and the Scheme of Salvation* 113–17. He interprets Need's speech as exposing the friars' philosophy of need, relates it to the controversy over the poverty of Christ, and suggests that the 'fyndyng' would remove the 'nede' that makes the friars dangerous. My own interpretation parallels Frank's at several points. A source in Job 41:13 for the conjoined appearances of Need (20.4–50) and Antichrist (20.52 *ad fin*) has been persuasively established by Adams 'The Nature of Need' 282–3. On the other hand, Bloomfield has held (unconvincingly, I believe) for the authority of Need (*'Piers Plowman' as a Fourteenth-Century Apocalypse* 135–43). Taking a view compatible with Bloomfield's are Robertson and Huppé *'Piers Plowman' and Scriptural Tradition* 227–9; Lawlor *'Piers Plowman': An Essay in Criticism* 178–9; and J.S. Wittig 'The Dramatic and Rhetorical Development of Long Will's Pilgrimage' *Neuphilologische Mitteilungen* 76 (1975) 74. Clopper's view of the Need episode 'as an appeal to the Wanderer's conscience in terms of a strict Franciscan absence of solicitude' is not easy to accept, in light of Need's repeated advice to 'take' (20.7, 9, 11, 20), 'by sleighte' if need be (20.14). This differs from the 'recklessness' that Patience urges on Haukyn, who, when he is hungry, cold, or thirsty, should conquer by patience, dying 'as god likeþ / Or þoruȝ hunger or þoruȝ hete, at his wille be it' (14.58–9). See L.M. Clopper 'Langland's Franciscanism' *Chaucer Review* 25 (1990) 64, 68.

51 Adams 'Nature of Need' 279. On the moral neutrality of Hunger, see also Mary Carruthers (Schroeder) *'Piers Plowman*: The Tearing of the Pardon' *Philological Quarterly* 49 (1970) 14.

52 Szittya *Antifraternal Tradition* 272

53 The 'kyng wiþ croune' (19.456), who confuses his being the authority from which 'law derives its ... positive legal value' with his being just (cf A.P. d'Entreves *The Medieval Contribution to Political Thought, Thomas Aquinas, Marsilius of Padua, Richard Hooker* [New York: Humanities 1959] esp 38–9), is presaged not only by the goliard's words to the king in the Prologue (139–42) but by the casually predatory cat of the fable.

54 Cf esp Adams 'Nature of Need' 278.

55 Cf esp ibid 286.

56 'Spede' here means to be satisfied (see R.E. Kaske review of Bloom-

field 'Piers Plowman' as a Fourteenth-Century Apocalypse in Journal of
English and Germanic Philology 62 [1963] 205). The gift of the 'copes'
surely does not increase the friars' neediness.

57   Hence, as Scase points out, 'The anticlerical objective must be to exclude from "need" the condition of voluntary mendicancy ...' ('Piers
Plowman' and the New Anticlericalism 66).

58   Pamela Gradon 'Langland and the Ideology of Dissent' Proceedings of
the British Academy 66 (1980) 203

59   Attrition and contrition here may match the 'two parts' of passus 20
that B.S. Lee notes in his fine discussion of its structure: 'Antichrist
and Allegory in Langland's Last Passus' University of Capetown Studies in English 2 (1971) 3.

60   Clopper interprets this 'fyndyng' as actually a disendowment of the
friars of their responsibility for the care of souls. It would re-establish
them, paradoxically, in 'a life of need' ('Langland's Franciscanism'
69–70). Clopper does not deal with Conscience's promise to the friars
of 'breed and cloþes / And oþere necessaries ynowe' (20.248–9).

61   Among explanations of Conscience's admitting Friar Flatterer, Goldsmith's seems to me the most apposite. She refers to Augustine's reminder that the blessing given to Moses and Aaron is reserved for
those who love their enemies. 'Langland, expressing the like belief,
does not want to expel the unruly friars from Piers's house, though
he exposes the appalling harm that they can do' (Figure of Piers
Plowman 131). However, see also Clopper 'Langland's Franciscanism'
69; Godden Making of 'Piers Plowman' 167; Priscilla Jenkins 'Conscience: The Frustration of Allegory' in Hussey ed 'Piers Plowman':
Critical Approaches 139–41; and Mary Carruthers (Schroeder) 'The
Character of Conscience in Piers Plowman' Studies in Philology 67
(1970) 24–9.

62   In what turns out to be the last glimpse of Piers, he is 'to þe plow'
(19.335). One tradition interprets the plow as symbolic of the cross:
see Jean Daniélou 'La Charrue symbole de la Croix (Irenée, Adv.
haer., IV. 34, 4)' Recherches de science religieuse 42 (1954) 193–203. Piers's
taking the plow in response, not just to the 'cros,' but to Christ's
'baptisme and blood,' 'hise peynes and his passion' (19.323, 326),
signifies conversion.

63   Although P.M. Kean speaks of 'the Dobest to which we have become
accustomed – the power over sin which arises because in it man and
God find a meeting place' ('Justice, Kingship and the Good Life in
the Second Part of Piers Plowman' in Hussey ed 'Piers Plowman': Criti-

cal Approaches 88), her interpretation is not close to mine. She interprets 'dobest' variously as the church, love, and grace (81–3).

64 As far back as Repentance's speech in passus 5, the notion that a person becomes like God because he or she 'manet in caritate' is transected by Christ's having become like 'vs synfulle' by experiencing 'sorwe' (5.491). For 'in oure secte was þe sorwe ...' (5.490). Cf *Patience* 296: 'he knawez Hym in care þat couþe not in sele' (in Malcolm Andrew and Ronald Waldron eds *The Poems of the 'Pearl' Manuscript* [Berkeley and Los Angeles: University of California Press 1978] 198).

65 Hence Godden's observation: 'The action of Conscience, and the feeling behind it, strongly recall the end of the second vision' (*Making of 'Piers Plowman'* 168).

66 The restlessness of Conscience at the end in crying aloud for grace and in undertaking ever to search for Piers may be precisely the inquietude that, for Aquinas and others, defines faith: see M.-D. Chenu 'La psychologie de la foi dans la théologie du XIIIe siècle' *Etudes d'histoire littéraire et doctrinale du XIIIe siècle* 2 (1932) 183–4. Walter Ong has written that faith, an 'essentially unsatisfying state,' leaves the mind 'restless and tense': 'Wit and Mystery: A Revaluation in Mediaeval Latin Hymnody' *Speculum* 22 (1947) 333; cf Philippe Delhaye *La problème de la conscience morale chez S. Bernard, étudié dans ses oeuvres et dans ses sources* Analecta Mediaevalia Namurcensia 9 (Louvain: Nauwelaerts 1957) 30. Although any suggestion that *Piers* anticipates the doctrine of 'sola fides' must await some comment on the *Visio*, one might suggest here that Conscience's becoming a pilgrim at the end simultaneously with his representing the conversion of the narrator foreshadows what Steven Ozment has called 'the most revolutionary aspect of Luther's theology' from the perspective of late medieval thought. Luther held that 'The *viator*-status of a Christian who must live between fear-inspiring judgment and hope-creating mercy is existentially and theologically overcome' through belief in Christ. Yet 'unlike the traditional *fides charitate formata*, Luther's *sola fides* unites the believer with God in Christ while still leaving him sinful in himself.' This suspends the viator-status and yet leaves the Christian 'very much a *viator*': 'Homo Viator: Luther and Late Medieval Theology' *Harvard Theological Review* 62 (1969): 287, 276, 287.

CHAPTER SIX

1 Cf Nevill Coghill 'The Pardon of Piers Plowman' *Proceedings of the*

British Academy 30 (1944) 322, 357, esp his treatment of Langland's revision of A (329–37); Rosemary Woolf 'The Tearing of the Pardon' in
S.S. Hussey ed *'Piers Plowman': Critical Approaches* (London: Methuen
1969) 75; and Geoffrey Shepherd 'The Nature of Alliterative Poetry in
Late Medieval England' *Proceedings of the British Academy* 56 (1970)
58, 70, 74.

2 See Konrad Burdach *Der Dichter des Ackermann aus Böhmen und seine
Zeit* (Berlin: Weidmann 1926–32) 314.

3 Cf Julia Bolton Holloway: 'Langland ... places Piers the Plowman in
one typological context after another, as Abraham, as Moses, as Christ,
as Pope' (*The Pilgrim and the Book: A Study of Dante, Langland, and
Chaucer* [New York, Berne, Frankfurt am Main: Peter Lang 1987] 164).

4 Margaret E. Goldsmith sees Piers as consistently the pattern of godliness or 'justitia.' The conception of this godliness changes (from 'the
righteousness of the patriarchs and the penitential hope of the
prophets to the Christian charity of the apostles') as Will's 'spiritual
education proceeds': *The Figure of Piers Plowman* (Cambridge: D.S.
Brewer 1981) 24. For a suggestion of earlier comment on the meaning
of Piers, see Elizabeth Z. Salter 'Medieval Poetry and the Figural
View of Reality' *Proceedings of the British Academy* 54 (1968) 91–2 and
her *'Piers Plowman', An Introduction* (Cambridge, Mass: Harvard University Press 1962) 88; Christopher Dawson 'The Vision of Piers
Plowman' in his *Medieval Essays* (London and New York: Sheed and
Ward 1953) 250, 257–9; S.B. James 'The Mad Poet of Malvern' *The
Month* 159 (1932) 226; H.W. Troyer 'Who is Piers Plowman?' *PMLA* 47
(1932) 368–84; Charles W. Stubbs *The Christ of English Poetry* (London
and New York: Dent 1906) 93–4; and Bernhard ten Brink *Geschichte
der Englischen Literatur* 2nd ed, ed A. Brandl, 2 vols (Strassburg: Trub-
ner 1890–1912) 1: 365.

5 See T.P. Dunning *'Piers Plowman,' An Interpretation of the A Text* 2nd
ed, ed T.P. Dolan (Oxford: Clarendon 1980) 115.

6 The nature of this point common to God and humanity and signified
by Piers has been variously described. Pamela Gradon identified it as
patient poverty, an essence shared by Christ and Piers: 'Langland
and the Ideology of Dissent' *Proceedings of the British Academy* 66
(1980) 198–9. For John Alford, Piers 'symbolizes the perfect conformity of wills that unites God and man': 'The Design of the Poem' in
J.A. Alford ed *A Companion to 'Piers Plowman'* (Berkeley: University
of California Press 1988) 55.

7 And therefore as metonymic for the mystical body: cf M.C. Davlin

'*Petrus, Id Est, Christus*: Piers the Plowman As "The Whole Christ,"' *Chaucer Review* 6 (1972) 280–92.

8 Augustine glosses the verse by saying, 'Non timebo mala, quoniam tu habitas in corde meo per fidem'; and his comment on the earlier verses emphasizes justification and conversion – 'non propter meritum meum, sed propter nomen suum': *Enarrationes in Psalmos I–L* Corpus Christianorum, Series Latina 38 (Turnhout, Belg: Brepols 1956) 134. Cf J.S. Wittig '*Piers Plowman* B, Passus IX–XII: Elements in the Design of the Inward Journey' *Traditio* 28 (1972) 278.

9 'Wil' here denotes contrition, while 'wordes' and 'werkes' mean confession and satisfaction. Cf John Chrysostom, as quoted by Peter Lombard *Sententiae* 4.16.1 (*Patrologia Latina* 192: 877). The poet names the three parts of penance elsewhere, eg, 14.16–21.

10 On this passage cf R.E. Kaske 'Patristic Exegesis in the Criticism of Medieval Literature: The Defense' in Dorothy Bethurum ed *Critical Approaches to Medieval Literature* (New York: Columbia University Press 1960) 42–8.

11 Bernard of Clairvaux *The Steps of Humility* tr George Bosworth Burch (Cambridge, Mass: Harvard University Press 1940) 137. Cf K.J. Woollcombe: 'Is it the case that God remembers His mercy, because He remembers His pain?' ('The Pain of God' *Scottish Journal of Theology* 20 [1967] 147).

12 See, for instance, 2.119–24, 129–33, and 3.122–4, 131–3. Philippa Tristram rightly observes that 'It is the use to which Meed is put, rather than her actual nature, which is at fault': *Figures of Life and Death* (London: Paul Elek 1976) 44. Cf, among others, Dunning '*Piers Plowman: An Interpretation of the A Text* 53. When Theology objects to a marriage between Meed and False Fickle-Tongue, he claims she is 'a maiden of goode' – and so the 'bona temporalia' are, in an unfallen world. But Meed is morally and politically dual; she is not simply neutral. The Fall itself is invoked metonymically by Holy Church in the 'Fals' she makes the father of Meed (2.25). After the Fall, cupidity is a habit. 'Meed' names this, so far as she not only denotes material wealth but connotes a habitual neglect of the just relationship between the giver and receiver of a gift, as that relationship is determined by the divine idea of both persons and their obligations. Meed as cupidity is the root of all the sins. But given the existence of the sins, Meed as bribery is the protection of them.

13 So Gerald Morgan sees Meed always representing 'material reward ... as an end of human endeavor':'The Status and Meaning of Meed

in the First Vision of *Piers Plowman' Neophilologus* 72 (1988) 458–9. Cf
A.G. Mitchell *Lady Meed and the Art of 'Piers Plowman'* (London: H.K.
Lewis 1956) 17–22. C.D. Benson has interestingly suggested that, in
the Meed episode, Langland also includes another perspective, 'from
which Meed can be seen to prefigure Christ himself': 'The Function
of Lady Meed in *Piers Plowman' English Studies* 61 (1980) 193–205;
quotation from 194.

14   See T.D. Hill 'Two Notes on Exegetical Allusion in Langland: *Piers
Plowman* B.XI.161–67 and B.I.115–24' *Neuphilologische Mitteilungen* 75
(1974) 94–7. Contrast P.M. Kean 'Justice, Kingship, and the Good Life
in the Second Part of *Piers Plowman'* in Hussey ed *'Piers Plowman':
Critical Approaches* esp 87; Mary Carruthers (Schroeder) *'Piers Plowman*: The Tearing of the Pardon' *Philological Quarterly* 49 (1970) 11–17;
and Mary Carruthers *The Search for St. Truth: A Study of Meaning in
'Piers Plowman'* (Evanston, Ill: Northwestern University Press 1973)
58. Kean misses the way in which love is central to the divine Law.
Carruthers is mistaken in thinking that there is 'no moral value' in
'the world of the *Visio*.'

15   Anna P. Baldwin *The Theme of Government in 'Piers Plowman'* (Cambridge: D.S. Brewer 1981) 16.

16   1.12–137 vs 1.140–209. But cf R.E. Kaske 'Holy Church's Speech and
the Structure of *Piers Plowman'* in Beryl Rowland ed *Chaucer and Middle English Studies in Honour of Rossell Hope Robbins* (London: Allen
and Unwin 1974) 320–1.

17   The priest never doubts that obedience to the Law in the first instance is preferable to forgiveness for disobedience ('demed þat
dowel Indulgences passeþ'). Cf John Reidy: 'Nobody then thinks that
Indulgences are better than a good life; why should they? Piers,
priest, and poet are in agreement' ('Piers the Ploughman, Whiche a
Pardoun He Hadde' *Papers of the Michigan Academy of Science, Arts,
and Letters* 50 [1965] 541).

18   The comparable line in B names neither conscience nor 'kynde wit'
(Prol 116), although 'kynde wit' appears shortly thereafter (Prol 118, 121).

19   But see D.W. Robertson and B.F. Huppé *'Piers Plowman' and Scriptural
Tradition* (Princeton: Princeton University Press 1951) 27–9.

20   Malcolm Godden *The Making of 'Piers Plowman'* (London and New
York: Longman 1990) 41

21   For a contrary view of the fable, see E.M. Orsten 'The Ambiguities in
Langland's Rat Parliament' *Medieval Studies* 23 (1961) 216–39.

22   Jill Mann observes that 'the larger problem of how mercy can be ex-

ercised without undermining justice ... occupies Langland throughout the poem': 'Eating and Drinking in *Piers Plowman' Essays and
Studies* ns 32 (1979) 30. Langland seems incapable, that is, of tolerat-
ing what Przemyslaw Mroczkowski called the 'paradox that the sub-
limity of the ideal ... rooted in charity does not make the discipline
enforced less strict': 'Piers and His Pardon, a Dynamic Analysis' in
M. Brahmer, S. Helsztyński, and J. Krzyżanowski eds *Studies in Language and Literature in Honour of Margaret Schlauch* (Warsaw: Polish
Scientific Publishers 1966) 277; cf 279. Cf R.W. Chambers *Man's Unconquerable Mind: Studies of English Writers from Bede to A.E. Housman
and W.P. Ker* (London and Toronto: Jonathan Cape 1939) 117; George
Kane *Middle English Literature: A Critical Study of the Romances, the Religious Lyrics, 'Piers Plowman'* (London: Methuen 1951) 193; and W.O.
Evans 'Charity in *Piers Plowman'* in Hussey ed *'Piers Plowman': Critical Approaches* 257. But contrast B.F. Huppé, who finds Piers learning
in the 'pardoun' that 'there is no use attempting to lead men to
goodness by the nose ...': 'The Authorship of the A and B Texts of
Piers Plowman' Speculum 22 (1947) 601. To put it another way, Langland learns the limits of satire: cf Steven Justice 'The Genres of *Piers
Plowman' Viator* 19 (1988) 295.

23 The next two lines – 'And þouȝ þow mowe amercy hem [viz, the
tenants] lat mercy be taxour / And mekenesse þi maister' – incorpo-
rate the same tension between justice and love.

24 Alfred North Whitehead *Religion in the Making* (1926; Cleveland and
New York: Meridian 1960) 16

25 See the observation of Hope at this point: 'Deus tu conuersus viuifi-
cabis nos' (5.506).

26 Langland's purpose, in Lee Patterson's view, 'is not to portray the
Sins as moved by contrition but to trace the vicissitudes of contrition
itself.' These vicissitudes evidently reach to Langland's uncertainty
about how large a role to assign Repentance. As George Russell
points out, in revising A, Langland added and 'notably emphasized'
Repentance in the confession of the sins. C, however, reduces his role.
See Lee Patterson 'Chaucerian Confession: Penitential Literature and
the Pardoner' *Mediaevalia et Humanistica* ns 7 (1976) 158; and G.H.
Russell 'The Poet as Reviser: The Metamorphosis of the Confession
of the Seven Deadly Sins in *Piers Plowman'* in Mary J. Carruthers and
Elizabeth D. Kirk eds. *Acts of Interpretation: The Text in Its Contexts,
700–1600: Essays on Medieval and Renaissance Literature in Honor of E.
Talbot Donaldson* (Norman, Okla: Pilgrim 1982) 57, 63.

27 Cf David Fowler 'A New Interpretation of the A and B Texts of *Piers Plowman' Modern Philology* 71 (1974) 395.

28 Anne Middleton 'Making a Good End: John But as a Reader of *Piers Plowman*' in E.D. Kennedy, Ronald Waldron, and J.S. Wittig eds *Medieval English Studies Presented to George Kane* (Wolfeboro NH and Woodbridge, Eng: D.S. Brewer 1988) 248. 'In the psychology of sin implicit in the medieval handbooks, in which the subject's capacity to tell the truth about himself is circumscribed by the empty recursiveness formed by his own *habitus*, such utterance is in practice equally capable of deflecting and deferring penitential contrition ...' (248). As against such critics as Coghill ('The Pardon of Piers Plowman' 356), A.H. Smith ('*Piers Plowman' and the Pursuit of Poetry* [London: H.K. Lewis 1952] 10), and J.A. Burrow ('The Action of Langland's Second Vision' *Essays in Criticism* 15 [1965] 248, 253), I would agree with G.W. Stone that the course of human life shown in the second vision 'is one of error followed by temporary repentance, succeeded by a second course of evil ways': 'An Interpretation of the A-Text of *Piers Plowman' PMLA* 53 (1938) 662.

29 Cf Dunning: Piers's 'doing the labor of the world dressed as a pilgrim symbolizes his looking upon corporal things in the light of eternity' ('*Piers Plowman': An Interpretation of the A Text* 100).

30 Stubbs (*The Christ of English Poetry* 81), Dunning ('*Piers Plowman': An Interpretation of the A Text* 100, 115), Goldsmith (*Figure of Piers Plowman* 34), and Myra Stokes (*Justice and Mercy in 'Piers Plowman'* [London and Canberra: Croom Helm 1984] 229) distinguish the work on the half-acre from a pilgrimage that is to ensue.

31 This is the view taken by R.W. Chambers ('The Authorship of *Piers Plowman' Modern Languge Review* 5 [1910] 13), R.W. Rauch ('Langland and Medieval Functionalism' *Review of Politics* 5 [1943] 449–50), David Mills ('The Role of the Dreamer in *Piers Plowman*' in Hussey ed *'Piers Plowman': Critical Approaches* 199), Lavinia Griffiths (*Personification in 'Piers Plowman'* [Cambridge: D.S. Brewer 1985] 9), and Godden (*Making of 'Piers Plowman'* 47–8). While understanding the language of plowing to be figurative, S.A. Barney takes the referent to be penance: 'The Plowshare of the Tongue: The Progress of a Symbol from the Bible to *Piers Plowman' Medieval Studies* 35 (1973) 288. For yet another metaphorical pilgrimage, see 15.182–3.

32 But see the suggestive comments by W.C. Strange 'The Willful Trope: Some Notes on Personification with Illustrations from *Piers* (A)' *Annuale Mediaevale* 9 (1968) 29–32.

33   Godden is therefore wrong to say that, on this allegorical route, 'even
     the worst of sinners can find mercy' (*Making of 'Piers Plowman'* 46).
     He is surely right, however, in remarking that 'here is no Augus-
     tinian insistence on the primacy of grace ...' (46).
34   By contrast, grace is a condition for keeping the Law at 7.201–6. The
     Tree of Charity reverses the path described by Piers. There the *root* of
     the Tree is mercy, while the leaves are 'lele wordes, þe lawe of holy
     chirche' (16.5–6). Cf Denise Baker: 'in the directions to Truth's castle
     which Piers gives the penitents, he claims that grace follows rather
     than precedes good works ...' ('From Plowing to Penitence: *Piers
     Plowman* and Fourteenth-Century Theology' *Speculum* 55 [1980] 721).
     Cf also Cindy L. Vitto *The Virtuous Pagan in Middle English Literature*
     in *Transactions of the American Philosophical Society* ns 79.5 (Philadel-
     phia: American Philosophical Society 1989) 87. In what has come to
     be known as the semi-Pelagian view, God convenants to reward with
     grace those who do the best they know how to do. That grace, con-
     ferring merit 'de congruo,' should therefore be a sequel to obedience
     would conform to this view: see Janet Coleman *'Piers Plowman' and
     the 'Moderni'* (Rome: Edizioni di Storia e Letteratura 1981) 38–9, 101.
     But grace in this 'court' is also given to those who have not done
     their best: ie, it comes at least sometimes from the intervention of
     'Mercy,' who is 'sib to alle synfulle' (5.635–6). That is, there is grace
     in this 'court' for those who, according to the allegory, never get
     there, but yet are urged to 'go bityme' (5.638). On the possibility of
     meriting grace 'de congruo,' see W.J. Courtenay 'Covenant and
     Causality in Pierre d'Ailly' *Speculum* 46 (1971) 107.
35   See, for instance, 6.83: 'For now I am old and hoor and *haue of myn owene.*'
36   Similarly, the Conscience of the *Visio* takes the view that one must
     either work or 'spille hymself with sleuþe' (3.310).
37   While the gloss to Piers's 'pardoun' teaches people to feed beggars
     indiscriminately (7.76–8), 'pardoun' itself is granted only to the invol-
     untarily poor (7.66). Similarly, Hunger urges that charity be granted
     only the involuntarily poor (6.218–28a). When Hunger takes the
     harder line, he may, as Robert Kaske has suggested, represent a 'bib-
     lical hunger ... after justice': 'The Character Hunger in *Piers Plowman'*
     in Kennedy, Waldron, and Wittig eds *Medieval English Studies Pre-
     sented to George Kane* 190. He may also, however, be taking the politi-
     cally necessary steps to keep himself alive.
38   On the amoral nature of Hunger, cf Carruthers *Search for St. Truth*
     75–6. A.C. Spearing calls him a materialist who emphasizes the mate-

rialist ethos of the passage: see 'The Development of a Theme in *Piers Plowman' Review of English Studies* ns 11 (1960) 244–6. David Aers sees the tearing of the 'pardoun' as Langland's rejection of something like materialism: Langland 'grasped that the dominant tendency of Passus V–VII could be promoting an ethos in which productive work ... was becoming the *official* goal and informing end of human existence.' This tendency conflicted with Langland's traditional idea of Christ's unity with 'the poor' (*'Piers Plowman* and Problems in the Perception of Poverty: A Culture in Transition' *Leeds Studies in English* ns 14 [1983] 16–17). In discussing the pardon scene, Stokes sees that Piers, and through him Langland, is discovering that there is 'something carnal and worldly' in the *Visio's* 'vision of Dowel,' 'a hard-working community, honestly earning its "lyflod,"' each taking no more than his due' (*Justice and Mercy* 242).

39   Godden *Making of 'Piers Plowman'* 200, 42. Cf esp 66–7.
40   By contrast with the 'god [who] bouȝte vs alle,' Piers habitually promotes here the interests of a vindictive God: 'Ac truþe shal teche yow his teme to dryue, / Or ye shul eten barly breed and of þe broke drynke' (6.134–5).
41   See Huppé 'Authorship of the A and B Texts' 593.
42   R.W. Frank 'The Pardon Scene in *Piers Plowman' Speculum* 26 (1951) 317
43   See esp c 9.159–61.
44   Dunning *'Piers Plowman': An Interpretation of the A Text* 115
45   John Lawlor *'Piers Plowman': An Essay in Criticism* (London: Edward Arnold 1962) 81
46   See eg, Francis Carnegy *The Relations between the Social and Divine Order in William Langland's 'Vision of William Concerning Piers the Plowman'* (Breslau: Priebatsch 1934) 17–18; R.W. Chambers, 'Incoherencies in the A- and B-Texts of *Piers Plowman* and Their Bearing on the Authorship' R.W. Chambers, A.H. Smith, and F. Norman eds *London Medieval Studies* 1.1 (London: University of London 1937) 29–30.
47   It is also the idea of some critics. Eg, Robert Adams has written of passus 7, 'The only pardon comes when you try to avoid offending God in the first place': 'Piers's Pardon and Langland's Semi-Pelagianism' *Traditio* 39 (1983) 417. That is, the sacrament of penance is in principle unnecessary. William J. Courtenay reports that the fourteenth-century Dominican Robert Holcot in effect took the same position, affirming 'that a *viator* in a state of grace could avoid all sin,

both venial and mortal': *Schools and Scholars in Fourteenth-Century England* (Princeton: Princeton University Press 1987) 297. Will, however, will shortly argue against two Franciscans 'That þoruȝ the fend and þe flessh and þe false worlde / Synneþ þe sadde man seuen siþes a day' (8.43–4). And the Franciscan Adam Wodeham might have been sympathetic. An intellectual like Holcot who flourished at Oxford in the decade after Ockham (1330–40), maintaining like Holcot that God would reward with grace people who did their best (Courtenay *Schools and Scholars* 296–7), Wodeham nevertheless held that the viator, 'unless he has special help from God, such as Mary received, cannot remain sinless throughout life' (Courtenay *Schools and Scholars* 297). If Langland thought pardon came only from never having offended God 'in the first place,' we would be hard pressed indeed to account for his preoccupation with the sacrament of penance (eg, in passus 14 and 20). Holcot, Wodeham, and theologians like them were similarly concerned. 'Penance was hardly a pretext for a discussion of other, more philosophical issues. It was that door through which one reentered a state of grace and again became a "friend of God"' (Courtenay *Schools and Scholars* 306).

48 See B 7.76–83a. Cf the C-Text revision of Hunger's speech, B 6.218–24a.

49 Cf Coghill 'Pardon of Piers Plowman' 319–20; Maureen Quilligan *The Language of Allegory: Defining the Genre* (Ithaca and London: Cornell University Press 1979) 69–70; Baker 'From Plowing to Penitence' 720; David Mills 'The Dreams of Bunyan and Langland' in Vincent Newey ed *'The Pilgrim's Progress': Critical and Historical Views* (Totowa: Barnes and Noble 1980) 164; and Godden *Making of 'Piers Plowman'* 57.

50 Middleton 'Making a Good End' 254

51 A.C. Hamilton 'The Visions of *Piers Plowman* and the *Faerie Queen'* in William Nelson ed *Form and Convention in the Poetry of Edmund Spenser: English Institute Essays* (New York: Columbia University Press 1961) 11. This line of comment has been perceptively extended by E.D. Kirk *The Dream Thought of 'Piers Plowman'* (New Haven: Yale University Press 1972) 71–100; Ruth H. Ames *The Fulfillment of the Scriptures: Abraham, Moses, and Piers* (Evanston, Ill: Northwestern University Press 1970) 48–9, 54–64; and Baker 'From Plowing to Penitence' 721–3.

52 See Coghill 'The Pardon of Piers Plowman' 318–19. John Lawlor rightly emphasizes this. Although insightful in many respects,

Lawlor's discussion of the pardon scene seems finally incoherent. Relatively good, Piers confronts in the 'pardoun' the standard by which all human endeavour falls short and is therefore culpable: '*Piers Plowman*: The Pardon Reconsidered' *Modern Language Review* 45 (1950) 450. He must turn 'to the comfort offered by simple dependence upon his Master' ('Pardon Reconsidered' 451; cf John Lawlor's 'The Imaginative Unity of *Piers Plowman*' *Review of English Studies* ns 8 [1957] 122; and his '*Piers Plowman*': *An Essay in Criticism* 79, 296). At other times, however, Lawlor suggests that Piers has conformed to 'riȝtful reson,' 'the Law expressed in the Commandments' ('*Piers Plowman*': *An Essay in Criticism* 299).

53 Howard Meroney 'The Life and Death of Long Will' ELH 17 (1950) 17-19. Cf Carruthers *Search for St. Truth* 69-74. Earlier critics often interpreted the tearing of the 'pardoun' as Piers's turn from the active to the contemplative life. E. Talbot Donaldson suggested that Piers ceases to pursue mere salvation and begins to seek perfection: '*Piers Plowman*': *The C-Text and Its Poet* (New Haven: Yale University Press 1949) 160-1. Similarly, Stokes sees Piers's speech after he has torn the 'pardoun' as 'the most vivid example of the receding point of perfection the poem represents the Christian as always chasing'; the good deeds required for salvation are re-envisaged as 'some distinterested act' that will succeed the merely preliminary economic labours (*Justice and Mercy* 244, 232). In Frank's thorough and judicious 'The Pardon Scene in *Piers Plowman*,' he notes that Piers promises to do penance, but fails to suggest, if Piers and many other folk indeed meet the conditions of the 'pardoun' (320), what the penance might be for. In Woolf's brilliant interpretation, the 'pardoun,' which 'turns out to be a threat and a symbol of the Day of Judgment,' becomes a pardon at the moment it is torn up ('Tearing of the Pardon' 69-70). However, she does not deal with the question of whether the threat also applies to Piers – and, if it does, how he can be 'Christ-like' in the tearing of it (72). Marshall Walker, among others, proposes that Piers tears the 'pardoun' because it misleadingly emphasizes the letter rather than the spirit: 'Piers Plowman's Pardon: A Note' *English Studies in Africa* 8 (1965) 64-70. Cf esp Goldsmith *Figure of Piers Plowman* 18-19, 46.

54 A.V.C. Schmidt believes that, at 6.253-60, Langland is pointing up a universal gluttony that captures even Piers: 'Langland's Structural Imagery' *Essays in Criticism* 30 (1980) 312.

55 Thus, Godden believes that Piers comes to know God in the consci-

entious work of 'sowing His seed and tending His beasts' (*Making of 'Piers Plowman'* 45).

56 'In the *Contra Gentiles*,' Coleman has remarked, '... Aquinas recognises a natural, spontaneously acquired, though vague, notion of God. But this is not the kind of knowledge of God, the cause of man's justification, that is sufficient for salvation. Rather, it is similar to the natural knowledge of "Truth" as Langland expresses it in the *Visio*' (*'Piers Plowman' and the 'Moderni'* 114).

57 One course of action that may have ended has been well described by J.S. Wittig: 'The *Visio* represents a double reform *manqué*, the effect of which is to deny the possibility of remaking society from the top down or from the outside in' ('The Dramatic and Rhetorical Development of Long Will's Pilgrimage' *Neuphilologische Mitteilungen* 76 [1975] 54).

58 With the 'tene,' Goldsmith adduces Augustine's construction of the anger in Psalms 4:4 as the pangs of contrition (*Figure of Piers Plowman* 44). See also A.V.C. Schmidt 'The Inner Dreams in *Piers Plowman*' *Medium Aevum* 55 (1986) 30.

59 Yves Congar 'The Idea of Conversion' tr A. Marzi *Thought* 33 (1958) 8–9

60 For another recent suggestion of a reason for the change, however, see Malcolm Godden 'Plowmen and Hermits in Langland's *Piers Plowman*' *Review of English Studies* ns 35 (1984) 156–7.

61 Thus, I believe Baker is right to speak of 'Piers's conversion in Passus VII' ('From Plowing to Penitence' 720). Cf Goldsmith *Figure of Piers Plowman* 45, 121.

62 Cf Kirk *Dream Thought of 'Piers Plowman'* 94.

Index